Workshop on Graph-based Methods for Natural Language Processing 2013

(TextGraphs-8)

Seattle, Washington, USA
18 October 2013

ISBN: 978-1-62993-550-8

Printed from e-media with permission by:

Curran Associates, Inc.
57 Morehouse Lane
Red Hook, NY 12571

Some format issues inherent in the e-media version may also appear in this print version.

Printed by Curran Associates, Inc. (2014)

For permission requests, please contact the Association for Computational Linguistics at the address below.

Association for Computational Linguistics
209 N. Eighth Street
Stroudsburg, Pennsylvania 18360

Phone: 1-570-476-8006
Fax: 1-570-476-0860

acl@aclweb.org

Additional copies of this publication are available from:

Curran Associates, Inc.
57 Morehouse Lane
Red Hook, NY 12571 USA
Phone: 845-758-0400
Fax: 845-758-2634
Email: curran@proceedings.com
Web: www.proceedings.com

Introduction to TextGraphs-8

For the past 7 years, the series of TextGraphs workshops have exposed and encouraged the synergy between the field of Graph Theory (GT) and Natural Language Processing (NLP). The mix between the two started small, with graph theoretical framework providing efficient and elegant solutions for NLP applications that focused on single documents for part-of-speech tagging, word sense disambiguation and semantic role labeling. It then got progressively larger with ontology learning and information extraction from large text collections, and have reached web scale through the new fields of research that focus on information propagation in social networks, rumor proliferation, e-reputation, multiple entity detection, language dynamics learning and future events prediction to name but a few.

The 8th edition of the TextGraphs workshop aimed to be a new step in the series, focused on issues and solutions for large-scale graphs, such as those derived for web-scale knowledge acquisition or social networks. We encouraged the description of novel NLP problems or applications that have emerged in recent years which can be addressed with graph-based solutions, as well as novel graph-based solutions to known NLP tasks. Continuing to bring together researchers interested in Graph Theory applied to Natural Language Processing, provides an environment for further integration of graph-based solutions into NLP tasks. A deeper understanding of new theories of graph-based algorithms is likely to help create new approaches and widen the usage of graphs for NLP applications.

This edition of the TextGraphs workshop took place on October 18th, 2013, in Seattle, WA, immediately preceding the Conference on Empirical Methods in Natural Language Processing – EMNLP 2013.

This volume contains papers accepted for presentation at the workshop. We issued calls for regular papers, short late–breaking papers, and demos. After careful review by the program committee of the 15 submissions received – 12 regular papers, 2 short papers and 1 demo – 8 regular papers, 2 short papers and 1 demo were accepted for presentation. The accepted papers address varied problems – from theoretical and general considerations, to NLP and also "real-world" applications - through interesting variations in known and also novel graph-based methods.

We are thankful to the members of the program committee, who have provided high quality reviews in a timely fashion despite the holiday season, and all submissions have benefited from this expert feedback.

We were lucky to have two excellent speakers for this year's event. We thank Oren Etzioni and Pedro Domingos for their enthusiastic acceptance and presentations.

Zornitsa Kozareva, Irina Matveeva, Gabor Melli, Vivi Nastase

October, 2013

Organizers:

Zornitsa Kozareva, ISI, University of South California (USA)
Irina Matveeva, NexLP (USA)
Gabor Melli, VigLink (USA)
Vivi Nastase, FBK (Italy)

Program Committee:

Patricio Barco, Universiry of Alicante (Spain)
Chris Biemann, Darmstadt University of Technology (Germany)
Razvan Bunescu, Ohio University (USA)
Guillaume Cleuziou, University of Orlèans (France)
Bruno Crémilleux, University of Caen (France)
Mona Diab, Columbia University (USA)
Aram Galystan, ISI (University of Southern California (USA)
Lise Getoor, University of Maryland (USA)
Filip Ginter, University of Turku (Finland)
Amit Goyal, Yahoo! Labs (USA)
Udo Hahn, University of Jena (Germany)
Liang Huang, City University of New York (USA)
Kristina Lerman, ISI, University of South California (USA)
Mausam, University of Washington (USA)
Sofus Macskassy, ISI, University of Southern California (USA)
Rada Mihalcea, University of North Texas (USA)
Gerard de Melo, University of Berkeley (USA)
Andres Montoyo, University of Alicante (Spain)
Alessandro Moschitti, University of Trento (Italy)
Animesh Mukherjee, Indian Institute of Technology (India)
Philippe Muller, Paul Sabatier University (France)
Rafael Munoz, University of Alicante (Spain)
Preslav Nakov, Qatar Foundation (Qatar)
Roberto Navigli, Sapienza, Universita di Roma (Italy)
Guenther Neumann, DFKI (Germany)
Zaiqing Nie, Microsoft (China)
Tae-Gil Noh, University of Heidelberg (Germany)
Arzucan Özgür, Bogazici University (Turkey)
Manuel Palomar, University of Alicante (Spain)
Simone Paolo Ponzetto, Sapienza Universita di Roma (Italy)
Octavian Popescu, FBK (Italy)
Alan Ritter, University of Washington (USA)
Paolo Rosso, Technical University of Valencia (Spain)
Stephen Soderland, University of Washington (USA)

Thamar Solorio, University of Alabama (USA)
Veselin Stoyanov, Johns Hopkins University (USA)
Mihai Surdeanu, University of Arizona (USA)
Paul Tarau, University of North Texas (USA)
Konstantin Voevodski, Google (USA)
Rui Wang, DFKI GmbH (Germany)
Fabio Massimo Zanzotto, University of Rome (Italy)

Invited Speakers:

Oren Etzioni, Allen Institute for Artificial Intelligence (USA)
Pedro Domingos, University of Washignton (USA)

Table of Contents

Workshop Program

Friday, October 18, 2013

7:30-8:50	Breakfast and Registration
8:50-9:00	Opening Remarks
	(9:00-10:30) Session One
9:00-10:05	Invited talk: Opportunities for Graph-based Machine Reading by Oren Etzioni
10:05–10:20	*Event-Centered Information Retrieval Using Kernels on Event Graphs* Goran Glavaš and Jan Šnajder
10:20–10:30	*JoBimText Visualizer: A Graph-based Approach to Contextualizing Distributional Similarity* Chris Biemann, Bonaventura Coppola, Michael R. Glass, Alfio Gliozzo, Matthew Hatem and Martin Riedl
10:30-11:00	Coffee Break and Demo
	(11:00-12:30) Session Two
11:00–11:25	*Merging Word Senses* Sumit Bhagwani, Shrutiranjan Satapathy and Harish Karnick
11:25–11:50	*Reconstructing Big Semantic Similarity Networks* Ai He, Shefali Sharma and Chun-Nan Hsu
11:50–12:15	*Graph-Based Unsupervised Learning of Word Similarities Using Heterogeneous Feature Types* Avneesh Saluja and Jiri Navratil
12:15–12:30	*From Global to Local Similarities: A Graph-Based Contextualization Method using Distributional Thesauri* Martin Riedl and Chris Biemann
12:30-2:00	Lunch Break

Friday, October 18, 2013 (continued)

(2:00-3:30) Session Three

2:00-3:05 Invited talk: Extracting Tractable Probabilistic Knowledge Graphs from Text by Pedro Domingos

3:05–3:30 *Understanding seed selection in bootstrapping*
Yo Ehara, Issei Sato, Hidekazu Oiwa and Hiroshi Nakagawa

3:30-4:00 Coffee Break

(4:00-5:40) Session Four

4:00–4:25 *Graph-Structures Matching for Review Relevance Identification*
Lakshmi Ramachandran and Edward Gehringer

4:25–4:50 *Automatic Extraction of Reasoning Chains from Textual Reports*
Gleb Sizov and Pinar Öztürk

4:50–5:15 *Graph-based Approaches for Organization Entity Resolution in MapReduce*
Hakan Kardes, Deepak Konidena, Siddharth Agrawal, Micah Huff and Ang Sun

5:15–5:40 *A Graph-Based Approach to Skill Extraction from Text*
Ilkka Kivimäki, Alexander Panchenko, Adrien Dessy, Dries Verdegem, Pascal Francq, Hugues Bersini and Marco Saerens

5:40-6:00 Closing Remarks

Event-Centered Information Retrieval Using Kernels on Event Graphs

Goran Glavaš and **Jan Šnajder**
University of Zagreb
Faculty of Electrical Engineering and Computing
Unska 3, 10000 Zagreb, Croatia
{goran.glavas, jan.snajder}@fer.hr

Abstract

Traditional information retrieval models assume keyword-based queries and use unstructured document representations. There is an abundance of event-centered texts (e.g., breaking news) and event-oriented information needs that often involve structure that cannot be expressed using keywords. We present a novel retrieval model that uses a structured event-based representation. We structure queries and documents as graphs of event mentions and employ graph kernels to measure the query-document similarity. Experimental results on two event-oriented test collections show significant improvements over state-of-the-art keyword-based models.

1 Introduction

The purpose of an information retrieval (IR) system is to retrieve the documents relevant to user's information need expressed in the form of a query. Many information needs are event-oriented, while at the same time there exists an abundance of event-centered texts (e.g., breaking news, police reports) that could satisfy these needs. Furthermore, event-oriented information needs often involve structure that cannot easily be expressed with keyword-based queries (e.g., *"What are the countries that President Bush has visited and in which has his visit triggered protests?"*). Traditional IR models (Salton et al., 1975; Robertson and Jones, 1976; Ponte and Croft, 1998) rely on shallow unstructured representations of documents and queries, making no use of syntactic, semantic, or discourse level information. On the other hand, models utilizing structured event-based representations have not yet proven useful in IR. However, significant advances in event extraction have been achieved in the last decade as the result of standardization efforts (Pustejovsky et al., 2003) and shared evaluation tasks (Verhagen et al., 2010), renewing the interest in structured event-based text representations.

In this paper we present a novel retrieval model that relies on structured event-based representation of text and addresses event-centered queries. We define an *event-oriented query* as a query referring to one or more real-world events, possibly including their participants, the circumstances under which the events occurred, and the temporal relations between the events. We account for such queries by structuring both documents and queries into *event graphs* (Glavaš and Šnajder, 2013b). The event graphs are built from individual event mentions extracted from text, capturing their protagonists, times, locations, and temporal relations. To measure the query-document similarity, we compare the corresponding event graphs using graph kernels (Borgwardt, 2007). Experimental results on two news story collections show significant improvements over state-of-the-art keyword-based models. We also show that our models are especially suitable for retrieval from collections containing topically similar documents.

2 Related Work

Most IR systems are a variant of the vector space model (Salton et al., 1975), probabilistic model (Robertson and Jones, 1976), or language model (Ponte and Croft, 1998), which do not account for associations between query terms. Recent models introduce co-occurrence-based (Park et al., 2011) and syntactic (Shinzato et al., 2012) dependencies. However, these dependencies alone in most cases cannot capture in sufficient detail the semantics of events.

A more comprehensive set of dependencies can be modeled with graph-based representations. Graph-based IR approaches come in two flavors: (1) the entire document collection is represented as a single graph in which queries are inserted as additional vertices (Mihalcea and Tarau, 2004); (2) each query and each document are represented as graphs of concepts, and the relevance of a document for a query is determined by comparing the corresponding graphs (Montes-y Gómez et al., 2000). Our approach fits into the latter group but we represent documents as graphs of events rather than graphs of concepts. In NLP, graph kernels have been used for question type classification (Suzuki, 2005), cross-lingual retrieval (Noh et al., 2009), and recognizing news stories on the same event (Glavaš and Šnajder, 2013b).

Event-based IR is addressed explicitly by Lin et al. (2007), who compare predicate-argument structures extracted from queries to those extracted from documents. However, queries have to be manually decomposed into semantic roles and can contain only a single predicate. Kawahara et al. (2013) propose a similar approach and demonstrate that ranking based on semantic roles outperforms ranking based on syntactic dependencies. Both these approaches target the problem of syntactic alternation but do not consider the queries made of multiple predicates, such as those expressing temporal relations between events.

3 Kernels on Event Graphs

Our approach consists of two steps. First, we construct event graphs from both the document and the query. We then use a graph kernel to measure the query-document similarity and rank the documents.

3.1 Event Graphs

An event graph is a mixed graph in which vertices represent the individual event mentions and edges represent temporal relations between them. More formally, an event graph is a tuple $G = (V, E, A, m, r)$, where V is the set of vertices, E is the set of undirected edges, A is the set of directed edges, $m : V \to M$ maps the vertices to event mentions, and $r : E \to R$ assigns temporal relations to edges.

We use a generic representation of a *factual* event mention, which consists of an event anchor and event arguments of four coarse types (*agent*, *target*, *time*, and *location*) (Glavaš and Šnajder, 2013a; Glavaš and Šnajder, 2013b). We adopt the set of temporal relations used in TempEval-2 (Verhagen et al., 2010) (*before*, *after*, and *overlap*), with additional temporal equivalence relation (*equal*).

To build an event graph, we first extract the event mentions and then extract the temporal relations between them. To extract the event anchors, we use a supervised model based on a rich feature set proposed by Glavaš and Šnajder (2013b), performing at 80% F1-score. We then use a robust rule-based approach from Glavaš and Šnajder (2013a) to extract event arguments. Finally, we extract the temporal relations using a supervised model with a rich feature set proposed by Glavaš and Šnajder (2013b). Relation classification performs at 60% F1-score.

To compute the product graph kernels, we must identify event mentions from the query that corefer with mentions from the document. To this end, we employ the model from Glavaš and Šnajder (2013a), which compares the anchors and four types of arguments between a pair of event mentions. The model performs at 67% F-score on the EventCorefBank dataset (Bejan and Harabagiu, 2008).

3.2 Product Graph Kernels

Graph kernels provide an expressive measure of similarity between graphs (Borgwardt, 2007). In this work, we use product graph kernel (PGK), a type of random walk graph kernel that counts the common walks between two graphs (Gärtner et al., 2003).

Product graph. The graph product of two labeled graphs, G and G', denoted $G_P = G \times G'$, is a graph with the vertex set

$$V_P = \{(v, v') \mid v \in V_G, v' \in V_{G'}, \delta(v, v')\}$$

where predicate $\delta(v, v')$ holds iff vertices v and v' are identically labeled (Hammack et al., 2011). Vertices of event graphs have the same label if the event mentions they denote corefer. The edge set of the product is conditioned on the type of the graph product. In the *tensor product*, an edge exists in the product iff the corresponding edges exist in both input graphs and have the same label, i.e., denote the same temporal relation. In the *conormal product*, an edge is introduced iff the corresponding edge exists in at least one input graph. A conormal product may compensate for omitted temporal relations in the input graphs but may introduce spurious edges that do not represent

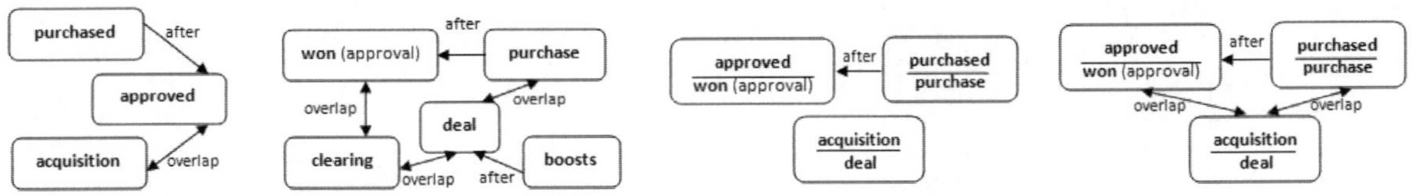

(a) Query graph (b) Document graph (c) Tensor product (d) Conormal product

Figure 1: Examples of event graphs and their products

true overlap between queries and documents. Fig. 1 shows an example of input graphs and their products.

PGK computation. The PGK for input graphs G and G' is computed as

$$k_{PG}(G, G') = \sum_{i,j=1}^{|V_P|} [(I - \lambda A_P)^{-1}]_{ij}$$

provided $\lambda < 1/d$, where d is the maximum vertex degree in the product graph G_P with the adjacency matrix A_P. In experiments, we set λ to $1/(d+1)$. PGK suffers from tottering (Mahé et al., 2005), a phenomenon due to the repetition of edges in a random walk. A walk that totters between neighboring vertices produces an unrealistically high similarity score. To prevent tottering between neighboring vertices, Mahé et al. (2005) transform the input graphs before computing the kernel score on their product: each edge (v_i, v_j) is converted into a vertex v_e; the edge itself gets replaced with edges (v_e, v_i) and (v_e, v_j). We experiment with Mahé extension for PGK, accounting for the increased probability of one-edge-cycle tottering due the small size of query graphs.

4 Experiments

Test Collections and Queries. To the best of our knowledge, there is no standard test collection available for event-centered IR that we could use to evaluate our models. Thus, we decided to build two such test collections, with 50 queries each: (1) a general collection of topically diverse news stories and (2) a topic-specific collection of news on Syria crisis. The first collection contains 25,948 news stories obtained from EMM News Brief, an online news clustering service.[1] For the topic-specific collection, we selected from the general collection 1387 documents that contain the word *"Syria"* or its derivations.

[1] http://emm.newsbrief.eu

General collection (news stories)	
q1:	*An ICT giant purchased the phone maker after the government approved the acquisition*
q2:	*The warship tried to detain Chinese fishermen but was obstructed by the Chinese vessels*
Topic-specific collection (Syria crisis)	
q3:	*Syrian forces killed civilians, torched houses, and ransacked stores, overrunning a farmer village*
q4:	*Rebels murdered many Syrian soldiers and the government troops blasted the town in central Syria*

Table 1: Example queries from the test collection

For each collection we asked an annotator to compile 50 queries. She was instructed to select at random a document from the collection, read the document carefully, and compile at least one query consisting of at least two event mentions, in such a way that the selected document is relevant for the query. Example queries are shown in Table 1. For instance, query **q1** (whose corresponding event graph is shown in Fig. 1a) was created based on the following document (whose event graph is shown in Fig. 1b):

> *Google Inc. won approval from Chinese regulators for its $12.5 billion purchase of Motorola Mobility Holdings Inc., clearing a final hurdle for a deal that boosts its patents portfolio...*

Relevance judgments. To create relevance judgments, we use the standard IR pooling method with two baseline retrieval models – a TF-IDF weighted vector space model (VSM) and a language model. Our graph-based model was not used for pooling because of time limitations (note that this favors the baseline models because pool-based evaluation is biased against models not contributing to the pool (Büttcher et al., 2007)). Given that EMM News Brief builds clusters of related news and that most EMM

	Model	Collection	
		General	Specific
Baselines	TF-IDF VSM	0.335	0.199
	Hiemstra LM	0.300	0.175
	In_expC2	0.341	0.188
	DFR_BM25	0.332	0.192
Graph-based	Tensor	**0.502**	0.407
	Conormal	0.434	0.359
	Mahé Tensor	0.497	**0.412**
	Mahé Conormal	0.428	0.362

Table 2: Retrieval performance (MAP)

clusters contain less than 50 news stories, we estimate that there are at most 50 relevant documents per query. To get an even better estimate of recall, for each query we pooled the union of top 75 documents retrieved by each of the two baseline models.

One annotator made the relevance judgments for all queries. We asked another annotator to provide judgments for two randomly chosen queries and obtained perfect agreement, which confirmed our intuition that determining relevance for complex event-centered queries is not difficult. The average number of relevant documents per query in the general and topic-specific collection is 12 and 8, respectively.[2]

Results. Table 2 shows the mean average precision (MAP) on both test collections for four graph kernel-based models (tensor/conormal product and with/without Mahé extension). We compare our models to baselines from the three traditional IR paradigms: a TF-IDF-weighted cosine VSM, the language model of Hiemstra (2001), and the best-performing models from the probabilistic Divergence from Randomness (DFR) framework (In_expC2 and DFR_BM25) (Amati, 2003; Ounis et al., 2006). We evaluate these models using the Terrier IR platform.[3]

Overall, all models perform worse on the topic-specific collection, in which all documents are topically related. Our graph kernel models outperform all baseline models ($p<0.01$ for tensor models and $p<0.05$ for conormal models; paired student's t-test) on both collections, with a wider margin on topic-specific than on the general collection. This result

[2]Available at http://takelab.fer.hr/data

[3]http://terrier.org

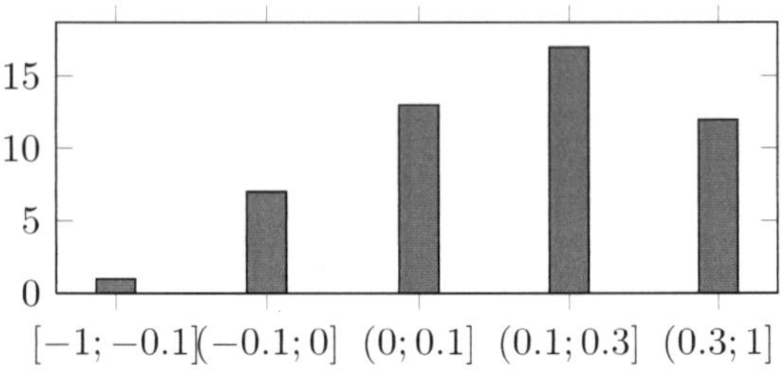

Figure 2: Histogram of AP differences

suggests that the graph-based models are especially suitable for retrieval over topic-specific collections. There is no significant difference between the tensor product and conormal product models, indicating that the conormal product introduces spurious edges more often than it remedies for incorrect extraction of temporal relations. The performance differences due to Mahé extension are not significant, providing no conclusive evidence on the effect of tottering.

To gain more insights into the performance of our event graph-based model, we analyzed per query differences in average precision between our best-performing model (Tensor) and the best-performing baseline (In_expC2) on queries from the general collection. Fig. 2 shows the histogram of differences. Our graph kernel-based model outperforms the baseline on 42 out of 50 queries. A closer inspection of the eight queries on which our model performs worse than the baseline reveals that this is due to (1) an important event mention not being extracted from the query (2 cases) or a (2) failure in coreference resolution between an event mention from the query and a mention from the document (6 cases).

5 Conclusion and Perspectives

We presented a graph-based model for event-centered information retrieval. The model represents queries and documents as event graphs and ranks the documents based on graph kernel similarity. The experiments demonstrate that for event-based queries our graph-based model significantly outperforms state-of-the-art keyword-based retrieval models. Our models are especially suitable for topic-specific collections, on which traditional IR models perform poorly.

An interesting topic for further research is the extension of the model with other types of dependencies between events, such as entailment, causality, and structural relations. Another direction concerns the effective integration of event graph-based and keyword-based models. We will also consider applications of event graphs on other natural language processing tasks such as text summarization.

Acknowledgments. This work has been supported by the Ministry of Science, Education and Sports, Republic of Croatia under the Grant 036-1300646-1986. We thank the reviewers for their comments.

References

Giambattista Amati. 2003. *Probability models for information retrieval based on divergence from randomness*. Ph.D. thesis, University of Glasgow.

Cosmin Adrian Bejan and Sanda Harabagiu. 2008. A linguistic resource for discovering event structures and resolving event coreference. In *Proc. of the LREC 2008*.

Karsten Michael Borgwardt. 2007. *Graph Kernels*. Ph.D. thesis, Ludwig-Maximilians-Universität München.

Stefan Büttcher, Charles LA Clarke, Peter CK Yeung, and Ian Soboroff. 2007. Reliable information retrieval evaluation with incomplete and biased judgements. In *Proc. of the ACM SIGIR*, pages 63–70. ACM.

Thomas Gärtner, Peter Flach, and Stefan Wrobel. 2003. On graph kernels: Hardness results and efficient alternatives. In *Learning Theory and Kernel Machines*, pages 129–143. Springer.

Goran Glavaš and Jan Šnajder. 2013a. Exploring coreference uncertainty of generically extracted event mentions. In *Proc. of the CICLing 2013*, pages 408–422. Springer.

Goran Glavaš and Jan Šnajder. 2013b. Recognizing identical events with graph kernels. In *Proc. of the ACL 2013*, pages 797–803.

Richard Hammack, Wilfried Imrich, and Sandi Klavžar. 2011. *Handbook of Product Graphs*. Discrete Mathematics and Its Applications. CRC Press.

Djoerd Hiemstra. 2001. *Using language models for information retrieval*. Taaluitgeverij Neslia Paniculata.

Daisuke Kawahara, Keiji Shinzato, Tomohide Shibata, and Sadao Kurohashi. 2013. Precise information retrieval exploiting predicate-argument structures. In *Proc. of the IJCNLP 2013*. In press.

Chia-Hung Lin, Chia-Wei Yen, Jen-Shin Hong, Samuel Cruz-Lara, et al. 2007. Event-based textual document retrieval by using semantic role labeling and coreference resolution. In *IADIS International Conference WWW/Internet 2007*.

Pierre Mahé, Nobuhisa Ueda, Tatsuya Akutsu, Jean-Luc Perret, and Jean-Philippe Vert. 2005. Graph kernels for molecular structure-activity relationship analysis with support vector machines. *Journal of Chemical Information and Modeling*, 45(4):939–951.

Rada Mihalcea and Paul Tarau. 2004. TextRank: Bringing order into texts. In *Proc. of the EMNLP 2004*, volume 4. Barcelona, Spain.

Manuel Montes-y Gómez, Aurelio López-López, and Alexander Gelbukh. 2000. Information retrieval with conceptual graph matching. In *Database and Expert Systems Applications*, pages 312–321. Springer.

Tae-Gil Noh, Seong-Bae Park, Hee-Geun Yoon, Sang-Jo Lee, and Se-Young Park. 2009. An automatic translation of tags for multimedia contents using folksonomy networks. In *Proc. of the ACM SIGIR 2009*, pages 492–499. ACM.

Iadh Ounis, Gianni Amati, Vassilis Plachouras, Ben He, Craig Macdonald, and Christina Lioma. 2006. Terrier: A high performance and scalable information retrieval platform. In *Proceedings of the OSIR Workshop*, pages 18–25.

Jae Hyun Park, W Bruce Croft, and David A Smith. 2011. A quasi-synchronous dependence model for information retrieval. In *Proc. of the 20th ACM International Conference on Information and Knowledge Management*, pages 17–26. ACM.

Jay Ponte and Bruce Croft. 1998. A language modeling approach to information retrieval. In *Proc. of the ACM SIGIR*, pages 275–281. ACM.

James Pustejovsky, José Castano, Robert Ingria, Roser Sauri, Robert Gaizauskas, Andrea Setzer, Graham Katz, and Dragomir Radev. 2003. TimeML: Robust specification of event and temporal expressions in text. *New Directions in Question Answering*, 3:28–34.

Stephen E Robertson and K Sparck Jones. 1976. Relevance weighting of search terms. *Journal of the American Society for Information science*, 27(3):129–146.

Gerard Salton, Anita Wong, and Chung-Shu Yang. 1975. A vector space model for automatic indexing. *Communications of the ACM*, 18(11):613–620.

Keiji Shinzato, Tomohide Shibata, Daisuke Kawahara, and Sadao Kurohashi. 2012. Tsubaki: An open search engine infrastructure for developing information access methodology. *Journal of Information Processing*, 20(1):216–227.

Jun Suzuki. 2005. Kernels for structured data in natural language processing. *Doctor Thesis, Nara Institute of Science and Technology*.

Marc Verhagen, Roser Sauri, Tommaso Caselli, and James Pustejovsky. 2010. SemEval-2010 Task 13: TempEval-2. In *Proc. of the SemEval 2010*, pages 57–62.

JoBimText Visualizer: A Graph-based Approach to Contextualizing Distributional Similarity

Alfio Gliozzo[1] **Chris Biemann**[2] **Martin Riedl**[2]
Bonaventura Coppola[1] **Michael R. Glass**[1] **Matthew Hatem**[1]
(1) IBM T.J. Watson Research, Yorktown Heights, NY 10598, USA
(2) FG Language Technology, CS Dept., TU Darmstadt, 64289 Darmstadt, Germany
{gliozzo,mrglass,mhatem}@us.ibm.com coppolab@gmail.com
{biem,riedl}@cs.tu-darmstadt.de

Abstract

We introduce an interactive visualization component for the JoBimText project. JoBimText is an open source platform for large-scale distributional semantics based on graph representations. First we describe the underlying technology for computing a distributional thesaurus on words using bipartite graphs of words and context features, and contextualizing the list of semantically similar words towards a given sentential context using graph-based ranking. Then we demonstrate the capabilities of this contextualized text expansion technology in an interactive visualization. The visualization can be used as a semantic parser providing contextualized expansions of words in text as well as disambiguation to word senses induced by graph clustering, and is provided as an open source tool.

1 Introduction

The aim of the JoBimText[1] project is to build a graph-based unsupervised framework for computational semantics, addressing problems like lexical ambiguity and variability, word sense disambiguation and lexical substitutability, paraphrasing, frame induction and parsing, and textual entailment. We construct a semantic analyzer able to self-adapt to new domains and languages by unsupervised learning of semantics from large corpora of raw text. At the moment, this analyzer encompasses contextualized similarity, sense clustering, and a mapping of senses to existing knowledge bases. While its primary target application is functional domain adaptation of Question Answering (QA) systems (Ferrucci et al., 2013), output of the semantic analyzer has been successfully utilized for word sense disambiguation (Miller et al., 2012) and lexical substitution (Szarvas et al., 2013). Rather than presenting the different algorithms and technical solutions currently implemented by the JoBimText community in detail, in this paper we will focus on available functionalities and illustrate them using an interactive visualization.

2 Underlying Technologies

While distributional semantics (de Saussure, 1959; Harris, 1951; Miller and Charles, 1991) and the computation of distributional thesauri (Lin, 1998) has been around for decades, its full potential has yet to be utilized in Natural Language Processing (NLP) tasks and applications. Structural semantics claims that meaning can be fully defined by semantic oppositions and relations between words. In order to perform a reliable knowledge acquisition process in this framework, we gather statistical information about word co-occurrences with syntactic contexts from very large corpora. To avoid the intrinsic quadratic complexity of the similarity computation, we have developed an optimized process based on MapReduce (Dean and Ghemawat, 2004) that takes advantage of the sparsity of contexts, which allows scaling the process through parallelization. The result of this computation is a graph connecting the most discriminative contexts to terms and explicitly linking the most similar terms. This graph represents local models of semantic relations *per term* rather than a model with fixed dimensions. This representation departs from the vector space metaphor (Schütze, 1993; Erk and Padó, 2008; Baroni and Zamparelli,

[1] `http://sf.net/projects/jobimtext/`

2010), commonly employed in other frameworks for distributional semantics such as LSA (Deerwester et al., 1990) or LDA (Blei et al., 2003).

The main contribution of this paper is to describe how we operationalize semantic similarity in a graph-based framework and explore this semantic graph using an interactive visualization. We describe a scalable and flexible computation of a distributional thesaurus (DT), and the contextualization of distributional similarity for specific occurrences of language elements (i.e. terms). For related works on the computation of distributional similarity, see e.g. (Lin, 1998; Lin and Dyer, 2010).

2.1 Holing System

To keep the framework flexible and abstract with respect to the pre-processing that identifies structure in language material, we introduce the holing operation, cf. (Biemann and Riedl, 2013). It is applied to observations over the structure of text, and splits these observations into a pair of two parts, which we call the "Jo" and the "Bim"[2]. All JoBim pairs are maintained in the bipartite First-Order JoBim graph $TC(T, C, E)$ with T set of terms (Jos), C set of contexts (Bims), and $e(t, c, f) \in E$ edges between $t \in T$, $c \in C$ with frequency f. While these parts can be thought of as language elements referred to as *terms*, and their respective *context features*, splits over arbitrary structures are possible (including pairs of terms for Jos), which makes this formulation more general than similar formulations found e.g. in (Lin, 1998; Baroni and Lenci, 2010). These splits form the basis for the computation of global similarities and for their contextualization. A Holing System based on dependency parses is illustrated in Figure 1: for each dependency relation, two JoBim pairs are generated.

2.2 Distributed Distributional Thesaurus Computation

We employ the Apache Hadoop MapReduce Framwork[3], and Apache Pig[4], for parallelizing and distributing the computation of the DT. We describe this computation in terms of graph transformations.

[2]arbitrary names to emphasize the generality, should be thought of as "term" and "context"

[3]`http://hadoop.apache.org`

[4]`http://pig.apache.org/`

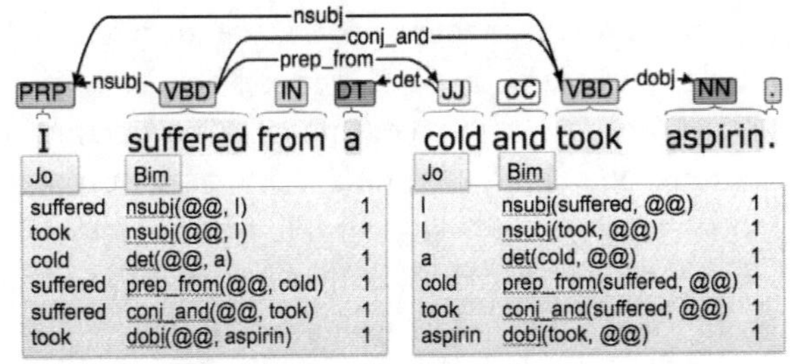

Figure 1: Jos and Bims generated applying a dependency parser (de Marneffe et al., 2006) to the sentence *I suffered from a cold and took aspirin.* The @@ symbolizes the hole.

Staring from the JoBim graph TC with counts as weights, we first apply a statistical test[5] to compute the significance of each pair (t, c), then we only keep the p most significant pairs per t. This constitutes our first-order graph for Jos FO_{JO}. In analogy, when keeping the p most significant pairs per c, we can produce the first-order graph for Bims FO_{BIM}. The second order similarity graph for Jos is defined as $SO_{JO}(T, E)$ with Jos $t_1, t_2 \in T$ and undirected edges $e(t_1, t_2, s)$ with similarity $s = |\{c|e(t_1, c) \in FO_{JO}, e(t_2, c) \in FO_{JO}\}|$, which defines similarity between Jos as the number of salient features two Jos share. SO_{JO} defines a distributional thesaurus. In analogy, SO_{BIM} is defined over the shared Jos for pairs of Bims and defines similarity of contexts. This method, which can be computed very efficiently in a few MapReduce steps, has been found superior to other measures for very large datasets in semantic relatedness evaluations in (Biemann and Riedl, 2013), but could be replaced by any other measure without interfering with the remainder of the system.

2.3 Contextualization with CRF

While the distributional thesaurus provides the similarity between pairs of terms, the fidelity of a particular expansion depends on the context. From the term-context associations gathered in the construction of the distributional thesaurus we effectively have a language model, factorized according to the holing operation. As with any language model, smoothing is critical to performance. There may be

[5]we use log-likelihood ratio (Dunning, 1993) or LMI (Evert, 2004)

many JoBim (term-context) pairs that are valid and yet under represented in the corpus. Yet, there may be some similar term-context pair that is attested in the corpus. We can find similar contexts by expanding the term arguments with similar terms. However, again we are confronted with the fact that the similarity of these terms depends on the context.

This suggests some technique of joint inference to expand terms in context. We use marginal inference in a conditional random field (CRF) (Lafferty et al., 2001). A particular world, $\mathbf{x}$ is defined as single, definite sequence of either original or expanded words. The weight of the world, $w(\mathbf{x})$ depends on the degree to which the term-context associations present in this sentence are present in the corpus and the general out-of-context similarity of each expanded term to the corresponding term in the original sentence. Therefore the probability associated with any expansion t for any position x_i is given by Equation 1. Where Z is the partition function, a normalization constant.

$$P(x_i = t) = \frac{1}{Z} \sum_{\{\mathbf{x} \mid x_i = t\}} e^{w(\mathbf{x})} \quad (1)$$

The balance between the plausibility of an expanded sentence according to the language model, and its per-term similarity to the original sentence is an application specific tuning parameter.

2.4 Word Sense Induction, Disambiguation and Cluster Labeling

The contextualization described in the previous subsection performs implicit word sense disambiguation (WSD) by ranking contextually better fitting similar terms higher. To model this more explicitly, and to give rise to linking senses to taxonomies and domain ontologies, we apply a word sense induction (WSI) technique and use information extracted by IS-A-patterns (Hearst, 1992) to label the clusters.

Using the aggregated context features of the clusters, the word cluster senses are assigned in context. The DT entry for each term j as given in $SO_{JO}(J, E)$ induces an open neighborhood graph $N_j(V_j, E_j)$ with $V_j = \{j' | e(j, j', s) \in E)$ and E_j the projection of E regarding V_j, consisting of similar terms to j and their similarities, cf. (Widdows and Dorow, 2002).

We cluster this graph using the Chinese Whispers graph clustering algorithm (Biemann, 2010), which finds the number of clusters automatically, to obtain induced word senses. Running shallow, part-of-speech-based IS-A patterns (Hearst, 1992) over the text collection, we obtain a list of extracted IS-A relationships between terms, and their frequency. For each of the word clusters, consisting of similar terms for the same target term sense, we aggregate the IS-A information by summing the frequency of hypernyms, and multiplying this sum by the number of words in the cluster that elicited this hypernym. This results in taxonomic information for labeling the clusters, which provides an abstraction layer for terms in context[6]. Table 1 shows an example of this labeling from the model described below. The most similar 200 terms for "jaguar" have been clustered into the car sense and the cat sense and the highest scoring 6 hypernyms provide a concise description of these senses. This information can be used to automatically map these cluster senses to senses in an taxonomy or ontology. Occurrences of ambiguous words in context can be disambiguated to these cluster senses comparing the actual context with salient contexts per sense, obtained by aggregating the Bims from the FO_{JO} graph per cluster.

sense	IS-A labels	similar terms
jaguar N.0	car, brand, company, automaker, manufacturer, vehicle	geely, lincoln-mercury, tesla, peugeot, ..., mitsubishi, cadillac, jag, benz, mclaren, skoda, infiniti, sable, thunderbird
jaguar N.1	animal, species, wildlife, team, wild animal, cat	panther, cougar, alligator, tiger, elephant, bull, hippo, dragon, leopard, shark, bear, otter, lynx, lion

Table 1: Word sense induction and cluster labeling example for "jaguar". The shortened cluster for the car sense has 186 members.

3 Interactive Visualization

3.1 Open Domain Model

The open domain model used in the current visualization has been trained from newspaper cor-

[6]Note that this mechanism also elicits hypernyms for unambiguous terms receiving a single cluster by the WSI technique.

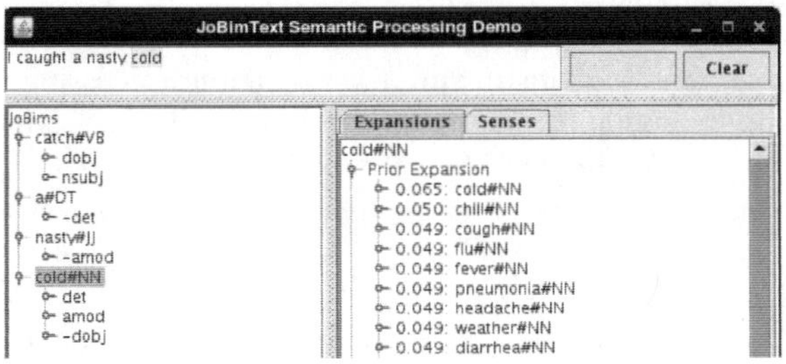

Figure 2: Visualization GUI with prior expansions for "cold". Jobims are visualized on the left, expansions on the right side.

pora using 120 million sentences (about 2 Gigawords), compiled from LCC (Richter et al., 2006) and the Gigaword (Parker et al., 2011) corpus. We constructed a UIMA (Ferrucci and Lally, 2004) pipeline, which tokenizes, lemmatizes and parses the data using the Stanford dependency parser (de Marneffe et al., 2006). The last annotator in the pipeline annotates *Jo*s and *Bim*s using the collapsed dependency relations, cf. Fig. 1. We define the lemmatized forms of the terminals including the part-of-speech as Jo and the lemmatized dependent word and the dependency relation name as Bim.

3.2 Interactive Visualization Features

Evaluating the impact of this technology in applications is an ongoing effort. However, in the context of this paper, we will show a visualization of the capabilities allowed by this flavor of distributional semantics. The visualization is a GUI as depicted in Figure 2, and exemplifies a set of capabilities that can be accessed through an API. It is straightforward to include all shown data as features for semantic preprocessing. The input is a sentence in natural language, which is processed into JoBim pairs as described above. All the Jos can be expanded, showing their paradigmatic relations with other words.

We can perform this operation with and without taking the context into account (cf. Sect. 2.3). The latter performs an implicit disambiguation by ranking similar words higher if they fit the context. In the example, the "common cold" sense clearly dominates in the prior expansions. However, "weather" and "chill" appear amongst the top-similar prior expansions.

We also have implemented a sense view, which displays sense clusters for the selected word, see Figure 3. Per sense, a list of expansions is provided together with a list of possible IS-A types. In this example, the algorithm identified two senses of "cold" as a temperature and a disease (not all cluster members shown). Given the JoBim graph of the context (as displayed left in Fig. 2), the particular occurrence of "cold" can be disambiguated to Cluster 0 in Fig. 3, since its Bims "amod(@@,nasty)" and "-dobj(catch, @@)" are found in FO_{JO} for far more members of cluster 0 than for members of cluster 1. Applications of this type of information include knowledge-based word sense disambiguation (Miller et al., 2012), type coercion (Kalyanpur et al., 2011) and answer justification in question answering (Chu-Carroll et al., 2012).

4 Conclusion

In this paper we discussed applications of the JoBimText platform and introduced a new interactive visualization which showcases a graph-based unsupervised technology for semantic processing. The implementation is operationalized in a way that it can be efficiently trained "off line" using MapReduce, generating domain and language specific models for distributional semantics. In its "on line" use, those models are used to enhance parsing with contextualized text expansions of terms. This expansion step is very efficient and runs on a standard laptop, so it can be used as a semantic text preprocessor. The entire project, including pre-computed data models, is available in open source under the ASL 2.0, and allows computing contextualized lexical expansion on arbitrary domains.

References

M. Baroni and A. Lenci. 2010. Distributional memory: A general framework for corpus-based semantics. *Comp. Ling.*, 36(4):673–721.

M. Baroni and R. Zamparelli. 2010. Nouns are vectors, adjectives are matrices: representing adjective-noun constructions in semantic space. In *Proc. EMNLP-2010*, pages 1183–1193, Cambridge, Massachusetts.

C. Biemann and M. Riedl. 2013. Text: Now in 2D! a framework for lexical expansion with contextual similarity. *Journal of Language Modelling*, 1(1):55–95.

C. Biemann. 2010. Co-occurrence cluster features for lexical substitutions in context. In *Proceedings of TextGraphs-5*, pages 55–59, Uppsala, Sweden.

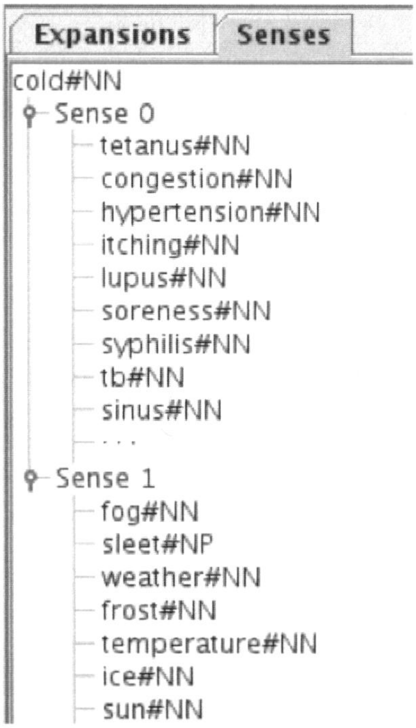

Figure 3: Senses induced for the term "cold".

D. M. Blei, A. Y. Ng, and M. I. Jordan. 2003. Latent dirichlet allocation. *J. Mach. Learn. Res.*, 3:993–1022, March.

J. Chu-Carroll, J. Fan, B. K. Boguraev, D. Carmel, D. Sheinwald, and C. Welty. 2012. Finding needles in the haystack: search and candidate generation. *IBM J. Res. Dev.*, 56(3):300–311.

M.-C. de Marneffe, B. MacCartney, and C. D. Manning. 2006. Generating typed dependency parses from phrase structure parses. In *Proc. LREC-2006*, Genova, Italy.

Ferdinand de Saussure. 1916. *Cours de linguistique générale*. Payot, Paris, France.

J. Dean and S. Ghemawat. 2004. MapReduce: Simplified Data Processing on Large Clusters. In *Proc. OSDI '04*, San Francisco, CA.

S. Deerwester, S. T. Dumais, G. W. Furnas, T. K. Landauer, and R. Harshman. 1990. Indexing by latent semantic analysis. *Journal of the American Society for Information Science*, 41(6):391–407.

T. Dunning. 1993. Accurate methods for the statistics of surprise and coincidence. *Computational Linguistics*, 19(1):61–74.

K. Erk and S. Padó. 2008. A structured vector space model for word meaning in context. In *Proc. EMNLP-2008*, pages 897–906, Honolulu, Hawaii.

S. Evert. 2004. *The statistics of word cooccurrences: word pairs and collocations*. Ph.D. thesis, IMS, Universität Stuttgart.

D. Ferrucci and A. Lally. 2004. UIMA: An Architectural Approach to Unstructured Information Processing in the Corporate Research Environment. In *Nat. Lang. Eng. 2004*, pages 327–348.

D. Ferrucci, A. Levas, S. Bagchi, D. Gondek, and E. T. Mueller. 2013. Watson: Beyond Jeopardy! *Artificial Intelligence*, 199-200:93–105.

Z. S. Harris. 1951. *Methods in Structural Linguistics*. University of Chicago Press, Chicago.

M. A. Hearst. 1992. Automatic acquisition of hyponyms from large text corpora. In *Proc. COLING-1992*, pages 539–545, Nantes, France.

A. Kalyanpur, J.W. Murdock, J. Fan, and C. Welty. 2011. Leveraging community-built knowledge for type coercion in question answering. In *Proc. ISWC 2011*, pages 144–156. Springer.

J. D. Lafferty, A. McCallum, and F. C. N. Pereira. 2001. Conditional random fields: Probabilistic models for segmenting and labeling sequence data. In *Proc. ICML 2001*, pages 282–289, San Francisco, CA, USA.

J. Lin and C. Dyer. 2010. *Data-Intensive Text Processing with MapReduce*. Morgan & Claypool Publishers, San Rafael, CA.

D. Lin. 1998. Automatic retrieval and clustering of similar words. In *Proc. COLING-98*, pages 768–774, Montréal, Quebec, Canada.

G. A. Miller and W. G. Charles. 1991. Contextual correlates of semantic similarity. *Language and Cognitive Processes*, 6(1):1–28.

T. Miller, C. Biemann, T. Zesch, and I. Gurevych. 2012. Using distributional similarity for lexical expansion in knowledge-based word sense disambiguation. In *Proc. COLING-2012*, pages 1781–1796, Mumbai, India.

R. Parker, D. Graff, J. Kong, K. Chen, and K. Maeda. 2011. *English Gigaword Fifth Edition*. Linguistic Data Consortium, Philadelphia.

M. Richter, U. Quasthoff, E. Hallsteinsdóttir, and C. Biemann. 2006. Exploiting the leipzig corpora collection. In *Proc. IS-LTC 2006*, Ljubljana, Slovenia.

H. Schütze. 1993. Word space. In *Advances in Neural Information Processing Systems 5*, pages 895–902. Morgan Kaufmann.

G. Szarvas, C. Biemann, and I. Gurevych. 2013. Supervised all-words lexical substitution using delexicalized features. In *Proc. NAACL-2013*, Atlanta, GA, USA.

D. Widdows and B. Dorow. 2002. A graph model for unsupervised lexical acquisition. In *Proc. COLING-2002*, pages 1–7, Taipei, Taiwan.

Merging Word Senses

Sumit Bhagwani, Shrutiranjan Satapathy, Harish Karnick
Computer Science and Engineering
IIT Kanpur, Kanpur - 208016, India
{sumitb,sranjans,hk}@cse.iitk.ac.in

Abstract

WordNet, a widely used sense inventory for Word Sense Disambiguation(WSD), is often too fine-grained for many Natural Language applications because of its narrow sense distinctions. We present a semi-supervised approach to learn similarity between WordNet synsets using a graph based recursive similarity definition. We seed our framework with sense similarities of all the word-sense pairs, learnt using supervision on human-labelled sense clusterings. Finally we discuss our method to derive coarse sense inventories at arbitrary granularities and show that the coarse-grained sense inventory obtained significantly boosts the disambiguation of nouns on standard test sets.

1 Introduction

With different applications requiring different levels of word sense granularity, producing sense clustered inventories with the requisite level of sense granularity has become important. The subtleties of sense distinctions captured by WordNet(Miller, 1995) are helpful for language learners (Snow et al., 2007) and in machine translation of languages as diverse as Chinese and English (Ng et al., 2003). On the other hand, for tasks like Document Categorization and Information Retrieval (Buitelaar, 2000), it may be sufficient to know if a given word belongs to a coarsely defined class of WordNet senses. Using the fine grained sense inventory of WordNet may be detrimental to the performance of these applications. Thus developing a framework which can generate sense inventories with different granularities can improve the performance of many applications.

To generate a coarse sense inventory, many researchers have focused on generating coarse senses for each word by merging the fine-grained senses (Chugur et al., 2002) (Navigli, 2006). This approach has two problems. First, it requires a stopping criterion for each word — for example the number of final classes. The right number of classes for each word cannot usually be predetermined even if the application is known. So such systems cannot be used to derive coarse senses for all the words. Second, inconsistent sense clusters are obtained because coarse senses are independently generated for each word. This leads to transitive closure errors and suggests that for deriving consistent coarse senses, instead of clustering senses for each word separately we should cluster synsets.

We propose a framework that derives a coarse sense inventory by learning a synset similarity metric. We focus on coarsening the noun synsets of WordNet and show that the obtained coarse-grained sense inventory greatly improves the noun sense disambiguation. Our approach closely resembles (Snow et al., 2007) for supervised learning of synset similarity. But to learn similarity between synset pairs which do not share a word we use a variant of the SimRank framework (Jeh and Widom, 2002) and avoid giving them zero similarity. Thus the similarity learnt is more than a binary decision and is reflective of a more comprehensive semantic similarity between the synsets. The use of SimRank for learning synset similarity is inspired by the success of graph-centrality algorithms in WSD. We do not modify the WordNet ontology, unlike (Snow et al., 2007), as it may introduce spurious relations and remove some manually encoded information.

In section 2, we discuss past work in sense clustering. In section 3 and 4, we describe our framework of learning synset similarity using SimRank. In section 5, we discuss our methodology of producing coarse senses using the learnt similarity metric. Section 6 describes the experimental setup and evaluates the framework described. Section 7 contains conclusions and discusses the directions for future work.

2 Related Work

A wide variety of automatic methods have been proposed for coarsening fine-grained inventories. The earliest attempt on WordNet include (Mihalcea and Moldovan, 2001) which merged synsets on semantic principles like sharing a *pertainym*, *antonym* or *verb group*. We discuss some of the ideas which are related to our work. Though promising, many of these techniques are severely limited by the amount of available manually annotated data.

(Chugur et al., 2002) constructed sense similarity matrices using *translation equivalences* in four languages. With the advent of WordNets being developed in multiple languages[1] as well as multilingual ontologies like BabelNet (Navigli and Ponzetto, 2012), this seems a promising area.

(McCarthy, 2006) estimated sense similarities using a combination of word-to-word distributional similarity combined with the JCN WordNet based similarity measure (Jiang and Conrath, 1997). They introduce a more relaxed notion of sense relatedness which allows the user to control the granularity for the application in hand.

(Navigli, 2006) produced a fixed set sense clusters by mapping WordNet word senses to Oxford English Dictionary(OED) word senses exploiting similarities in glosses and semantic relationships in the sense inventories. It is expected that the different WordNet senses that are semantically close mapped to the same sense in the other ontology via an efficient mapping that is able to capture the semantic similarity between the concepts in both the ontologies. The drawback of this method is the generation of inconsistent sense clusters.

(Snow et al., 2007) presented a novel supervised approach in which they train a Support Vector Machine(SVM) using features derived from WordNet and other lexical resources, whose predictions serve as a distance measure between synsets. Assuming zero similarity between synset pairs with no common words, they cluster synsets using average link agglomerative clustering and the synset similarity model learnt.

3 SimRank

SimRank (Jeh and Widom, 2002) is a graph based similarity measure applicable in any domain with object-to-object relationships. It uses the intuition that "*two objects are similar if they are related to similar objects*". Since SimRank has a recursive structure, the base cases play an important role.

Let us denote the SimRank similarity between objects α and β by $s(\alpha, \beta)$. It is defined as 1 if $\alpha = \beta$, otherwise it is given by:

$$s(\alpha,\beta) = \frac{C}{|I(\alpha)||I(\beta)|} \sum_{i=1}^{|I(\alpha)|} \sum_{j=1}^{|I(\beta)|} s(I_i(\alpha), I_j(\beta)) \tag{1}$$

where $C \in (0, 1)$ is a constant decay factor and $I(v)$ is the set consisting of in-neighbours of node v, whose individual members are referred to as $I_j(v)$, $1 \leq j \leq |I(v)|$.

3.1 Solution and its Properties

(Jeh and Widom, 2002) proved that a solution $s(*, *)$ to the SimRank equations always exists and is unique. For a graph $G(V, E)$, the solution is reached by iteration to a fixed-point. For each iteration k, we keep $|V|^2$ entries $S_k(*, *)$, where $S_k(\alpha, \beta)$ is the estimate of similarity between α and β at the kth iteration. We start with $S_0(*, *)$ which is 1 for singleton nodes like (x, x), 0 otherwise. We successively compute $S_{k+1}(*, *)$ based on $S_k(*, *)$ using equation 1.

Regarding the convergence of the above computation process, (Lizorkin et al., 2010) proved that the difference between the SimRank theoretical scores

[1] GlobalWordNet lists the WordNets available in the public domains: http://www.globalwordnet.org/gwa/wordnet_table.html.

and iterative similarity scores decreases exponentially in the number of iterations and uniformly for every pair of nodes i.e.

$$s(\alpha,\beta) - S_k(\alpha,\beta) \leq C^{k+1} \quad \forall \alpha,\beta \in V;\ k = 0,1,2\ldots \tag{2}$$

3.2 Personalizing SimRank

In many scenarios we do not have complete information about the objects and thus have similarities for only some pairs of objects. These similarities may be independently learnt and may not directly conform with the underlying graph. In such situations, we would like to get a more complete and consistent similarity metric between objects while simultaneously using the existing information. For this we propose a personalized framework for SimRank where we bias the SimRank by changing the initialization. If we know similarities of some pairs, we fix them in our set of equations and let the rest of the values be automatically learnt by the system.

Let us call the map of node pairs to their similarity values as $InitStore$. It also contains all the singleton nodes like (x, x) which have values equal to 1. For other node pairs, the system of equations is the same as equation 1. In the personalized framework, we have no constraints on the initialization as long as all values initialized are in the range $[0, C]$.

3.3 Learning Synset Similarity using SimRank

The Personalized SimRank framework requires an underlying graph $G(V, E)$, where V is the set of objects to be clustered and E is the set of semantic links connecting these objects and an $InitStore$ containing the similarity values over some pairs from $V \times V$ learnt or known otherwise. Note that the values in the $InitStore$ have an upper bound of C.

For learning synset similarity, V is the set of synsets to be clustered and E is the set of WordNet relations connecting these synsets. We use the *Hypernymy*, *Hyponymy*, *Meronymy* and *Holonymy* relations of WordNet as the semantic links. The method for seeding the $InitStore$ is described in section 4 and can be summed up as follows:

- We train the SVMs from synset-merging data from OntoNotes (Hovy et al., 2006) to predict the similarity values of all the synset pairs which share at least one word.
- We estimate the posterior probabilities from the SVM predictions by approximating the posterior by a sigmoid function, using the method discussed in (Lin et al., 2003).
- We scale the posterior probabilities obtained to range between $[0, C]$ by linear scaling, where C is the SimRank decay parameter.

4 Seeding SimRank with supervision

4.1 Outline

We learn semantic similarity between different senses of a word using supervision, which allows us to intelligently combine and weigh the different features and thus give us an insight into how humans relate word senses. We obtain pairs of synsets which human-annotators have labeled as "merged" or "not merged" and describe each pair as a feature vector. We learn a synset similarity measure by using an SVM on this extracted dataset, where positive examples are the pairs which were merged and negative examples are the ones which were not merged by the annotators. We then calculate the posterior probability using the classifier score which is used as an estimate of the similarity between synsets constituting the pair.

4.2 Gold standard sense clustering dataset

Since our methodology depends upon the availability of labelled judgements of synset relatedness, a dataset with a high Inter-Annotator agreement is required. We use the manually labelled mappings from the Omega ontology[2] (Philpot et al., 2005) to the WordNet senses, provided by the OntoNotes project (Hovy et al., 2006).

The OntoNotes dataset creation involved a rigorous iterative annotation process producing a coarse sense inventory which guarantees at least 90% Inter-Tagger agreement on the sense-tagging of the sample sentences used in the annotation process. Thus we expect the quality of the final clustering of senses and the derived labelled judgements to be reasonably high.

[2] http://omega.isi.edu/

We use OntoNotes Release 3.0 [3] for extracting WordNet sense clusters.[4]. The dataset consists of senses for selected words in sense files. The senses in OntoNotes are mapped to WordNet senses, if a good mapping between senses exists. The steps involved in extraction are as follows:

1. OntoNotes has mappings to 4 WordNet versions: 1.7, 2.0, 2.1 and 3.0. We mapped all the senses[5] to WordNet 3.0.

2. Validating clusters on WN3.0:
   - We removed the sense files which did not contain all the senses of the word i.e. the clustering was not complete.
   - We removed the sense files in which the clusters had a clash i.e. one sense belonged to multiple clusters.

3. We removed instances that were present in both positive and negative examples. This situation arises because the annotators were working with word senses and there were inconsistent sense clusters.

Statistics	Nouns	Verbs
# of Word Sense File Before Processing	2033	2156
# of Word Sense Files After Processing	1680	1951
Distinct Offsets encountered	4930	6296
Positive Examples	1214	6881
Negative Examples	11974	20899
Percentage of Positive examples	9.20	24.76

Table 1: Statistics of Pairwise Classification Dataset obtained from OntoNotes

4.3 Feature Engineering

In this section, we describe the feature space construction. We derive features from the structure of WordNet and other available lexical resources. Our features can be broadly categorized into two parts: derived from WordNet and derived from other corpora. Many of the listed features are motivated by (Snow et al., 2007) and (Mihalcea and Moldovan, 2001).

4.3.1 Features derived from WordNet

WordNet based features are further subdivided into similarity measures and features. Among the WordNet similarity measures, we used Path Based Similarity Measures: WUP (Wu and Palmer, 1994), LCH (Leacock et al., 1998); Information Content Based Measures: RES (Resnik, 1995), JCN (Jiang and Conrath, 1997), LIN (Lin, 1998); Gloss Based Heuristics (variants of Lesk (Lesk, 1986)): Adapted Lesk (Banerjee and Pedersen, 2002), Adapted Lesk Tanimoto and Adapted Lesk Tanimoto without hyponyms[6]

Other synset and sense based features include number of lemmas common in two synsets, SenseCount: maximum polysemy degree among the lemmas shared by the synsets, SenseNum: number of lemmas having maximum polysemy degree among the lemmas shared by the synsets, whether two synsets have the same lexicographer file, number of common hypernyms, autohyponymy: whether the two synsets have a hyponym-hypernym relation between them and merging heuristics by (Mihalcea and Moldovan, 2001).[7]

4.3.2 Features derived from External Corpora

- eXtended WordNet Domains Project (González et al., 2012) provides us the score of a synset with respect to 169 hierarchically organized domain-labels(excluding factotum label). We obtain a representation of a synset in the domain label space and use cosine similarity, L1 distance and L2 distance computed over the weight representations of the synsets as features.

- BabelNet (Navigli and Ponzetto, 2012) provides us with the translation of noun word senses in 6 languages namely: English, German, Spanish, Catalan, Italian and French and the mapping of noun synsets to DBpedia[8] entries. For features we use counts of common

[3] http://www.ldc.upenn.edu/Catalog/docs/LDC2009T24/OntoNotes-Release-3.0.pdf

[4] The OntoNotes groupings will be available through the LDC at http://www.ldc.upenn.edu

[5] We dropped WN1.7 as there were very few senses and the mapping from WN1.7 to WN3.0 was not easily available.

[6] We call the lesk variants as AdapLesk, AdapLeskTani and AdapLeskTaniNoHypo.

[7] We divide mergeSP1_2 into two features: The strict heuristic checks whether all the hypernyms are shared or not whereas the relaxed heuristic checks if the synsets have at least 1 common hypernym.

[8] http://dbpedia.org/About

lemmas in all 6 languages and count of common DBpedia entries.

- SentiWordNet (Baccianella et al., 2010) provides us with a mapping from a synset to a triad of three weights. The weights correspond to the score given to a synset based on its objectivity and subjectivity(positive and negative). We use cosine similarity, L1 distance and L2 distance of the weight representations of the synsets as features.
- We use the sense clusterings produced by mapping WordNet senses to OED senses by the organizers of the coarse-grained AW task in SemEval-2007[9] (Navigli et al., 2007). For each pair of synsets, we check if there are senses in the synsets that belong to the same cluster in the OED mapping.

4.4 Classifier and Training

We train SVMs using the features above on the synset pairs extracted from OntoNotes, where every synset pair is given either a "merged" or "not-merged" label. Because of the skewed class distribution in the dataset, we randomly generated balanced datasets (equal number of positive and negative instances) and then divided them in a ratio of 7:3 for training and testing respectively. We repeated the process multiple number of times and report the average.

To train the SVMs we used an implementation by (Joachims, 1998), whose java access is provided by JNI-SVMLight [10] library. For all experiments reported, we use the linear kernel with the default parameters provided by the library. [11]

We scale the ranges of all the features to a common range [-1,1]. The main advantage offered by scaling is that it prevents domination of attributes with smaller numeric ranges by those with greater numeric ranges. It also avoids numerical difficulties like overflow errors caused by large attribute values. Note that both training and testing data should be scaled with the same parameters.

[9] http://lcl.uniroma1.it/coarse-grained-aw/

[10] JNI-SVMLight: http://adrem.ua.ac.be/~tmartin/

[11] We also tested our system with an RBF kernel but the best results were obtained with the linear kernel(Bhagwani, 2013)

4.5 Estimating Posterior Probabilities from SVM Scores

For seeding SimRank, we need an estimate of the posterior probability $Pr(y = +1|x)$ instead of the class label. (Platt, 1999) proposed approximating the posterior by a sigmoid function

$$Pr(y = +1|x) \approx P_{A,B}(f(x)) \equiv \frac{1}{1+exp(Af(x)+B)}$$

We use the method described in (Lin et al., 2003), as it avoids numerical difficulties faced by (Platt, 1999).

5 Coarsening WordNet

We construct an undirected graph $G(V, E)$ where the vertex set V contains the synsets of WordNet and edge set E comprises of edges obtained by thresholding the similarity metric learnt using the personalized SimRank model (see section 3.2). On varying the threshold, we obtain different graphs which differ in the number of edges. On these graphs, we find connected components[12], which gives us a partition over synsets. All the senses of a word occurring in the same component are grouped as a single coarse sense. We call our approach Connected Components Clustering(CCC).

For lower thresholds, we obtain denser graphs and thus fewer connected components. This small number of components translates into more coarser senses. Therefore, using this threshold as a parameter of the system, we can control the granularity of the coarse senses produced.

6 Experimental Setup and Evaluation

6.1 Feature Analysis

We analyze the feature space used for SVMs in two ways. We evaluate Information Gain(IG) and Gain Ratio(GR) functions over the features and do a feature ablation study. The former tries to capture the discrimination ability of the feature on its own and the latter measures how a feature corroborates with other features in the feature space.

[12] a connected component of an undirected graph is a subgraph in which any two vertices are connected to each other by paths, and which is connected to no additional vertices in the supergraph.

We extracted all the features over the complete OntoNotes dataset without any normalization and evaluated them using IG and GR functions. We report the top 7 features of both the evaluators in table 2[13].

Feature	GR	IG
LCH	0.0129	**0.0323**
WUP	0.0148	**0.0290**
JCN	**0.0215**	0.0209
AdapLesk	0.0169	**0.0346**
AdapLeskTani	**0.0231**	**0.0360**
AdapLeskTaniNoHypo	0.0168	**0.0301**
mergeSP1_2_strict	**0.0420**	0.0010
mergeSP1_2_relaxed	**0.0471**	0.0012
number of Common Hypernyms	**0.0883**	0.0096
Domain-Cosine Similarity	**0.0200**	**0.0442**
OED	**0.0326**	**0.0312**

Table 2: Information Gain and Gain Ratio Based Evaluation

We divide our features into 6 broad categories and report the average F-Score of both the classes observed by removing that category of features from our feature space. The SVMs are trained with features normalized using MinMax Normalization for this study.

Features Removed	FScore Pos	FScore Neg
WordNet Similarity Measures	0.6948	0.6784
WordNet Based Features	0.7227	0.7092
BabelNet Features	0.7232	0.7127
Domain Similarity Features	0.6814	0.6619
OED Feature	0.6957	0.7212
SentiWordNet Features	0.7262	0.7192
Without Removing Features	0.7262	0.7192

Table 3: Feature Ablation Study

From tables 2 and 3, we observe that the most significant contributors in SVM performance are WordNet similarity measures and domain cosine similarity. The former highlights the importance of the ontology structure and the gloss definitions in WordNet. The latter stresses the fact that approximately matching the domain of two senses is a strong cue about whether the two senses are semantically related enough to be merged.

Other notable observations are the effectiveness of the OED feature and the low Information Gain and Gain Ratio of multilingual features. We also found that SentiWordNet features were non-discriminatory as most of the noun synsets were described as objective concepts.

6.2 Estimating Posterior Probabilities from SVM Scores

We learn parameters A and B of the sigmoid that transforms SVM predictions to posterior probabilities (see section 4.5). Since using the same data set that was used to train the model we want to calibrate will introduce unwanted bias we calibrate on an independently generated random balanced subset from OntoNotes.

The values of A and B obtained are -1.1655 and 0.0222 respectively. Using these values, the SVM prediction of value 0 gets mapped to 0.4944.

6.3 Semi-Supervised Similarity Learning

We learn similarity models using the SimRank variant described in section 3. (Jeh and Widom, 2002) use $C = 0.8$ and find that 5-6 iterations are enough. (Lizorkin et al., 2010) suggest lower values of C or more number of iterations. We vary the values for C between 0.6, 0.7 and 0.8 and we run all systems for 10 iterations to avoid convergence issues.

6.4 Coarsening WordNet

We assess the effect of automatic synset clustering on the English all-words task at Senseval-3 (Snyder and Palmer, 2004) [14]. The task asked WSD systems to select the apt sense for 2,041 content words in running texts comprising of 351 sentences. Since the BabelNet project provided multilingual equivalences for only nouns, we focussed on nouns and used the 890 noun instances.

We consider the three best performing WSD systems: GAMBL (Decadt et al., 2004), SenseLearner (Mihalcea and Faruque, 2004) and Koc University (Yuret, 2004) - and the best unsupervised system: IRST-DDD (Strapparava et al., 2004) submitted in the task. The answer by the system is given full

[13]Table lists only 11 features as 3 features are common in top 7 features of both the evaluators

[14]This evaluation is similar to the evaluation used by (Navigli, 2006) and (Snow et al., 2007)

C	System	F-Score	Threshold	CCC	Random	Improvement
0.6	GAMBL	0.7116	0.36	0.9031	0.8424	0.0607
	SenseLearner	0.7104	0.37	0.8824	0.8305	0.0518
	KOC University	0.7191	0.37	0.8924	0.8314	0.0610
	IRST-DDD	0.6367	0.35	0.8731	0.8013	0.0718
0.7	GAMBL	0.7116	0.52	0.8453	0.7864	0.0589
	SenseLearner	0.7104	0.49	0.8541	0.8097	0.0444
	KOC University	0.7191	0.52	0.8448	0.7911	0.0538
	IRST-DDD	0.6367	0.49	0.7970	0.7402	0.0568
0.8	GAMBL	0.7116	0.59	0.8419	0.7843	0.0577
	SenseLearner	0.7104	0.56	0.8439	0.7984	0.0455
	KOC University	0.7191	0.59	0.8414	0.7879	0.0535
	IRST-DDD	0.6367	0.47	0.8881	0.8324	0.0557

Table 4: Improvement in Senseval-3 WSD performance using Connected Component Clustering Vs Random Clustering at the same granularity

credit if it belongs to the cluster of the correct answer.

Observe that any clustering will only improve the WSD performance. Therefore to assess the improvement obtained because of our clustering, we calculate the expected F-Score, the harmonic mean of expected precision and expected recall, for a random clustering at the same granularity and study the improvement over the random clustering.

Let the word to be disambiguated have N senses, each mapped to a unique synset. Let the clustering of these N synsets on a particular granularity give us k clusters $C_1, \ldots C_k$. The expectation that an incorrectly chosen sense and the actual correct sense would belong to same cluster is

$$\frac{\sum_{i=1}^{k} |C_i|(|C_i|-1)}{N(N-1)} \qquad (3)$$

We experiment with C = 0.6, 0.7 and 0.8. The SVM probability boundaries when scaled to $[0, C]$ for these values are 0.30, 0.35 and 0.40. To find the threshold giving the best improvement against the random clustering baseline, we use the search space $[C - 0.35, C]$. The performance of the systems at these thresholds for different values of C is reported in table 4.

Commenting theoretically about the impact of C on the performance is tough as by changing C we are changing all the $|V|^2$ simultaneous equations to be solved. Empirically, we observe that across all systems improvements over the baseline keep decreasing as C increases. This might be due to the slow convergence of SimRank for higher values of C.

Figure 1 shows that by varying thresholds the improvement of the Connected Components Clustering over the random clustering baseline at the same granularity first increases and then decreases. This behaviour is shared by both supervised and unsupervised systems. Similar figures are obtained for other values of C (0.7 and 0.8), but are omitted because of lack of space.

Across supervised and unsupervised systems, we observe higher improvements for unsupervised systems. This could be because the unsupervised system was underperforming compared to the supervised systems in the fine grained WSD task setting.

7 Conclusions and Future Work

We presented a model for learning synset similarity utilizing the taxonomy information and information learnt from manually obtained sense clustering. The framework obtained is generic and can be applied to other parts of speech as well. For coarsening senses, we used one of the simplest approaches to cluster senses but the generic nature of the similarity gives us the flexibility to use other clustering algorithms

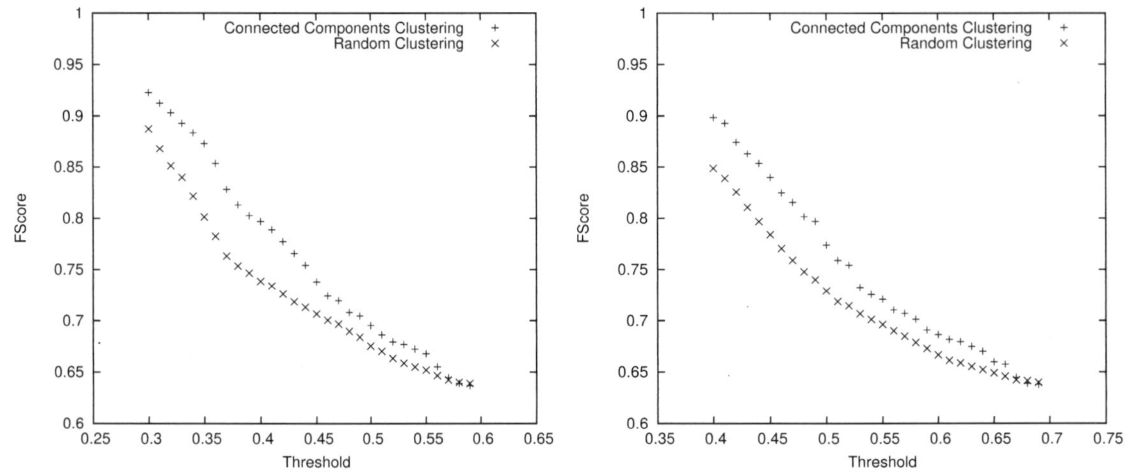

(a) (b)

Figure 1: Improvement in (a) average performance of best 3 Supervised Systems and (b) performance of best Unupervised System in Senseval-3 using Connected Component Clustering Vs Random Clustering at the same granularity with C = 0.6

for experimentation. We show that the clustering obtained by partitioning synsets in connected components gives us a maximum improvement of 5.78% on supervised systems and 7.18% on an unsupervised system. This encourages us to study graph based similarity learning methods further as they allow us to employ available wide-coverage knowledge bases.

We use the WordNet relations *Hypernymy*, *Hyponymy*, *Meronymy* and *Holonymy* without any differentiation. If we can grade the weights of the relations based on their relative importance we can expect an improvement in the system. These weights can be obtained by annotator feedback from cognitive experiments or in a task based setting. In addition to the basic WordNet relations, we can also enrich our relation set using the Princeton WordNet Gloss Corpus[15], in which all the WordNet glosses have been sense disambiguated. Any synset occuring in the gloss of a synset is directly related to that synset via the *gloss* relation. This relation helps make the WordNet graph denser and richer by capturing the notion of *semantic relatedness*, rather than just the notion of *semantic similarity* captured by the basic WordNet relations.

[15] http://wordnet.princeton.edu/glosstag.shtml

Acknowledgments

The authors would like to thank the anonymous reviewers for their valuable comments and suggestions to improve the quality of the paper.

References

Stefano Baccianella, Andrea Esuli, and Fabrizio Sebastiani. 2010. Sentiwordnet 3.0: An enhanced lexical resource for sentiment analysis and opinion mining. In *Proceedings of LREC*.

Satanjeev Banerjee and Ted Pedersen. 2002. An adapted lesk algorithm for word sense disambiguation using wordnet. In *Proceedings of CICLing 2002*.

Sumit Bhagwani. 2013. Merging word senses. Master's thesis, Indian Institute of Technology Kanpur.

Paul Buitelaar. 2000. Reducing lexical semantic complexity with systematic polysemous classes and underspecification. In *NAACL-ANLP 2000 Workshop: Syntactic and Semantic Complexity in Natural Language Processing Systems*, pages 14–19. Association for Computational Linguistics.

Irina Chugur, Julio Gonzalo, and Felisa Verdejo. 2002. Polysemy and sense proximity in the senseval-2 test suite. In *Proceedings of the ACL 2002 WSD workshop*.

Bart Decadt, Véronique Hoste, Walter Daelemans, and Antal Van den Bosch. 2004. Gambl, genetic algorithm optimization of memory-based wsd. In *Proceedings of ACL/SIGLEX Senseval-3*.

Aitor González, German Rigau, and Mauro Castillo. 2012. A graph-based method to improve wordnet domains. In *Proceedings of CICLing 2012*.

Eduard Hovy, Mitchell Marcus, Martha Palmer, Lance Ramshaw, and Ralph Weischedel. 2006. Ontonotes: the 90% solution. In *Proceedings of HLT-NAACL 2006*.

Glen Jeh and Jennifer Widom. 2002. Simrank: A measure of structural-context similarity. In *KDD*, pages 538–543.

Jay J. Jiang and David W. Conrath. 1997. Semantic similarity based on corpus statistics and lexical taxonomy. In *Proceedings of ROCLING'97*.

Thorsten Joachims. 1998. Making large-scale support vector machine learning practical.

Claudia Leacock, George A. Miller, and Martin Chodorow. 1998. Using corpus statistics and wordnet relations for sense identification. *Comput. Linguist.*, 24(1):147–165, March.

Michael Lesk. 1986. Automatic sense disambiguation using machine readable dictionaries: how to tell a pine cone from an ice cream cone. In *Proceedings of SIGDOC 1986*.

Hsuan-tien Lin, Chih-Jen Lin, and Ruby C. Weng. 2003. A note on platt's probabilistic outputs for support vector machines.

Dekang Lin. 1998. An information-theoretic definition of similarity. In *Proceedings of ICML 1998*.

Dmitry Lizorkin, Pavel Velikhov, Maxim Grinev, and Denis Turdakov. 2010. Accuracy estimate and optimization techniques for simrank computation. *The VLDB Journal*, 19(1):45–66, February.

Diana McCarthy. 2006. Relating wordnet senses for word sense disambiguation. *Making Sense of Sense: Bringing Psycholinguistics and Computational Linguistics Together*, 17.

Rada Mihalcea and Ehsanul Faruque. 2004. Senselearner: Minimally supervised word sense disambiguation for all words in open text. In *Proceedings of ACL/SIGLEX Senseval-3*.

Rada Mihalcea and Dan Moldovan. 2001. Ez.wordnet: principles for automatic generation of a coarse grained wordnet. In *Proceedings of Flairs 2001*, pages 454–459.

George A Miller. 1995. Wordnet: a lexical database for english. *Communications of the ACM*, 38(11):39–41.

Roberto Navigli and Simone Paolo Ponzetto. 2012. BabelNet: The automatic construction, evaluation and application of a wide-coverage multilingual semantic network. *Artificial Intelligence*, 193:217–250.

Roberto Navigli, Kenneth C. Litkowski, and Orin Hargraves. 2007. Semeval-2007 task 07: Coarse-grained english all-words task. In *Proceedings of SemEval-2007*, pages 30–35. Association for Computational Linguistics, June.

Roberto Navigli. 2006. Meaningful clustering of senses helps boost word sense disambiguation performance. In *Proceedings of COLING-ACL*, pages 105–112.

Hwee Tou Ng, Bin Wang, and Yee Seng Chan. 2003. Exploiting parallel texts for word sense disambiguation: an empirical study. In *Proceedings of ACL 2003*.

Andrew Philpot, Eduard Hovy, and Patrick Pantel. 2005. The omega ontology. In *Proceedings of the ONTOLEX Workshop at IJCNLP 2005*.

John C. Platt. 1999. Probabilistic outputs for support vector machines and comparisons to regularized likelihood methods. In *ADVANCES IN LARGE MARGIN CLASSIFIERS*, pages 61–74. MIT Press.

Philip Resnik. 1995. Using information content to evaluate semantic similarity in a taxonomy. In *Proceedings of IJCAI 1995*.

Rion Snow, Sushant Prakash, Daniel Jurafsky, and Andrew Y. Ng. 2007. Learning to Merge Word Senses. In *Proceedings of EMNLP-CoNLL*, pages 1005–1014, June.

Benjamin Snyder and Martha Palmer. 2004. The english all-words task. In *Proceedings of ACL/SIGLEX Senseval-3*, pages 41–43.

Carlo Strapparava, Alfio Gliozzo, and Claudiu Giuliano. 2004. Pattern abstraction and term similarity for word sense disambiguation: Irst at senseval-3. In *Proceedings of ACL/SIGLEX Senseval-3*.

Zhibiao Wu and Martha Palmer. 1994. Verbs semantics and lexical selection. In *Proceedings of ACL 1994*.

Deniz Yuret. 2004. Some experiments with a naive bayes wsd system. In *Proceedings of ACL/SIGLEX Senseval-3*.

Reconstructing Big Semantic Similarity Networks

Ai He, Shefali Sharma
*Information Sciences Institute
University of Southern California
4676 Adminralty Way
Marina del Rey, CA 90292
{aihe|sharma}@isi.edu

Chun-Nan Hsu[*,†]
†Division of Biomedical Informatics
Department of Medicine
University of California, San Diego
La Jolla, CA 92093
chunnan@ucsd.edu

Abstract

Distance metric learning from high (thousands or more) dimensional data with hundreds or thousands of classes is intractable but in NLP and IR, high dimensionality is usually required to represent data points, such as in modeling semantic similarity. This paper presents algorithms to scale up learning of a Mahalanobis distance metric from a large data graph in a high dimensional space. Our novel contributions include random projection that reduces dimensionality and a new objective function that regularizes intra-class and inter-class distances to handle a large number of classes. We show that the new objective function is convex and can be efficiently optimized by a stochastic-batch subgradient descent method. We applied our algorithm to two different domains; semantic similarity of documents collected from the Web, and phenotype descriptions in genomic data. Experiments show that our algorithm can handle the high-dimensional big data and outperform competing approximations in both domains.

1 Introduction

According to Yang (2006), distance metric learning learns a distance metric from data sets that consists of pairs of points of the same or different classes while at the same time preserving the adjacency relations among the data points. Usually, it is easier to let the user label whether a set of data is in the same class than directly assign a distance between each pair or classify whether a pair of data points is a match or not. Learning a good distance metric in the feature space is essential in many real-world NLP and IR applications. For example, Web news article clustering applying hierarchical clustering or k-means requires that the distance between the two feature vectors extracted from the news articles faithfully reflect the semantic similarity between them for these algorithms to perform well.

Studies on distance metric learning over the past few years show that the learned metric can outperform Euclidean distance metric. The constraints of training examples in learning usually comes from the global or local adjacency information. Data points with the same class labels are supposed to be connected while those with different classes labels disconnected. Supervised algorithms aim to learn the distance metric to make the adjacency relationships in the training examples preserved.

One of the most common approaches to distance metric learning is to learn a Mahalanobis distance metric. Example algorithms to learn a Mahalanobis distance metric include (Xing et al., 2002; Goldberger et al., 2004; Shaw et al., 2011).

A common limitation shared by these algorithms is that they fail to scale up to high dimensional data sets. When those algorithms run on high dimensional data sets, they usually run out of memory. However, many NLP applications depend on tens of thousands of features to perform well. Dimensionality reduction and approximation have been suggested, but they usually degrade performance. Other issues occur when the data sets consists of a large number of disjoint classes. In this case, the learned distance metric must map the data points to a space where the data points cluster unevenly into a large number of small groups, which makes the learning problem harder and may require special treatments.

In this paper, we present a new scalable approach to distance metric learning that addresses the scalability issues mentioned above. To deal with high dimensionality, one approach is to factorize the metric matrix in the Mahalanobis distance metric into low-rank matrix. This reduces the number of parameters that must be learned during the learning phase. However, the learning problem becomes non-convex. Different initializations may result in drastically different performance due to local optima. We solve this problem by introducing random projection, which projects data points to a low dimensional space before learning a low dimensional full-rank metric matrix. We show that this strategy not only is more robust than the low-rank approximation, but also outperforms the Principal Component Analysis (PCA), a common approach to dimensionality reduction.

Another contribution that our approach offers is new regularization terms in the objective function of learning. The new terms specify that one should learn to minimize the distance for data points in the same classes and maximize those in different ones. We found that minimization but not maximization would lead to the best performance, so we kept only the minimization term.

We evaluated our new approach with data sets from two problem domains. One domain is about learning semantic similarity between Web pages. This domain was studied in (Shaw et al., 2011) and involves moderately high dimensional data sets of bag-of-words. The other is about matching semantically related phenotype variables across different genome-wide association studies (GWAS) (Hsu et al., 2011). This problem domain requires extremely high dimensional data for a learner to perform well. Our experimental results show that our new algorithm consistently outperform the previous ones in both the domains.

2 Distance Metric Learning

Let $\mathbf{X} \in \mathbb{R}^{d \times n}$ be the feature matrix of input data points. For any two data points $x_i,\ x_j \in \mathbb{R}^{d \times 1}$ in $\mathbf{X}$, the (square of) the Mahalanobis distance between x_i and x_j is defined as

$$D_M^{i,j} = (x_i - x_j)^\intercal \mathbf{M}(x_i - x_j),$$

where $\mathbf{M} \in \mathbb{R}^{d \times d}$ is a metric matrix. The distance is always non-negative because $\mathbf{M}$ is required to be positive semidefinite (PSD).

Xing (2002) used semidefinite programming to learn a Mahalanobis distance metric for clustering. It was a convex optimization problem, which allowed them to derive local optima free algorithms. Weinberger (2005) learned a Mahalanobis distance metric for the k-nearest neighbor classifier by maintaining a margin between data points in different classes, *i.e.*, enforcing the neighbors of the same class to be closer than all others. As in the support vector machines, the learning problem was reduced to convex optimization based on hinge loss. Yang (2006) presented a comprehensive survey on distance metric learning.

Recently, Shaw *et al.* (2011) followed the preceding approaches but reformulated the problem, as an instance of the on-line learning algorithm PEGASOS (Shalev-Shwartz et al., 2011), albeit a complex construction. In a way, it scaled up the traditional metric learning method to a larger amount of data points. They also reformulated the margin mentioned above as triplets over the data set and clarify the derivation of the objective function. Each training example used here is a triplet (x_i, x_j, x_k), consisting of a pair x_i and x_j in the same class and x_k that is in a different class. Learning in this case ensures that the learned distance between x_i and x_j is less than their distance to x_k. In comparison, one may formulate the distance learning problem as binary classification, where the objective is to minimize the match probability of data point pairs in different classes and maximize those in the same ones. Since there will always be much more data point pairs in different classes than those in the same ones, this formulation always lead to an unbalanced classification problem.

3 Strategies for Scaling Up Learning

Shaw *et al.* (2011) suggested various strategies to scale up the algorithm for high dimensional multi-class data. In this section, we will review these strategies and their weaknesses, and then, present our approach that addresses these weaknesses.

3.1 Dimensional Reduction

Four strategies were suggested to handle the high dimensional data sets:

- Diagonal Approximation,
- Principal Component Analysis (PCA),
- Low Rank Decomposition,
- Random Projection.

Diagonal approximation requires the metric matrix $\mathbf{M}$ to be diagonal, thus it consists of only d parameters to learn, instead of $d \times d$. It indeed shrinks the number of parameters to learn, but also ignores the feature-feature interaction and might harm the expressiveness of the model.

Dimensionality reduction using PCA as a preprocessing step is a common way to deal with high dimensional data. However, it does not always work satisfactorily, especially when the data set does not have an apparent intrinsic low dimensional structure. It usually fails to perform well for those data sets.

Shaw *et al.* (2011) suggested a low-rank decomposition to scale up distance metric learning. The idea is to decompose $\mathbf{M}$ into $\mathbf{L}^\intercal\mathbf{L}$, where $\mathbf{L}$ is a $r \times d$ matrix and $r \ll d$ is a predefined low-rank degree. This approach reduces computational cost but results in a non-convex problem that suffers from local minima. Previously, low-rank decomposition has been proposed for other machine learning problems. For example, Rennie *et al.* (2005) applied it to scale up Maximum Margin Matrix Factorization (MMMF) (Srebro et al., 2004). Originally, MMMF was formulated as a convex semi-definite programming (SDP) problem and solved by a standard SDP solver, but it is no longer applicable for the non-convex low-rank decomposition. Therefore, they solved the non-convex problem by Conjugate Gradient (CG) (Fletcher and Reeves, 1964), but still there is no guarantee that CG will converge at a global minimum.

Our choice is to use *random projection* $\mathbf{L}^\intercal\mathbf{R}\mathbf{L}$, where $\mathbf{L}$ is a random $r \times d$ ($r \ll d$) matrix, with all of its element in $(0, 1)$. Random projection theory has been developed by Johnson and Lindenstrauss(1984). The theory shows that a set of n points in a high dimensional (d) Euclidean space can be mapped into a low-dimensional ($r \ll d$) Euclidean space such that the distance between any two points will be well-persevered (*i.e.*, changes by only a tiny factor ϵ if r is greater than a function of n and ϵ). Let $\mathbf{R}$ be a $r \times r$ PSD matrix to be learned from data. Distance between x_i and x_j becomes

$$D_R^{i,j} = (x_i - x_j)^\intercal \mathbf{L}^\intercal\mathbf{R}\mathbf{L}(x_i - x_j).$$

There are two possible strategies to generate a random projection matrix $\mathbf{L}$. One is completely random projection, where all elements are generated independently; the other one is orthonormal random projection, which requires that $\mathbf{L}_{r\times d}$ be a matrix with r orthonormal random column vectors. The Gram-Schmidt process (Golub and Van Loan, 1996) generates such a matrix, in which one starts by generating a random column and then the next columns, though generated randomly, too, must be orthonormal with regard to other columns. In both strategies, all of the elements must be in $(0, 1)$.

Consider $\mathbf{L}$ to be a matrix which compresses x_i with dimension d by $v_i = \mathbf{L}x_i$ with dimension r. Hence,

$$D_R^{i,j} = (v_i - v_j)^\intercal \mathbf{R}(v_i - v_j) \tag{1}$$

This distance metric can be learned by searching for $\mathbf{R}$ that minimizes the following objective function:

$$\mathcal{F}(\mathbf{R}) = \frac{1}{|S|} \sum_{(i,j,k)\in S} Z_+(D_R^{i,j} - D_R^{i,k} + \xi), \tag{2}$$

where $Z_+(x)$ is the hinge loss function. It can be shown that this new objective function is convex. As in Shaw *et al.*, the training examples are given as a hinge loss function over triplets.

$$S = \{(i,j,k)|\mathbf{A}_{ij} = 1, \mathbf{A}_{ik} = 0\}$$

is the set of all triplets where $\mathbf{A}$ is the adjacency matrix of $\mathbf{X}$. ξ is a predefined constant margin. The hinge loss function will penalize a candidate $\mathbf{R}$ when the resulting distance between x_i and x_j plus the margin is greater than the distance between x_i and x_k.

3.2 Intra and Inter-Class Distance

One challenge in distance metric learning is dealing with data sets that can be clustered into a large number of distinct classes. The hinge loss term in Eq. (2) does not consider this because it only keeps a margin of data points in one class against points in other classes. In our approach, we would like to learn a distance metric such that the entire set data points in the same class are close to each other and away from those in other classes. This idea is realized by adding additional regularization terms to the objective function. These new regularization terms are proved to be useful to handle problem domains where data points form a large number of mutually-exclusive classes.

The formula for intra-class distance regularization is given as

$$\mathcal{I}_1(\mathbf{R}) = \frac{1}{|S_1|} \sum_{(i,j)\in S_1} D_R^{i,j},\ S_1 = \{(i,j)|\mathbf{A}_{ij} = 1\}, \tag{3}$$

while the formulation for inter-class distance regularization is

$$\mathcal{I}_2(\mathbf{R}) = \frac{1}{|S_2|} \sum_{(i,k)\in S_2} D_R^{i,k},\ S_2 = \{(i,k)|\mathbf{A}_{ik} = 0\}. \tag{4}$$

3.3 Algorithm

Combining the regularization, the hinge loss, intra-class and the inter-class item, we get the complete objective function as Eq. (5).

$$\begin{aligned}\mathcal{F}(\mathbf{R}) = &\frac{\lambda}{2}\|\mathbf{R}\|_F^2 + \\ &\frac{1}{|S|} \sum_{(i,j,k)\in S} Z_+(D_R^{i,j} - D_R^{i,k} + \xi) \\ &+ \frac{1}{|S_1|} \sum_{(i,j)\in S_1} D_R^{i,j} - \frac{1}{|S_2|} \sum_{(i,k)\in S_2} D_R^{i,k}\end{aligned} \tag{5}$$

It is also possible to assign weights to terms above. According to Vandenberghe (1996), Eq. (5) can be expressed as a convex semidefinite programming problem. By construction, Eq. (5) can also be reformulated as an instance of PEGASOS algorithm, which basically employs a sub-gradient descent algorithm to optimize with a stochastic batch selection, and a smart step size selection. The sub-gradient of $\mathcal{F}$ in terms of $\mathbf{R}$ is then:

$$\begin{aligned}\nabla\mathcal{F} = &\lambda\mathbf{R} + \frac{1}{|S^+|} \sum_{(i,j,k)\in S^+} \mathbf{LXC}^{(i,j,k)}\mathbf{X}^\intercal\mathbf{L}^\intercal \\ &+ \frac{1}{|S_1|} \sum_{(i,j)\in S)1} \mathbf{LXC_1}^{(i,j)}\mathbf{X}^\intercal\mathbf{L}^\intercal \\ &- \frac{1}{|S_2|} \sum_{(i,k)\in S_2} \mathbf{LXC_2}^{(i,k)}\mathbf{X}^\intercal\mathbf{L}^\intercal, \\ S^+ = &\{(i,j,k)|D_R^{i,j} + \xi - D_R^{i,k} > 0\}\end{aligned} \tag{6}$$

Here the sparse symmetric matrix $\mathbf{C}$ is defined such that

$$\mathbf{C}_{jj}^{(i,j,k)} = \mathbf{C}_{ik}^{(i,j,k)} = \mathbf{C}_{ki}^{(i,j,k)} = 1,$$
$$\mathbf{C}_{ij}^{(i,j,k)} = \mathbf{C}_{ji}^{(i,j,k)} = \mathbf{C}_{kk}^{(i,j,k)} = -1,$$

and zero elsewhere. Similarly, $\mathbf{C_1}$ is given by

$$\mathbf{C_1}_{ii}^{(i,j)} = \mathbf{C_1}_{jj}^{(i,j)} = 1,$$
$$\mathbf{C_1}_{ij}^{(i,j)} = \mathbf{C_1}_{ji}^{(i,j)} = -1,$$

and zero elsewhere. $\mathbf{C_2}$ is

$$\mathbf{C_2}_{ii}^{(i,k)} = \mathbf{C_2}_{kk}^{(i,k)} = 1,$$
$$\mathbf{C_2}_{ik}^{(i,k)} = \mathbf{C_2}_{ki}^{(i,k)} = -1,$$

and zero elsewhere. It is easy to verify that

$$tr(\mathbf{C}^{(i,j,k)}\mathbf{X}^\intercal\mathbf{L}^\intercal\mathbf{RLX}) = D_R^{i,j} - D_R^{i,k}.$$

The derivation is from (Petersen and Pedersen, 2006):

$$\frac{\partial tr(\mathbf{C}^{(i,j,k)}\mathbf{X}^\intercal\mathbf{L}^\intercal\mathbf{RLX})}{\partial\mathbf{R}} = \mathbf{LXC}^{(i,j,k)}\mathbf{X}^\intercal\mathbf{L}^\intercal$$

Using the same method for intra-class and inter-class terms, the subgradient of $\mathcal{F}$ at $\mathbf{R}$ can be derived as

$$\begin{aligned}\nabla\mathcal{F} = \lambda\mathbf{R} + \mathbf{LX}\Bigg(&\sum_{(i,j,k)\in S^+} \mathbf{C}^{(i,j,k)} \\ &+ \frac{1}{|S_1|} \sum_{(i,j)\in S_1} \mathbf{C_1}^{(i,j)} \\ &- \frac{1}{|S_2|} \sum_{(i,k)\in S_2} \mathbf{C_2}^{(i,k)}\Bigg)\mathbf{X}^\intercal\mathbf{L}^\intercal.\end{aligned} \tag{7}$$

According to the PEGASOS algorithm, instead of using all elements in S, S_1 and S_2 to optimize $\mathcal{F}(\mathbf{R})$, we randomly sample subsets of S, S_1 and S_2 with size of B, B_1 and B_2 in each iteration. The full detail of the algorithm is given as procedure LEARN_METRIC.

```
procedure LEARN_METRIC(A ∈ 𝔹^{n×n}, X ∈ 𝔹^{n×d}, λ, S, S_1, S_2, B, B_1, B_2, T, ξ)
    L ← rand(r, d)
    R_1 ← zeros(r, r)
    for t ← 1 − T do
        η_t ← 1/(λt)
        C, C_1, C_2 ← zeros(n, n)
        for b ← 1 to B do
            (i, j, k) ← Sample from S
            if D_R^{i,j} − D_R^{i,k} + ξ ≥ 0 then
                C_jj ← C_jj + 1, C_ik ← C_ik + 1
                C_ki ← C_ki + 1, C_ij ← C_ij + 1
                C_ji ← C_ji + 1, C_kk ← C_kk + 1
            end if
        end for
        for b ← 1 to B_1 do
            (i, j) ← Sample from S_1
            C_{1,ii} ← C_{1,ii} + 1, C_{1,jj} ← C_{1,jj} + 1
            C_{1,ij} ← C_{1,ij} − 1, C_{1,ji} ← C_{1,ji} − 1
        end for
        for b ← 1 to B_2 do
            (i, k) ← Sample from S_2
            C_{2,ii} ← C_{2,ii} + 1, C_{2,kk} ← C_{2,kk} + 1
            C_{2,ik} ← C_{2,ik} − 1, C_{2,ki} ← C_{2,ki} − 1
        end for
        ∇_t ← λR + LX(C + C_1 − C_2)XᵀLᵀ
        R_{t+1} ← R_t − η_t ∇_t
        R_{t+1} ← [R_{t+1}]^+ Optional PSD projection
    end for
    return L, R_T
end procedure
```

4 Experimental Results

We applied our approach in two different problem domains. One involves a small amount of data points with moderately high dimensions (more than 1,000 and less than 10,000); the other involves a large number of data points with very high dimensions (more than 10,000). The results show that our approach can perform well in both cases.

4.1 Wikipedia Articles

In this domain, the goal is to predict semantic distances between Wikipedia documents about "Search Engine" and "Philosophy Concept". The data sets are available from Shaw *et al.* (2011). They manually labeled these pages to decide which pages should be linked, and extracted bag-of-words features from Web documents after preprocessing steps. Each data set forms a sub-network of all related documents.

The problem here is to learn the metric matrices $\mathbf{L}^\intercal\mathbf{R}\mathbf{L}$ according to the sub-network described above. The random projection matrix $\mathbf{L}$ was randomly initialized in the beginning and $\mathbf{R}$ was obtained by optimization, as described in Section 3.

Tables 1 shows the statistics about the Wikipedia documents data sets.

Table 1: Wikipedia pages dataset

Data set	n	m	d
Search Engine	269	332	6695
Philosophy Concept	303	921	6695

In this table, n denotes the number of data points, m, the number of edges, and d, feature dimensionality.

We split this data set $80/20$ for training and testing, where 20% of the nodes are randomly chosen for evaluations. The remaining 80% of data were used in a five-fold cross-validation to select the best performing hyper-parameters, *e.g.*, λ in Eq. (5). We then trained the model with these hyper-parameters.

With the held-out evaluation data, we applied the learned distance metric to compute the distance between each pair of data points. Then we ranked all distances and measured the quality of ranking using the Receiver Operator Characteristic (ROC) curve. The area under the curve (AUC) was then used to compare the performance of various algorithms.

The list below shows the alternatives of the objective functions used in the algorithms compared in the experiment. Note that HL denotes the hinge loss term, parameterized by either $\mathbf{M}$, the full-rank metric matrix, $\mathbf{L}$, the low-rank approximation matrix, or $\mathbf{R}$, dimensionally-reduced metric matrix after random projection. $\mathcal{I}_1$ denotes the intra-class distances as given in Eq. (3) and $\mathcal{I}_2$ inter-class distances in Eq. (4). Algorithms A, B, C and D are diagonal approximation. Algorithm E implements the low rank decomposition with reduced dimension $r = 300$. Algorithms F, G, H, and I are variations of our approach with combinations of random projection and/or intra/inter-class regularization. The reduced dimension of the new feature space was also 300 and $\mathbf{R}$ is a full matrix. Algorithm J uses PCA to reduce the dimension to 300 and $\mathbf{M}$ here is a full matrix.

In all algorithms, elements in the random projection matrix $\mathbf{L}$ were generated at random independently except for algorithm L, where $\mathbf{L}$ was generated such that its columns are orthonormal.

A $\frac{\lambda}{2}||\mathbf{M}||_F^2 + HL(\mathbf{M})$

B $\frac{\lambda}{2}||\mathbf{M}||_F^2 + HL(\mathbf{M}) + \mathcal{I}_1(\mathbf{M})$

C $\frac{\lambda}{2}||\mathbf{M}||_F^2 + HL(\mathbf{M}) - \mathcal{I}_2(\mathbf{M})$

D $\frac{\lambda}{2}||\mathbf{M}||_F^2 + HL(\mathbf{M}) + \mathcal{I}_1(\mathbf{M}) - \mathcal{I}_2(\mathbf{M})$

E $\frac{\lambda}{2}||\mathbf{L}||_F^2 + HL(\mathbf{L})$

F $\frac{\lambda}{2}||\mathbf{R}||_F^2 + HL(\mathbf{R})$

G $\frac{\lambda}{2}||\mathbf{R}||_F^2 + HL(\mathbf{R}) + \mathcal{I}_1(\mathbf{R})$

H $\frac{\lambda}{2}||\mathbf{R}||_F^2 + HL(\mathbf{R}) - \mathcal{I}_2(\mathbf{R})$

I $\frac{\lambda}{2}||\mathbf{R}||_F^2 + HL(\mathbf{R}) + \mathcal{I}_1(\mathbf{R}) - \mathcal{I}_2(\mathbf{R})$

J $\frac{\lambda}{2}||\mathbf{M}||_F^2 + HL(\mathbf{M})$ (PCA dimension reduction)

L $\frac{\lambda}{2}||\mathbf{R}||_F^2 + HL(\mathbf{R}) + \mathcal{I}_1(\mathbf{R})$ (orthonormal projection)

Table 2: Performance Comparison on Wikipedia Documents

	Search Engine	Philosophy Concept
A	0.7297	0.6935
B	0.6169	0.5870
C	0.5817	0.6808
D	0.6198	0.6704
E*	0.6952	0.4832
F	0.6962	0.6849
G	**0.7909**	**0.7264**
H	0.5744	0.6903
I	0.5984	0.6966
J	0.3509	0.4525
L	**0.7939**	**0.7174**

* Algorithm E performed unstably in this experiment even when all initial hyper-parameters were the same.

The running time for combined training and evaluation for A, B, C, D was around 15 seconds(s), for E about 300s, for F, G, H and I 200s and J 300s. All ran on a MacBook Pro notebook computer with 8GB of memory. Learning full-rank $\mathbf{M}$ is impossible because it ran out of memory.

Table 2 shows that algorithm G performs better than others in terms of the AUC metric, suggesting that the distances of two points in the same class is likely to be small and similar to some degree while the ones in the different classes vary a lot, as we speculated. Algorithm A also performs well probably because the bag-of-words features tend to be independent of each other and lack for word-to-word (feature-to-feature) interactions. As a result, diagonal approximation is sufficient to model the semantic similarity here. The low rank approximation algorithm E is unstable. Different trial runs resulted in drastically different AUCs. The AUC reported here is the best observed, but still not the best compared to other algorithms. In contrast, random projection algorithms rarely suffer this problem. PCA with dimensionality reducing to 300 hurt the performance significantly. This might be because there is too much information loss for such a low dimensionality, compared to the original one. However, using random $\mathbf{L}$ to project the feature vectors to 300 dimensions did not seem to have the same problem, according our results of algorithm F.

Comparing different strategies to generate the random projection matrix $\mathbf{L}$, we found that algorithms F and L basically performs similarly, yet variations of the performance of algorithm F in different trials are slightly higher than L, though the variations for both algorithms are negligible.

4.2 Phenotype Similarity

The second dataset comes from a project supported by NIH, with the objective of matching semantically related phenotype variables across studies. For training, phenotype variables that are semantically similar are categorized to be in the same class. The data set that we used here contained annotated data from the harmonization effort in the CARe (the Candidate Gene Association Resource) consortium, led by Prof. Leslie Lange from the University of North Carolina. This data set is comprised of 3,700 phenotypes that were manually classified into 160 categories. We note that previous works in distance metric learning usually used test data sets with less than 30 classes or categories.

A phenotype variable is given as a tuple of a condition description and an expert-assigned category. For example

1. ⟨`Forced Vital ...`
   `... Capacity (Litres),`
   `Forced Expiratory Volume`⟩

2. ⟨`MAX MID-EXPIR'Y FLOW RATE ...`
   `... FR MAX CURVE,`
   `Forced Expiratory Volume`⟩

3. ⟨`Age at natural menopause,`
   `Menopause`⟩

If we regard condition descriptions as data points and expert-assigned categories as class labels, each tuple above can be considered to be a node with a label in a graph. Hence, nodes with the same labels should be a match (be linked) to form a semantic network. For example, phenotype 1 and 2 forms a match because they have the same category ``Forced Expiratory Volume.''

Previously, we applied the Maximum Entropy model (MaxEnt) to predict the match on pairs, which were labeled according to the annotated data by considering variables in the same category as semantically similar (*i.e.*, a match), and those across categories as dissimilar (Hsu et al., 2011). We extracted features from each pair, such as whether a keyword appear in both phenotype descriptions, and trained a MaxEnt model to predict whether a given pair is a match. To evaluate the performance, we split variables into training and test sets and paired variables within each set as the training and test data sets.

After careful observation of the descriptions of the phenotype variables, we found that they are in general short and non-standardized. To standardize them, and detect their semantic similarity, we expanded the descriptions using UMLS (Unified Medical Language System, `http://www.nlm.nih.gov/research/umls/`). We search UMLS with a series of n-grams constructed from the variable descriptions. For example, for a variable description: "Age Diagnosed Coronary Bypass". The n-gram words will be "age diagnosed coronary bypass", "age diagnosed coronary", "diagnosed coronary bypass", "age diagnosed", "diagnosed coronary", "coronary bypass". We query UMLS for concepts corresponding to these n-grams. The definitions thus returned are appended to the original variable description. We reused the feature set described in (Hsu et al., 2008) for the BioCreative 2 Gene Mention Tagging task, but removed all char-gram features. This features set was carefully designed and proved to be effective for the gene mention tagging task, but results in a very high dimensional data set. Note that this feature set is different from the one used in our previous work (Hsu et al., 2011).

To make the configurations of our experiment exactly comparable with what described in Sharma *et al.* (2012), we modified the algorithms to be pairwise oriented. We randomly divided the annotated phenotype variable description data into three folds and created pairs for this experiment. The statistics of these folds is shown in Table 3. We trained our models on connected and disconnected training pairs in two folds and then evaluated with the pairs in the other fold. Again, after we used the trained model to predict the distances of all test pairs, we ranked them and compared the quality of the ranking using the ROC curves as described earlier. The evaluation metric is the average of their AUC scores for the three folds.

Table 3: Phenotype dataset

Fold	train+	train−	test+	test−
$Fold_1$	98,964	2,824,398	24,550	705,686
$Fold_2$	99,607	2,823,755	25,386	704,850
$Fold_3$	98,013	2,825,349	23,892	706,344

a. The number of data points is 2,484 and dimension here is 18,919.
b. In this table, train+ denotes number of connected (positive) pairs in training data, $train-$ number of disconnected (negative) pairs in training data, test+ number of connected pairs in testing data, test− number of disconnected pairs in testing data.

We compared algorithms A, E, G, H, I, J and L listed earlier with the same configurations except that the reduced dimensionality $r = 500$. Performance of the MaxEnt algorithm was also reported as K. Their AUC scores are shown in Table 4.

Training and evaluation processes took each fold for algorithm A around 500 seconds(s) , for algorithm E around 1400s , for algorithms F, G, H, I and L around 900s , for J 1400s, and for K 1200s.

The experimental results shows that random projection (algorithm F) outperformed diagonal approximation (algorithm A) by reserving feature-feature interactions with merely 500 dimensions, compared

Table 4: Performance Comparison on Phenotype Data

	AUC_1	AUC_2	AUC_3	AUC*
A	0.7668	0.7642	0.7627	0.7646
E*	0.9612	0.9617	0.9689	**0.9639**
F	0.8825	0.8953	0.8684	0.8820
G	0.9461	0.9545	0.9293	**0.9433**
H	0.7149	0.7272	0.7299	0.7240
I	0.8930	0.8888	0.8809	0.8876
J	0.7582	0.7357	0.7481	0.7473
K	0.8884	0.9107	0.8996	0.8996
L	0.9505	0.9580	0.9527	**0.9537**

$AUC_{1,2,3}$ denote the AUC performance of $Fold_{1,2,3}$ respectively. AUC* is the average AUC score.

* Results of algorithm E varied wildly in each running. For example, using $Fold_1$ with a fixed hyper-parameter setting, its AUC scores were 0.9612, 0.9301, 0.9017 and 0.8920 in different trails, respectively.

to the original dimensionality of nearly $19K$. Again, the best performer is algorithm G, which combines random projection with intra-class regularization. The intra-class term was beneficial but the inter-class term was not. One speculation is that the distance between data points in the same class may be confined in a small range while those in different classes may vary widely. Maximizing inter-class distance here might have distorted the learned feature space. The low rank decomposition (algorithm E) behaved unstably in this data sets. The result shown here is the best-chosen one. In fact, the non-convex low-rank decomposition results in drastically different AUC in each trial run. We speculate that the best result observed here is an overfitting. Diagonal approximation (algorithm A) and PCA (algorithm J) performed similarly, unlike the results for the Web documents.

Finally, when comparing different strategies to generate the random projection matrix **L**, we had the same conclusion as for the Wikipedia domain that orthonormal random projection (algorithm L) has a slight advantage in terms of low variations in different trials over completely indepndent random project (algorithm F).

5 Discussions and Future Work

We have proposed a convex, input-size free optimization algorithm for distance metric learning. This algorithm combines random projection and intra-class regularization that addresses the weaknesses presenting in the previous works. When the dimension d is in tens of thousands, as in many NLP and IR applications, **M** will be hundreds of millions in size, too large and intractable to handle for any existing approaches. Our approach addresses these issues, making the learning not only scalable, but also more accurate.

In the future, we will investigate theoretical properties that explain why the synergy of random projection and intra-class regularization works well and robust. We would also like to investigate how to use unlabeled data to regulate the learning to accomplish semi-supervised learning.

Acknowledgments

Research reported in this publication was supported in part by the National Human Genome Research Institute of the National Institutes of Health (NIH) under Award Number U01HG006894. The content is solely the responsibility of the authors and does not necessarily represent the official views of NIH.

References

John Blitzer, Kilian Q Weinberger, and Lawrence K Saul. 2005. Distance metric learning for large margin nearest neighbor classification. In *Advances in neural information processing systems*, pages 1473–1480.

Reeves Fletcher and Colin M Reeves. 1964. Function minimization by conjugate gradients. *The computer journal*, 7(2):149–154.

Jacob Goldberger, Sam Roweis, Geoff Hinton, and Ruslan Salakhutdinov. 2004. Neighbourhood components analysis.

G.H. Golub and C.F. Van Loan. 1996. *Matrix Computations*. Johns Hopkins Studies in the Mathematical Sciences. Johns Hopkins University Press.

Chun-Nan Hsu, Yu-Ming Chang, Cheng-Ju Kuo, Yu-Shi Lin, Han-Shen Huang, and I-Fang Chung. 2008. Integrating high dimensional bi-directional parsing models for gene mention tagging. *Bioinformatics*, 24(13):i286–i294.

Chun-Nan Hsu, Cheng-Ju Kuo, Congxing Cai, Sarah Pendergrass, Marylyn Ritchie, and Jose Luis Ambite.

2011. Learning phenotype mapping for integrating large genetic data. In *Proceedings of BioNLP 2011 Workshop*, pages 19–27, Portland, Oregon, USA, June. Association for Computational Linguistics.

William B Johnson and Joram Lindenstrauss. 1984. Extensions of lipschitz mappings into a hilbert space. *Contemporary mathematics*, 26(189-206):1.

Kaare Brandt Petersen and Michael Syskind Pedersen. 2006. The matrix cookbook.

Jasson DM Rennie and Nathan Srebro. 2005. Fast maximum margin matrix factorization for collaborative prediction. In *Proceedings of the 22nd international conference on Machine learning*, pages 713–719. ACM.

Shai Shalev-Shwartz, Yoram Singer, Nathan Srebro, and Andrew Cotter. 2011. Pegasos: Primal estimated subgradient solver for svm. *Mathematical Programming*, 127(1):3–30.

Shefali Sharma, Leslie Lange, Jose Luis Ambite, Yigal Arens, and Chun-Nan Hsu. 2012. Exploring label dependency in active learning for phenotype mapping. In *BioNLP: Proceedings of the 2012 Workshop on Biomedical Natural Language Processing*, pages 146–154, Montréal, Canada, June. Association for Computational Linguistics.

Blake Shaw, Bert Huang, and Tony Jebara. 2011. Learning a distance metric from a network. In *Advances in Neural Information Processing Systems*, pages 1899–1907.

Nathan Srebro, Jason Rennie, and Tommi S Jaakkola. 2004. Maximum-margin matrix factorization. In *Advances in neural information processing systems*, pages 1329–1336.

Lieven Vandenberghe and Stephen Boyd. 1996. Semidefinite programming. *SIAM review*, 38(1):49–95.

Eric P Xing, Michael I Jordan, Stuart Russell, and Andrew Ng. 2002. Distance metric learning with application to clustering with side-information. In *Advances in neural information processing systems*, pages 505–512.

Liu Yang and Rong Jin. 2006. Distance metric learning: A comprehensive survey. *Michigan State Universiy*, pages 1–51.

Graph-Based Unsupervised Learning of Word Similarities Using Heterogeneous Feature Types

Avneesh Saluja*
Carnegie Mellon University
avneesh@cmu.edu

Jiří Navrátil
IBM Research
jiri@us.ibm.com

Abstract

In this work, we propose a graph-based approach to computing similarities between words in an unsupervised manner, and take advantage of heterogeneous feature types in the process. The approach is based on the creation of two separate graphs, one for words and one for features of different types (alignment-based, orthographic, etc.). The graphs are connected through edges that link nodes in the feature graph to nodes in the word graph, the edge weights representing the importance of a particular feature for a particular word. High quality graphs are learned during training, and the proposed method outperforms experimental baselines.

1 Introduction

Data-driven approaches in natural language processing (NLP) have resulted in a marked improvement in a variety of NLP tasks, from machine translation to part-of-speech tagging. Such methods however, are generally only as good as the quality of the data itself. This issue becomes highlighted when there is a mismatch in domain between training and test data, in that the number of out-of-vocabulary (OOV) words increases, resulting in problems for language modeling, machine translation, and other tasks. An approach that specifically replaces OOV words with their synonyms from a restricted vocabulary (i.e., the words already contained in the training data) could alleviate this OOV word problem.

Vast ontologies that capture semantic similarities between words, also known as *WordNets*, have been carefully created and compiled by linguists for different languages. A WordNet-based solution could be implemented to fill the gaps when an OOV word is encountered, but this approach is not scalable in that it requires significant human effort for a number of languages in which the WordNet is limited or does not exist. Thus, a practical solution to this problem should ideally require as little human supervision and involvement as possible.

Additionally, words can be similar to each other due to a variety of reasons. For example, the similarity between the words *optimize* and *optimal* can be captured via the high orthographical similarity between the words. However, relying too much on a single feature type may result in false positives, e.g., suggestions of antonyms instead of synonyms. Valuable information can be gleaned from a variety of feature types, both monolingual and bilingual. Thus, any potential solution to an unsupervised or mildly supervised word similarity algorithm should be able to take into account *heterogeneous* feature types and combine them in a globally effective manner when yielding the final solution.

In this work, we present a graph-based approach to impute word similarities in an unsupervised manner and takes into account heterogeneous features. The key idea is to maintain two graphs, one for words and one for the all the features of different types, and attempt to promote concurrence between the two graphs in an effort to find a final solution. The similarity graphs learned during training are generally of high quality, and the testing approach proposed outperforms the chosen baselines.

*This work was done during the first author's internship at the IBM T.J. Watson Research Center, Yorktown Heights, NY in 2012.

2 Approach

The eventual goal is to compute the most similar word to a given OOV word from a restricted, pre-existing vocabulary. We propose a graph-based solution for this problem, relying on undirected graphs to represent words and features as well as the similarities between them. The solution can be broadly divided into two distinct sub-problems, the training and testing components.

2.1 Learning the Graph

The intuition of our approach is best expressed through a small example problem. Figure 1 shows an example graph of words (shaded) and features (unshaded). For exposition, let v_1 = optimize, v_2 = optimal, and v_3 = ideal, while f_1 = orth_|opti, i.e., an orthographic feature corresponding to the substring "opti" at the beginning of a word, and f_5 = align_idéal, i.e., a bilingual feature corresponding to the alignment of the word "optimal" to the French word "idéal" in the training data[1].

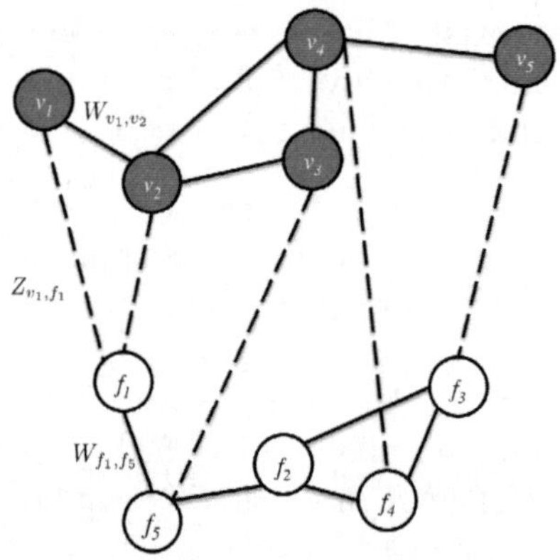

Figure 1: An example graph for explanatory purposes. The nodes in red constitute the word graph, and the nodes in white the feature graph.

There are three types of edges in this scenario. Edges between word nodes (e.g., W_{v_1,v_2}) represent word similarities, and edges between features (e.g., W_{f_1,f_5}) represent feature similarities. Edges between words and features (e.g., Z_{v_1,f_1}, the dashed lines) represent pertinent or active features for a given word when computing its similarity with other words, with the edge weight reflecting the degree of importance.

We restrict the values of all similarities to be between 0 and 1, as negative-valued edges in undirected graphs are significantly more complicated and would make subsequent computations more intricate. In an ideal situation, the similarity matrices that represent the word and feature graphs should be positive semi-definite, which provides a nice probabilistic interpretation due to connections to covariance matrices of multivariate distributions, but this constraint is not enforced here. Future work will focus on improved optimization techniques that respect the positive semi-definiteness constraint.

2.1.1 Objective Function

To learn the graph, the following objective function is minimized:

$$\Omega(\mathbf{W}_\mathcal{V}, \mathbf{W}_\mathcal{F}, \mathbf{Z}) = \alpha_0 \sum_{f_p, f_q \in \mathcal{F}} (W_{f_p,f_q} - W^*_{f_p,f_q})^2 \quad (1)$$

$$+ \alpha_1 \sum_{v_i \in \mathcal{V}} \sum_{f_p \in \mathcal{F}} (Z_{v_i,f_p} - Z^*_{v_i,f_p})^2 \quad (2)$$

$$+ \alpha_2 \sum_{v_i,v_j \in \mathcal{V}} \sum_{f_p,f_q \in \mathcal{F}} Z_{v_i,f_p} Z_{v_j,f_q} (W_{v_i,v_j} - W_{f_p,f_q})^2 \quad (3)$$

$$+ \alpha_3 \sum_{v_i,v_j \in \mathcal{V}} \sum_{f_p,f_q \in \mathcal{F}} W_{v_i,v_j} W_{f_p,f_q} (Z_{v_i,f_p} - Z_{v_j,f_q})^2 \quad (4)$$

where W_{f_p,f_q} is the current similarity between feature f_p and feature f_q (with corresponding initial value $W^*_{f_p,f_q}$), W_{v_i,v_j} is the current similarity between word v_i and word v_j, Z_{v_i,f_p} is the current importance weight of feature f_p for word v_i (with corresponding initial value $Z^*_{v_i,f_p}$), and α_0 to α_3 are parameters (that sum to 1) which represent the importance of a given term in the objective function.

The intuition of the objective function is straightforward. The first two terms correspond to minimizing the ℓ_2-norm between the initial and current values of W_{f_p,f_q} and Z_{v_i,f_p} (for further details on initialization, see Section 2.1.2). The intuition behind the third term is to minimize the difference between the word similarity of words v_i and v_j and the feature similarity of features f_p and f_q in proportion to how important those features are for words v_i and v_j respectively. If two features have high importance weights for two words, and those features are very similar to each other, then the corresponding words should also be similar. The fourth term has a similar rationale, in that it minimizes the difference between importance weights in proportion to the similarities. In other words, we attempt to promote parameter concurrence between the word and feature

[1]such word alignments can be extracted through standard word alignment algorithms applied to a parallel corpus in two different languages.

graphs, which in turn ensures smoothness over the two graphs.

The basic idea of minimizing two quantities of the graph in proportion to their link strength has been used before, for example (but not limited to) graph-based semi-supervised learning and label propagation (Zhu et al., 2003) where the concept is applied to node labels (as opposed to edge weights as presented in this work). In such methods, the idea is to ensure that the function varies smoothly over the graph (Zhou et al., 2004), i.e., to promote parameter concurrence *within* a graph, whereas we promote parameter concurrence *across* two graphs. In that sense, the α parameters as control the trade-off between respecting initial values vs. achieving consistency between the two graphs.

While not necessary, we decided to tie the parameters together, such that α_0 and α_2 (representing feature similarity preference for initial values vs. preference for consistency) sum to 0.5, and α_1 and α_3 sum to 0.5 as well, implicitly giving equal weight to feature similarities and importance weights. In the future, a more appropriate method of learning these α parameters will be explored.

2.1.2 Initialization

In many unsupervised algorithms, e.g., EM, the initialization of parameters is of paramount importance, as these initial values guide the algorithm in its attempt to minimize a proposed objective function. In our problem, initial estimates for word similarities do not exist (otherwise the problem would be considerably easier!). Instead, word similarities are seeded from the initial feature similarities and initial importance weights, and all three quantities are then iteratively refined.

The initial importance weight values are computed from the co-occurrence statistics between words and features, by taking the geometric mean of the conditional probabilities (feature given word and word given feature) in both directions: $Z^*_{v_i,f_p} = \sqrt{\mathbb{P}(v_i|f_p)\mathbb{P}(f_p|v_i)}$. For the initial feature similarity values, the pointwise mutual information (PMI) vector for each feature is first computed, by taking the log ratio of the joint probability with each word to the marginal probabilities of the feature and the word (also done through the co-occurrence statistics). Subsequently, the initial similarity is then computed as the normalized dot product between feature vectors: $\frac{\text{PMI}_{f_p} \cdot \text{PMI}_{f_q}}{\|\text{PMI}_{f_p}\|\|\text{PMI}_{f_q}\|}$.

After computing the initial feature similarity and weights matrices, we remove features that are densely connected in the feature similarity graph by trimming high entropy features (normalizing edge weights and treating the resulting values as a probability distribution). This pruning was done in order to speed up the optimization procedure, and we found that results were not affected by pruning away the top one percentile of features sorted by entropy.

2.1.3 Optimization

The objective function (Equations 1 to 4) is convex and differentiable with respect to the individual variables W_{v_i,v_j}, W_{f_p,f_q}, and Z_{v_i,f_p}. Hence, one way to minimize it is to evaluate the derivatives of the objective function with respect to these variables, set to 0 and solve. The final update equations are provided in the Appendix.

The entire training pipeline is captured in Figure 2. We first compute the word similarities from the initial feature similarities and importance weights, and then update those values in turn, based on the alternating minimization method (Csiszár and Tusnády, 1984). The process is repeated till convergence.

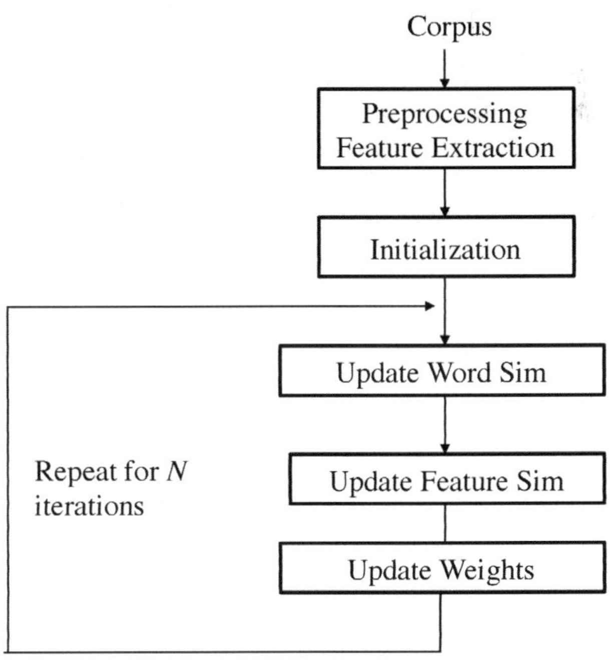

Figure 2: Flowchart for the training pipeline described in Section 2.1.3. The number of iterations N is determined beforehand.

2.2 Link Prediction

Given a learned word similarity graph (along with a learned feature similarity graph and the edges between the two graphs) and an OOV word with associated features, the proposed solution should also generate a list of synonyms. In a graph-based setting, this is analogous to the link prediction problem: given a graph and a new node that needs to be embedded in the graph, which links, or edges, do we add between the new node and all the existing ones?

We experimented with two different approaches for link prediction. The first computes word similarities in the same manner as in training, as per Equation 5. However, since the learned importance weights Z_{v_i,f_p} (or Z_{v_j,f_q}) are specific to a given word, importance weights for the OOV word are initialized in the same manner as in Section 2.1.2 for the words in the training data. Thus, for a given OOV word, we obtain word similarities with all words in the vocabulary through Equation 5, and output the most similar words by this metric.

The second method is based on a random walk approach, similar to (Kok and Brockett, 2010), wherein a probabilistic interpretation is imposed on the graphs by row-normalizing all of the matrices involved (word similarity, feature similarity, and importance weights), implying that the transition probability, say from node v_i to v_j, is proportional to the similarity between the two nodes. For this approach, only the *active* features for a given OOV word, i.e., the features that have at least one non-zero Z edge between the feature and a word, are used (see Section 2.3 for more details on active and inactive features). First, M random walks are initialized from each active feature node, each walk of maximum length T. For every walk, the number of steps needed to hit a word node in the word similarity graph for the first time is recorded. After averaging across the M runs, we need to average the hitting times across all of the active features, which is done by weighting the hitting times of each active feature f^* by $\sum_{v_i} Z_{v_i,f^*}$, i.e., the sum across all rows of a given feature (represented by a column) in the importance weights matrix.

The random walk-based approach introduces three new parameters: M, the number of random walks per active feature, T, the maximum length of each random walk, and β, a parameter that controls how often a random walk should take a Z edge (thereby transitioning from one graph to the other) or a W edge (thereby staying within the same graph). If a node has both Z and W edges, then β is the parameter for a simple Bernoulli distribution that samples whether to take one type of edge or the other; if the node has only one type of edge, then the walk traverses only that type.

2.3 Sparsification

There is a crucial point regarding Equations 1 to 4, namely that restricting the inputted values to between 0 and 1 does not guarantee that the resulting similarity or weight value will also be between 0 and 1, due to the difference in terms in the numerator of the equations. In order to bypass this problem, a projection step is employed subsequent to an update, wherein the value obtained is projected into the correct part of the n-dimensional Euclidean space, namely the positive orthant. Although slightly more involved in the multidimensional case, i.e., where $n > 1$, since the partial derivatives as computed in Equations 5 to 7 are with respect to a single element, orthant projection in the unidimensional case amounts to nothing more than setting the value to 0 if it is less than 0. This effectively sparsifies the resulting matrix, and is similar to the soft-thresholding effect that comes about due to ℓ_1-norm regularization. Further exploration of this link is left to future work.

However, the sparsification of the graphs/matrices is problematic for the random walk-based approach, in that an OOV word may consist of features that are all *inactive*, i.e., none of the features have a non-zero Z edge to the word similarity graph. In this case, we cannot compute which words in our vocabulary are similar to the OOV word. One method to alleviate this drawback is to add back Z edges that were removed during training with their initial weights. Yet, we found that adding back all of the features for a test word was worse than filtering out the features with the highest entropy (i.e., with the most edges to other features) out of the features to add back. The latter approach was thus adopted and is the setup used in Section 3.5.

3 Experiments & Results

In our experiments, we looked at both the quality of the similarity graphs learned from the data, as well as the performance of the link prediction techniques.

Corpus	Sentences	Words
EuroParl+ NewsComm (Train)	1.64 million+	40.6 million+
WMT2010 (Test)	2034	44,671

Table 1: Corpus statistics for the datasets used in evaluation.

3.1 Dataset

Table 1 summarizes the statistics of the training and test sets used. We used the standard WMT 2010 evaluation dataset, and the training data consists of a combination of European Parliament and news commentary bitext, while the test set is from the news domain. Note that a parallel corpus is not needed as only the English side is used. While the current experiment is restricted to English, any language can be used in principle.

3.2 Features

During the feature extraction phase, we first filtered the 30 most common words from the corpus and do not extract features for those words. However, these common words are still used when extracting distributional features. The following features are used:

- Orthographic: all substrings of length 3, 4, and 5 for a given word are extracted. For example, the feature "orth_|opt", corresponding to the substring "opt" at the beginning of a word, would be extracted from the word "optimal".

- Distributional (a.k.a., contextual): for a given word, we extract the word immediately preceding and succeeding it as well as words within a window of 5. These features are extracted from a corpus without the 30 most common words filtered. An example of such a feature is "LR_the+cost", representing an instance of a preceding and succeeding word for "optimal", extracted from the phrase "the optimal cost". Lastly, all distributional features that occur less than 5 times are removed.

- Part-of-Speech (POS): for example, "pos_JJ" is a POS feature extracted for the word "optimal".

- Alignment (a.k.a., bilingual): alignment features are extracted from alignment matrices across languages. For every word, we filter all words in the target language (treating English, our working language, as the source) that have a lexical probability less than half the maximum lexical probability, and use the resulting aligned words as features. For example, "align_idéal" would be a feature for the word "optimal", since the French word "idéal" is aligned (with high probability) to the word "optimal". Note that the assumption during test time is that alignment features are not available for OOV words; if they were, then the word would not be OOV. Nonetheless, alignment information can be utilized indirectly in the link prediction stage from random walk traversals of in-vocabulary nodes.

Statistics on the number of features broken down by type are presented in Table 2, for 3 different vocabulary sizes. In the experiments, we concentrated on the 10,000 and 50,000 size vocabularies.

3.3 Baselines

When selecting the baselines, we had two goals in mind. Firstly, we wanted to compare the proposed approach against simpler alternatives for generating word similarities. The baselines were also chosen so as to correspond in some way to the various feature types, since a main advantage of our approach is that it effectively combines various feature types to yield global word similarity scores. This choice of baselines also provides insight into the impact of the various feature types chosen; the idea is that a baseline corresponding to a particular feature type would be indicative of word similarity performance using just that type. Three baselines were initially selected:

- Distributional: a PMI vector is computed for each word over the various distributional features. The inner product of two PMI vectors is computed to evaluate the similarity of two words. We found that this baseline performed poorly relative to the other ones, and thus decided not to include it in the final evaluation.

- Orthographic: based on a simple edit distance-based approach, where all words within an edit distance of 25% of the length of the test word are retrieved.

- Alignment: we compose the alignment matrices in both directions to generate an English to English matrix (using German as the pivot language), from which the three most similar

Vocabulary	Words	Features	Alignment	Distributional	Orthographic	POS
Full	93,011	780,357	325,940	206,253	248,114	50
50k-vocab	50,000	569,890	222,701	204,266	142,873	50
10k-vocab	10,000	301,555	61,792	199,256	40,457	50

Table 2: Statistics on the number of features extracted based on the number of words, broken down by feature type. Note that the distributional features are only those with count 5 and above.

words (as per the lexical probabilities in the matrices) are extracted.

3.4 Evaluation

Automatic evaluation of an algorithm that computes similarities between words is tricky. The judgment on whether two words are synonyms is still done best by a human, requiring significant manual effort. Therefore, during the experimentation and parameter selection process we developed an intermediate form of evaluation wherein a human annotator assisted in creating a pseudo "ground truth". Prior to creating the ground truth, all OOV words in the test set were identified (i.e., no match in our vocabulary), resulting in 978 OOV words. Named entities were then manually filtered, resulting in a final test set of 312 words for evaluation purposes.

To create the ground truth, we generated for each test OOV word a set of possible synonyms using the alignment and orthographic baselines, as per Section 3.3. Naturally, many of the words generated were not legitimate synonyms; human evaluators thus removed all words that were not synonyms or near synonyms, ignoring mild grammatical inconsistencies, like singular vs. plural. Generally, a synonym was considered valid if substituting the word with the synonym preserved meaning in a sentence.

The final evaluation was performed by a human evaluator. The two baselines and the proposed approach generated the top three synonym candidates for a given OOV test word and both 1-best and 3-best results were evaluated (as in Table 3). Final performance was evaluated using precision and recall. Recall is defined as the percentage of words for which at least one synonym was generated, and precision evaluates the number of correct synonyms from the ones generated.

3.5 Results

Figure 3 looks at the neighborhood of words around the word "guardian". Note that while only two different α parameter configurations are compared in

Test Word	Synonym 1	Synonym 2	Synonym 3
pubescent	puberty	adolescence	nanotubes
sportswoman	sportswomen	athlete	draftswoman
briny	salty	saline	salinity

Table 3: Example of the annotation task. The suggested synonyms are real output from our algorithm.

the figure, we investigated a variety of settings and found that $\alpha_0 = 0.3, \alpha_1 = 0.4, \alpha_2 = 0.2, \alpha_3 = 0.1$ worked best from a final evaluation perspective.

The first point to note is that the graph in Figure 3b is generally more dense than that of Figure

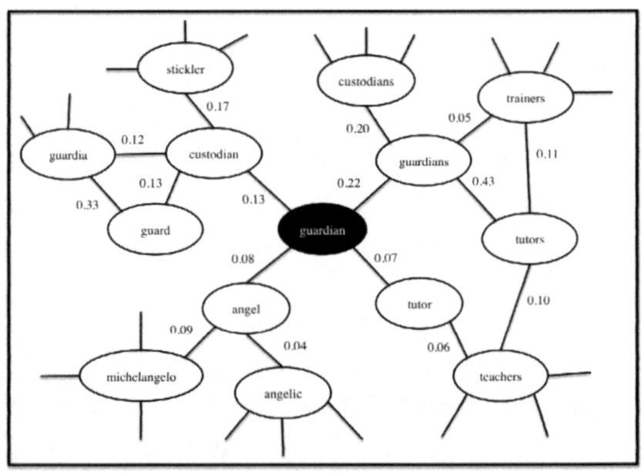

(a) $\alpha_0 = 0.3, \alpha_1 = 0.4, \alpha_2 = 0.2, \alpha_3 = 0.1$

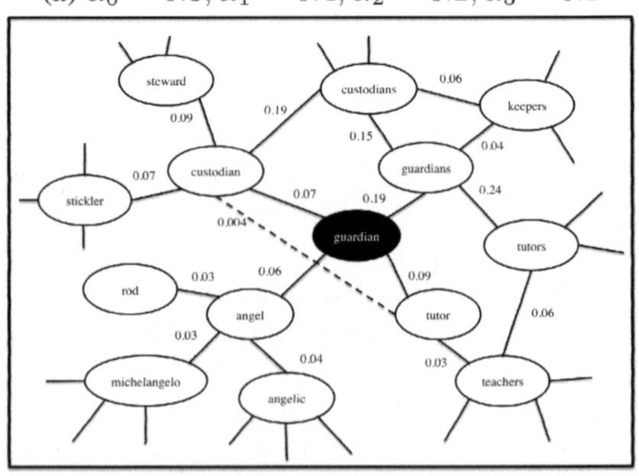

(b) $\alpha_0 = 0.4, \alpha_1 = 0.4, \alpha_2 = 0.1, \alpha_3 = 0.1$

Figure 3: A snapshot of a portion of the learned graph for two different parameter settings. The graph in 3b is more dense.

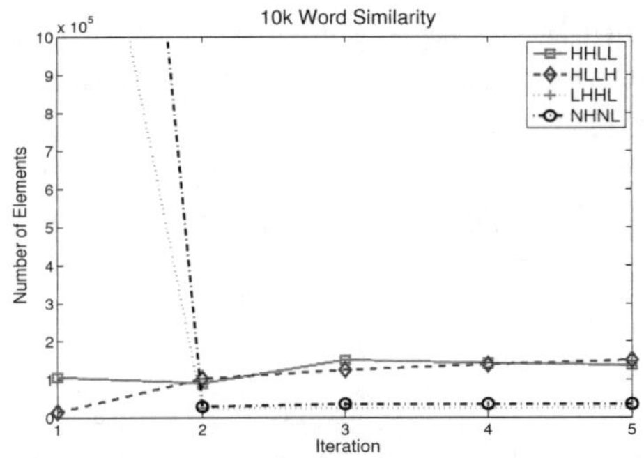

(a) Word similarity matrix sparsity

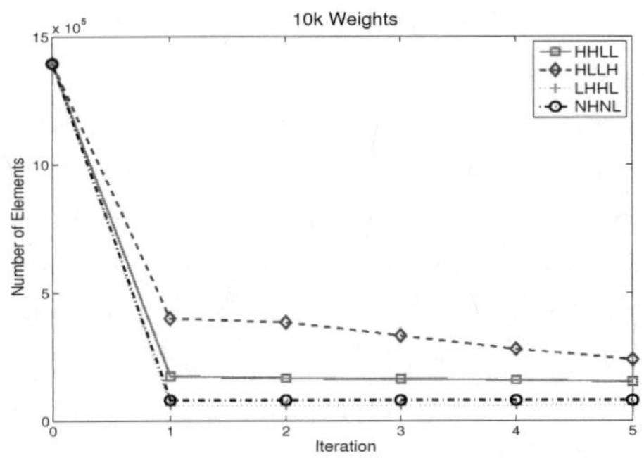

(b) Weights matrix sparsity

Figure 4: Word similarity and weights matrices sparsities for 10,000-word vocabulary.

Configuration	α_0	α_1	α_2	α_3
HHLL	0.4	0.4	0.1	0.1
NHNL	0.3	0.4	0.2	0.1
HLLH	0.4	0.1	0.1	0.4
LHHL	0.1	0.4	0.4	0.1

Table 4: Legend for the charts in Figures 4 and 5. H corresponds to "high", L to "low", and N to "neutral".

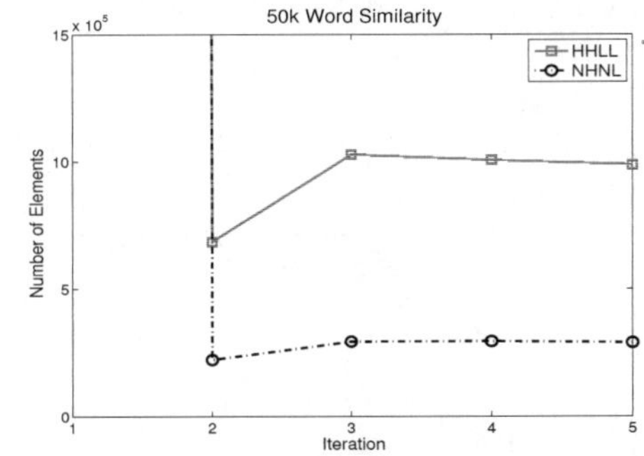

(a) Word similarity matrix sparsity

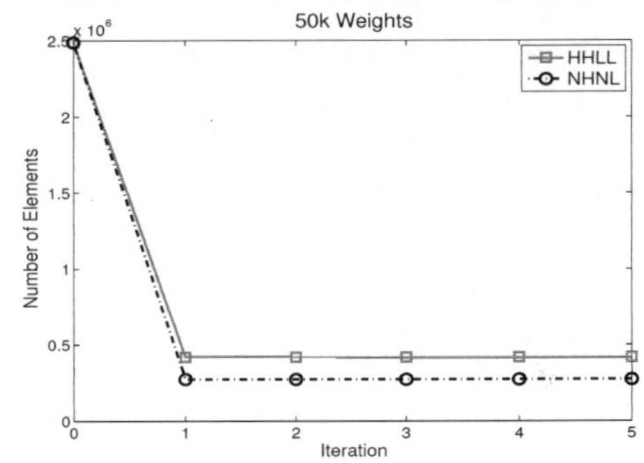

(b) Weights matrix sparsity

Figure 5: Word similarity and weights matrices sparsities for 50,000-word vocabulary.

3a. For example, Figure 3b contains an edge between "custodian" and "custodians", whereas Figure 3a does not. In the latter graph, there is a higher preference for smoothness over the graph and thus the idea is that "custodian" and "custodians" are linked via the smooth transition "custodian" $\rightarrow$ "guardian" $\rightarrow$ "guardians" $\rightarrow$ "custodians", whereas in the former, there is a higher preference to respect the initial values, which generates this additional edge. We also observed weak edges between words like "custodian" and "tutor" in Figure 3b but not in Figure 3a. The effect of the parameters on the sparsity of the graph is definitely apparent, but generally the learned graphs are of high quality. A further analysis reveals that for many of the words in the corpus, the highest weighted features are usually alignment features; their heavy use allows the algorithm to produce interesting synonym candidates, and emphasizes the importance of bilingual features.

To underscore the point regarding impact of parameters on graph sparsity, Figures 4 and 5 present the number of elements in the resulting word similarity and weights matrices (graphs) vs. iteration for vocabulary sizes of 10,000 and 50,000 respectively, with Table 4 providing a legend to the curves in those figures. Higher α weights for terms 1 and 2 in the objective function result in less sparse solutions. The density of the matrices also drops drastically after a few iterations and stabilizes thereafter.

Lastly, Tables 5 and 6 present the final results of the evaluation, as assessed by a human evaluator, on the 312 OOV words in the test set. While the results on the 1-best front are marginally better than the edit distance-based baseline, 3-best the performance of our approach is comfortably better than the baselines. Testing was done with the word similarity update method.

The performance of the random walk-based link

Method	Precision	Recall	F-1
τ matrix	31.1%	67.0%	42.5%
orthographic	37.5%	92.3%	53.3%
50k-nhnl	37.2%	100%	**54.2%**

Table 5: 1-best evaluation results on WMT 2010 OOV words trained on a 50,000-word vocabulary. Our best approach ("50k-nhnl") is bolded

Method	Precision	Recall	F-1
τ matrix	96.7%	67.0%	79.1%
orthographic	89.9%	92.3%	91.1%
50k-nhnl	92.6%	100%	**96.2%**

Table 6: 3-best evaluation results on WMT 2010 OOV words trained on a 50,000-word vocabulary. Our best approach ("50k-nhnl") is bolded

prediction approach was sub-optimal for several reasons. Firstly, it was difficult to use the learned importance weights as is, since the resulting weights matrix was so sparse that many test words simply did not have active features. This issue resulted in the vanilla variant of the random walk approach to have very low recall. Therefore, we adopted a "mixed weights" strategy, where we selectively introduced a number of features previously inactive for a test word, not including the features that had high entropy. Yet in this case, the random walks get stuck traversing certain edges, and a good sampling of similar words was not properly achievable.

A general issue that arose during link prediction is that the orthographic features tend to dominate the candidate synonyms list since alignment features are not utilized. If instead we assume that alignment features are accessible during testing, then the random walk-based approaches do marginally better than the word similarity update method, but further investigation is warranted before drawing any definitive conclusions.

4 Related Work

We used the objective function and basic formulation of (Muthukrishnan et al., 2011), but corrected their derivation of the optimization and introduced methods to handle the resulting complications. In addition, (Muthukrishnan et al., 2011) implemented their approach on just one feature type and with far fewer nodes, since their word similarity graph was actually over documents and their feature similarity graph was over words. Recently, an alternative graph-based approach for the same problem was presented in (Minkov and Cohen, 2012). However, in addition to requiring a dependency parse of the corpus, the emphasis of that work is more on the testing side. Indeed, we can incorporate some of the ideas presented in that work to improve our link prediction during query time. The label propagation-based approaches of (Tamura et al., 2012; Razmara et al., 2013), wherein "seed distributions" are extracted from bilingual corpora and are propagated around a similarity graph, can also be easily integrated into our approach as a downstream method specific to machine translation.

Another approach to handle OOVs, particularly in the translation domain, is (Zhang et al., 2005), wherein the authors leveraged the web as an expanded corpus for OOV mining. If web access is unavailable however, then this method would not work.

The general problem of combining multiple views of similarity (i.e., across different feature types) can also be tackled through multiple kernel learning (MKL) (Bach et al., 2004). However, most of the work in this field has been on supervised MKL, whereas we required an unsupervised approach.

An area that has seen a recent resurgence in popularity is deep learning, especially in its applications to continuous embeddings. Embeddings of word distributions have been explored in (Mnih and Hinton, 2007; Turian et al., 2010; Weston et al., 2008).

Lastly, while not directly relevant to our work, the idea of using a graph-based framework to combine both monolingual and bilingual features was also presented in (Das and Petrov, 2011).

5 Conclusion & Future Work

In this work, we presented a graph-based approach to computing word similarities, based on dual word and feature similarity graphs, and the edges that go between the graphs, representing importance weights. We introduced an objective function that promotes parameter concurrence between the two graphs, and minimized this function with a simple alternating minimization-based approach. The resulting optimization recovers high quality word similarity graphs, primarily due to the bilingual features, and improves over the baselines during the link prediction stage.

In the future, on the training side we would like to optimize the proposed objective function in a better manner, while enforcing the positive semi-definiteness constraints. Other link prediction techniques should be explored, as the current techniques have pitfalls. Richer features that model more refined aspects can be introduced. In particular, features from a dependency parse of the data would be very useful in this situation.

References

Francis R. Bach, Gert R. G. Lanckriet, and Michael I. Jordan. 2004. Multiple kernel learning, conic duality, and the smo algorithm. In *Proceedings of the twenty-first international conference on Machine learning*, ICML '04.

I. Csiszár and G. Tusnády. 1984. Information geometry and alternating minimization procedures. *Statistics and Decisions*, Supplement Issue 1:205–237.

Dipanjan Das and Slav Petrov. 2011. Unsupervised part-of-speech tagging with bilingual graph-based projections. In *Proceedings of the 49th Annual Meeting of the Association for Computational Linguistics: Human Language Technologies - Volume 1*, HLT '11, pages 600–609.

Stanley Kok and Chris Brockett. 2010. Hitting the right paraphrases in good time. In *Human Language Technologies: The 2010 Annual Conference of the North American Chapter of the Association for Computational Linguistics*, HLT '10, pages 145–153.

Einat Minkov and William W. Cohen. 2012. Graph based similarity measures for synonym extraction from parsed text. In *TextGraphs-7: Graph-based Methods for Natural Language Processing*.

Andriy Mnih and Geoffrey Hinton. 2007. Three new graphical models for statistical language modelling. In *Proceedings of the 24th international conference on Machine learning*, ICML '07, pages 641–648.

Pradeep Muthukrishnan, Dragomir R. Radev, and Qiaozhu Mei. 2011. Simultaneous similarity learning and feature-weight learning for document clustering. In *TextGraphs-6: Graph-based Methods for Natural Language Processing*, pages 42–50.

Majid Razmara, Maryam Siahbani, Gholamreza Haffari, and Anoop Sarkar. 2013. Graph propagation for paraphrasing out-of-vocabulary words in statistical machine translation. In *Proceedings of the 51st Annual Meeting of the Association for Computational Linguistics*, ACL '13.

Akihiro Tamura, Taro Watanabe, and Eiichiro Sumita. 2012. Bilingual lexicon extraction from comparable corpora using label propagation. In *Proceedings of the 2012 Joint Conference on Empirical Methods in Natural Language Processing and Computational Natural Language Learning*, EMNLP-CoNLL '12, pages 24–36, Stroudsburg, PA, USA. Association for Computational Linguistics.

Joseph Turian, Lev Ratinov, and Yoshua Bengio. 2010. Word representations: a simple and general method for semi-supervised learning. In *Proceedings of the 48th Annual Meeting of the Association for Computational Linguistics*, ACL '10, pages 384–394.

Jason Weston, Frédéric Ratle, and Ronan Collobert. 2008. Deep learning via semi-supervised embedding. In *ICML*, pages 1168–1175.

Ying Zhang, Fei Huang, and Stephan Vogel. 2005. Mining translations of oov terms from the web through cross-lingual query expansion. In *Proceedings of the 28th annual international ACM SIGIR conference on Research and development in information retrieval*, SIGIR '05, pages 669–670.

Dengyong Zhou, Olivier Bousquet, Thomas Navin Lal, Jason Weston, and Bernhard Schölkopf. 2004. Learning with local and global consistency. In Sebastian Thrun, Lawrence Saul, and Bernhard Schölkopf, editors, *Advances in Neural Information Processing Systems 16*. MIT Press, Cambridge, MA.

Xiaojin Zhu, Z. Ghahramani, and John Lafferty. 2003. Semi-supervised learning using gaussian fields and harmonic functions. In *Proceedings of the Twentieth International Conference on Machine Learning (ICML-2003)*, volume 20, page 912.

A Final Equations for Parameter Updates

$$W_{v_i,v_j} = \frac{1}{C_1}\Bigg(\sum_{f_p,f_q\in\mathcal{F}} \alpha_2 Z_{v_i,f_p} Z_{v_j,f_q} W_{f_p,f_q} - \frac{\alpha_3}{2} W_{f_p,f_q}(Z_{v_i,f_p} - Z_{v_j,f_q})^2\Bigg) \tag{5}$$

$$W_{f_p,f_q} = \frac{1}{C_2}\Bigg(\sum_{v_i,v_j\in\mathcal{V}} \big(\alpha_2 Z_{v_i,f_p} Z_{v_j,f_q} W_{v_i,v_j} - \frac{\alpha_3}{2} W_{v_i,v_j}(Z_{v_i,f_p} - Z_{v_j,f_q})^2\big) + \alpha_0 W^*_{f_p,f_q}\Bigg) \tag{6}$$

$$Z_{v_i,f_p} = \frac{1}{C_3}\Bigg(\sum_{v_i\in\mathcal{V}}\sum_{f_p\in\mathcal{F}} \big(\alpha_3 Z_{v_j,f_q} W_{v_i,v_j} W_{f_p,f_q} - \frac{\alpha_2}{2} Z_{v_j,f_q}(W_{v_i,v_j} - W_{f_p,f_q})^2\big) + \alpha_1 Z^*_{v_i,f_p}\Bigg) \tag{7}$$

where

$$C_1 = \alpha_2 \sum_{f_p, f_q \in \mathcal{F}} Z_{v_i, f_p} Z_{v_j, f_q}$$

$$C_2 = \alpha_0 + \alpha_2 \sum_{v_i, v_j \in \mathcal{V}} Z_{v_i, f_p} Z_{v_j, f_q}$$

$$C_3 = \alpha_1 + \alpha_3 \sum_{v_i \in \mathcal{V}} \sum_{f_p \in \mathcal{F}} W_{v_i, v_j} W_{f_p, f_q}$$

From Global to Local Similarities: A Graph-Based Contextualization Method using Distributional Thesauri

Chris Biemann and **Martin Riedl**
Computer Science Department, Technische Universität Darmstadt
Hochschulstrasse 10, D-64289 Darmstadt, Germany
{riedl,biem}@cs.tu-darmstadt.de

Abstract

After recasting the computation of a distributional thesaurus in a graph-based framework for term similarity, we introduce a new contextualization method that generates, for each term occurrence in a text, a ranked list of terms that are semantically similar and compatible with the given context. The framework is instantiated by the definition of term and context, which we derive from dependency parses in this work. Evaluating our approach on a standard data set for lexical substitution, we show substantial improvements over a strong non-contextualized baseline across all parts of speech. In contrast to comparable approaches, our framework defines an unsupervised generative method for similarity in context and does not rely on the existence of lexical resources as a source for candidate expansions.

1 Introduction

Following (de Saussure, 1916) we consider two distinct viewpoints: *syntagmatic* relations consider the assignment of values to a linear sequence of terms, and the *associative (also: paradigmatic)* viewpoint assigns values according to the commonalities and differences to other terms in the reader's memory. Based on these notions, we automatically expand terms in the linear sequence with their paradigmatically related terms.

Using the distributional hypothesis (Harris, 1951), and operationalizing similarity of terms (Miller and Charles, 1991), it became possible to compute term similarities for a large vocabulary (Ruge, 1992). Lin (1998) computed a *distributional thesaurus (DT)* by comparing context features defined over grammatical dependencies with an appropriate similarity measure for all reasonably frequent words in a large collection of text, and evaluated these automatically computed word similarities against lexical resources. Entries in the DT consist of a ranked list of the globally most similar terms for a *target* term. While the similarities are dependent on the instantiation of the context feature as well as on the underlying text collection, they are global in the sense that the DT aggregates over all occurrences of target and its similar elements. In our work, we will use a DT in a graph representation and move from a global notion of similarity to a contextualized version, which performs context-dependent text expansion for all word nodes in the DT graph.

2 Related Work

The need to model semantics just in the same way as local syntax is covered by the n-gram-model, i.e. trained from a background corpus sparked a large body of research on semantic modeling. This includes computational models for topicality (Deerwester et al., 1990; Hofmann, 1999; Blei et al., 2003), and language models that incorporate topical (as well as syntactic) information, see e.g. (Boyd-Graber and Blei, 2008; Tan et al., 2012). In the Computational Linguistics community, the vector space model (Schütze, 1993; Turney and Pantel, 2010; Baroni and Lenci, 2010; Pucci et al., 2009; de Cruys et al., 2013) is the prevalent metaphor for representing word meaning.

While the computation of semantic similarities on the basis of a background corpus produces a global model, which e.g. contains semantically similar words for different word senses, there are a number of works that aim at contextualizing the information held in the global model for particular occurrences. With his predication algorithm, Kintsch (2001) contextualizes LSA (Deerwester et al., 1990) for N-VP constructions by spreading activation over neighbourhood graphs in the latent space.

In particular, the question of operationalizing semantic compositionality in vector spaces (Mitchell and Lapata, 2008) received much attention. The lexical substitution task (McCarthy and Navigli, 2009) (LexSub) sparked several approaches for contextualization. While LexSub participants and subsequent works all relied on a list of possible substitutions as given by one or several lexical resources, we describe a graph-based system that is knowledge-free and unsupervised in the sense that it neither requires an existing resource (we compute a DT graph for that), nor needs training for contextualization.

3 Method

3.1 Holing System

For reasons of generality, we introduce the holing operation (cf. (Biemann and Riedl, 2013)), to split any sort of observations on the syntagmatic level (e.g. dependency relations) into pairs of term and context features. These pairs are then both used for the computation of the global DT graph similarity and for the contextualization. This holing system is the only part of the system that is dependent on a pre-processing step; subsequent steps operate on a unified representation. The representation is given by a list of pairs `<t,c>` where `t` is the term (at a certain offset) and `c` is the context feature. The position of `t` in `c` is denoted by a hole symbol '@'. As an example, the dependency triple $(\texttt{nsub;gave}_2\texttt{;I}_1)$ could be transferred to $<\texttt{gave}_2\texttt{, (nsub;@;I}_1\texttt{)}>$ and $<\texttt{I}_1\texttt{, (nsub;gave}_2\texttt{;@)}>$.

3.2 Distributional Similarity

Here, we present the computation of the distributional similarity between terms using three graphs. For the computation we use the Apache Hadoop Framework, based on (Dean and Ghemawat, 2004).

We can describe this operation using a bipartite "term"-"context feature" graph $TC(T, C, E)$ with T the set terms, C the set of context features and $e(t, c, f) \in E$ edges between $t \in T$, $c \in C$ with $f = count(t, c)$ frequency of co-occurrence. Additionally, we define $count(t)$ and $count(c)$ as the counts of the term, respectively as the count of the context feature. Based on the graph TC we can produce a first-order graph $FO(T, C, E)$, with $e(t, c, sig) \in E$. First, we calculate a significance score sig for each pair (t, c) using Lexicographer's Mutual Information (LMI): $score(t, c) = LMI(t, c,) = count(t, c) \log_2(\frac{count(t,c)}{count(t)count(c)})$ (Evert, 2004). Then, we remove all edges with $score(t, c) < 0$ and keep only the p most significant pairs per term t and remove the remaining edges. Additionally, we remove features which co-occur with more then 1000 words, as these features do not contribute enough to similarity to justify the increase of computation time (cf. (Rychlý and Kilgarriff, 2007; Goyal et al., 2010)). The second-order similarity graph between terms is defined as $SO(T, E)$ for $t_1, t_2 \in T$ with the similarity score $s = |\{c|e(t_1, c) \in FO, e(t_2, c) \in FO\}|$, which is the number of salient features two terms share. SO defines a distributional thesaurus.

In contrast to (Lin, 1998) we do not count how often a feature occurs with a term (we use significance ranking instead), and do not use cosine or other similarities (Lee, 1999) to calculate the similarity over the feature counts of each term, but only count significant common features per term. This constraint makes this approach more scalable to larger data, as we do not need to know the full list of features for a term pair at any time. Seemingly simplistic, we show in (Biemann and Riedl, 2013) that this measure outperforms other measures on large corpora in a semantic relatedness evaluation.

3.3 Contextual Similarity

The contextualization is framed as a ranking problem: given a set of candidate expansions as provided by the SO graph, we aim at ranking them such that the most similar term in context will be ranked higher, whereas non-compatible candidates should be ranked lower.

First, we run the holing system on the lexical material containing our target word $tw \in T' \subseteq T$ and select all pairs $<tw, c_i>$ $c_i \in C' \subseteq C$ that are instantiated in the current context. We then define a new graph $CON(T', C', S)$ with context features $c_i \in C'$. Using the second-order similarity graph $SO(T, E)$ we extract the top n similar terms $T'=\{t_i, \ldots, t_n\} \subseteq T$ from the second-order graph SO for tw and add them to the graph CON. We add edges $e(t, c, sig)$ between all target words and context features and label the edge with the significance score from the first order graph FO. Edges $e(t, c, sig)$, not contained in FO, get a significance score of zero. We can then calculate a ranking score for each t_i with the harmonic mean, using a plus one smoothing: $rank(t_i) = \frac{\prod_{c_j} (sig(t_i,c_j)+1)/count(term(c_j))}{\sum_{c_j} (sig(t_i,c_j)+1)/count(term(c_j))}$ ($term(c_j)$ extracts the term out of the context notation). Using that ranking score we can re-order the entries $t_1, \ldots, t_n$ according to their ranking score.

In Figure 1, we exemplify this, using the target word tw= "cold" in the sentence "I caught a nasty cold.". Our dependency parse-based

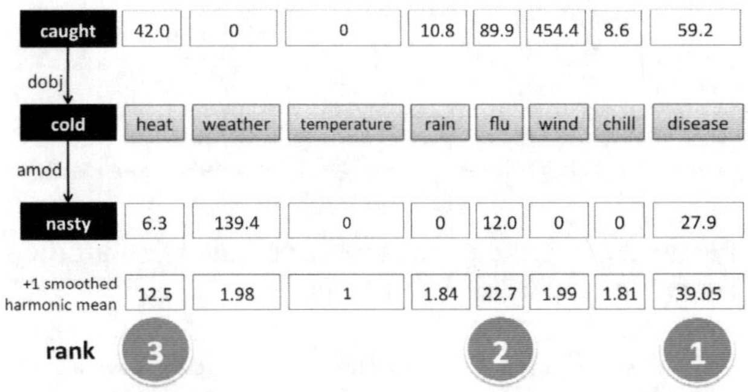

Figure 1: Contextualized ranking for target "cold" in the sentence "I caught a nasty cold" for the 10 most similar terms from the DT.

holing system produced the following pairs for "cold": <cold$_5$, (amod;@;nasty$_4$)>, <cold$_5$, (dobj;caught$_2$;@)>. The top 10 candidates for "cold" are T'={heat, weather, temperature, rain, flue, wind, chill, disease}. The scores per pair are e.g. <heat, (dobj;caught;@)> with an LMI score of 42.0, <weather , (amod;@;nasty)> with a score of 139.4. The pair <weather, (dobj;caught;@)> was not contained in our first-order data. Ranking the candidates by their overall scores as given in the figure, the top three contextualized expansions are "disease, flu, heat", which are compatible with both pairs. For the top 200 words, the ranking of fully compatible candidates is: "virus, disease, infection, flu, problem, cough, heat, water", which is clearly preferring the disease-related sense of "cold" over the temperature-related sense.

In this way, each candidate `t'` gets as many scores as there are pairs containing `c'` in the holing system output. An overall score per t' then given by the harmonic mean of the add-one-smoothed single scores – smoothing is necessary to rank candidates `t'` that are not compatible to all pairs. This scheme can easily be extended to expand all words in a given sentence or paragraph, yielding a two-dimensional contextualized text, where every (content) word is expanded by a list of globally similar words from the distributional thesaurus that are ranked according to their compatibility with the given context.

4 Evaluation

The evaluation of contextualizing the thesaurus (CT) was performed using the LexSub dataset, introduced in the Lexical Substitution task at Semeval 2007 (McCarthy and Navigli, 2009). Following the setup provided by the task organizers, we tuned our approach on the 300 trial sentences, and evaluate it on the official remaining 1710 test sentences. For the evaluation we used the out of ten (oot) precision and oot mode precision. Both measures calculate the number of detected substitutions within ten guesses over the complete subset. Whereas entries in the oot precision measures are considered correct if they match the gold standard, without penalizing non-matching entries, the oot mode precision includes also a weighting as given in the gold standard[1]. For comparison, we use the results of the DT as a baseline to evaluate the contextualization. The DT was computed based on newspaper corpora (120 million sentences), taken from the Leipzig Corpora Collection (Richter et al., 2006) and the Gigaword corpus (Parker et al., 2011). Our holing system uses collapsed Stanford parser dependencies (Marneffe et al., 2006) as context features. The contextualization uses only context features that contain words with part-of-speech prefixes V,N,J,R. Furthermore, we use a threshold for the significance value of the LMI values of 50.0, p=1000, and the most similar 30 terms from the DT entries.

5 Results

Since out contextualization algorithm is dependent on the number of context features containing the target word, we report scores for targets with at least two and at least three dependencies separately. In the Lexical Substitution Task 2007 dataset (LexSub) test data we detected 8 instances without entries in the gold standard and 19 target words without any

[1]The oot setting was chosen because it matches the expansions task better than e.g. precision@1

dependency, as they are collapsed into the dependency relation. The remaining entries have at least one, 49.2% have at least two and 26.0% have at least three dependencies. Furthermore, we also evaluated the results broken down into separate part-of-speeches of the target. The results on the LexSub test set are shown in Table 1.

		Precision			Mode Precision		
min. # dep.		1	2	3	1	2	3
POS	Alg.						
noun	CT	**26.64**	**26.55**	**28.36**	**38.68**	**38.24**	**37.68**
noun	DT	25.35	25.09	28.07	34.96	34.31	36.23
verb	CT	**23.39**	**23.75**	**23.05**	**32.05**	**33.09**	**33.33**
verb	DT	22.46	22.13	21.32	29.17	28.78	28.25
adj.	CT	**32.65**	**34.75**	**36.08**	**45.09**	**48.24**	**46.43**
adj.	DT	32.13	33.25	35.02	43.56	43.53	42.86
adv.	CT	20.47	**29.46**	**36.23**	30.14	**40.63**	**100.00**
adv.	DT	**28.91**	26.75	29.88	**41.63**	34.38	66.67
ALL	CT	26.46	**26.43**	**26.61**	**37.21**	**37.40**	**37.38**
ALL	DT	**27.06**	24.83	25.24	36.96	33.06	33.11

Table 1: Results of the LexSub test dataset.

Inspecting the results for all POS (denoted as ALL), we only observe a slight decline for the precision score with at least only one dependency, which is caused by adverbs. For targets with more than one dependency, we observe overall improvements of 1.6 points in precision and more than 4 points in mode precision.

Regarding the results of different part-of-speech tags, we always improve over the DT ranking, except for adverbs with only one dependency. Most notably, the largest relative improvements are observed on verbs, which is a notoriously difficult word class in computational semantics. For adverbs, at least two dependencies seem to be needed; there are only 7 adverb occurrences with more than two dependencies in the dataset. Regarding performance on the original lexical substitution task (McCarthy and Navigli, 2009), we did not come close to the performance of the participating systems, which range between 32–50 precision points, respectively 43–66 mode precision points (only taking systems without duplicate words in the result set into account). However, all participants used one or several lexical resources for generating substitution candidates, as well as a large number of features. Our system, on the other hand, merely requires a holing system – in this case based on a dependency parser – and a large amount of unlabeled text, and a very small number of contextual clues.

For an insight of the coverage for the entries delivered by the DT graph, we extended the oot precision measure, to consider not only the first 10 entries, but the first X={1,10,50,100,200} entries (see Figure 2). Here we also show the coverage for different sized

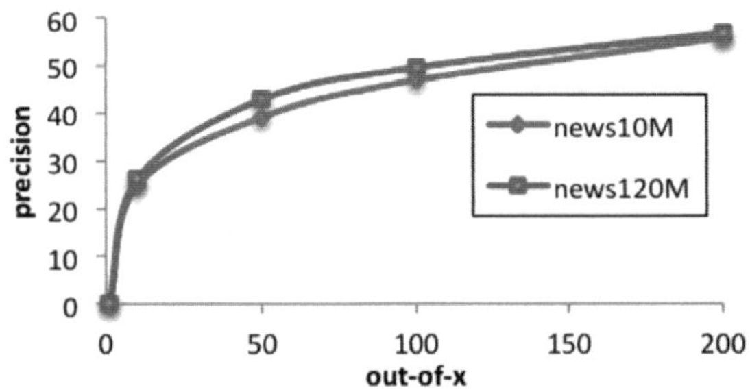

Figure 2: Coverage on the LexSub test dataset for different DT graphs, using *out of X* entries.

datasets (10 and 120 million sentences). Amongst the 200 most similar words from the DT, a coverage of up to 55.89 is reached. DT quality improves with corpus size, especially due to increased coverage. This shows that there is considerable headroom for optimization for our contextualization method, but also shows that our automatic candidate expansions can provide a coverage that is competitive to lexical resources.

6 Conclusion

We have provided a way of operationalizing semantic similarity by splitting syntagmatic observations into terms and context features, and representing them a first-order and second-order graph. Then, we introduced a conceptually simple and efficient method to perform a contextualization of semantic similarity. Overall, our approach constitutes an unsupervised generative model for lexical expansion in context. We have presented a generic method on contextualizing distributional information, which retrieves the lexical expansions from a target term from the DT graph, and ranks them with respect to their context compatibility. Evaluating our method on the LexSub task, we were able to show improvements, especially for expansion targets with many informing contextual elements. For further work, we will extend our holing system and combine several holing systems, such as e.g. n-gram contexts.

Additionally, we would like to adapt more advanced methods for the contextualization (Viterbi, 1967; Lafferty et al., 2001) that yield an all-words simultaneous expansion over the whole sequence, and constitutes a probabilistic model of lexical expansion.

References

M. Baroni and A. Lenci. 2010. Distributional memory: A general framework for corpus-based semantics. *Computational Linguistics*, 36(4):673–721.

Chris Biemann and Martin Riedl. 2013. Text: Now in 2D! a framework for lexical expansion with contextual similarity. *Journal of Language Modelling*, 1(1):55–95.

D. M. Blei, A. Y. Ng, and M. I. Jordan. 2003. Latent dirichlet allocation. *J. Mach. Learn. Res.*, 3:993–1022.

J. Boyd-Graber and D. M. Blei. 2008. Syntactic topic models. In *Neural Information Processing Systems*, Vancouver, BC, USA.

T. Van de Cruys, T. Poibeau, and A. Korhonen. 2013. A tensor-based factorization model of semantic compositionality. In *Proc. NAACL-HLT 2013*, Atlanta, USA.

F. de Saussure. 1916. *Cours de linguistique générale*. Payot, Paris, France.

J. Dean and S. Ghemawat. 2004. MapReduce: Simplified Data Processing on Large Clusters. In *Proc. of Operating Systems, Design & Implementation*, pages 137–150, San Francisco, CA, USA.

S. Deerwester, S. T. Dumais, G. W. Furnas, T. K. Landauer, and R. Harshman. 1990. Indexing by latent semantic analysis. *Journal of the American Society for Information Science*, 41(6):391–407.

S. Evert. 2004. *The statistics of word cooccurrences: word pairs and collocations*. Ph.D. thesis, IMS, Universität Stuttgart.

A. Goyal, J. Jagarlamudi, H. Daumé, III, and T. Venkatasubramanian. 2010. Sketch techniques for scaling distributional similarity to the web. In *Proc. of the 2010 Workshop on GEometrical Models of Nat. Lang. Semantics*, pages 51–56, Uppsala, Sweden.

Z. S. Harris. 1951. *Methods in Structural Linguistics*. University of Chicago Press, Chicago, USA.

Thomas Hofmann. 1999. Probabilistic latent semantic indexing. In *Proc. 22nd ACM SIGIR*, pages 50–57, New York, NY, USA.

W. Kintsch. 2001. Predication. *Cognitive Science*, 25(2):173–202.

J. D. Lafferty, A. McCallum, and F. C. N. Pereira. 2001. Conditional random fields: Probabilistic models for segmenting and labeling sequence data. In *Proc. of the 18th Int. Conf. on Machine Learning*, ICML '01, pages 282–289, San Francisco, CA, USA.

L. Lee. 1999. Measures of distributional similarity. In *Proc. of the 37th ACL*, pages 25–32, College Park, MD, USA.

D. Lin. 1998. Automatic retrieval and clustering of similar words. In *Proc. COLING'98*, pages 768–774, Montreal, Quebec, Canada.

M.-C. De Marneffe, B. Maccartney, and C. D. Manning. 2006. Generating typed dependency parses from phrase structure parses. In *Proc. of the Int. Conf. on Language Resources and Evaluation*, Genova, Italy.

D. McCarthy and R. Navigli. 2009. The english lexical substitution task. *Language Resources and Evaluation*, 43(2):139–159.

G. A. Miller and W. G. Charles. 1991. Contextual correlates of semantic similarity. *Language and Cognitive Processes*, 6(1):1–28.

J. Mitchell and M. Lapata. 2008. Vector-based models of semantic composition. In *Proceedings of ACL-08: HLT*, pages 236–244, Columbus, OH, USA.

R. Parker, D. Graff, J. Kong, K. Chen, and K. Maeda. 2011. *English Gigaword Fifth Edition*. Linguistic Data Consortium, Philadelphia, USA.

D. Pucci, M. Baroni, F. Cutugno, and R. Lenci. 2009. Unsupervised lexical substitution with a word space model. In *Workshop Proc. of the 11th Conf. of the Italian Association for Artificial Intelligence*, Reggio Emilia, Italy.

M. Richter, U. Quasthoff, E. Hallsteinsdóttir, and C. Biemann. 2006. Exploiting the leipzig corpora collection. In *Proceesings of the IS-LTC 2006*, Ljubljana, Slovenia.

G. Ruge. 1992. Experiments on linguistically-based term associations. *Information Processing & Management*, 28(3):317 – 332.

P. Rychlý and A. Kilgarriff. 2007. An efficient algorithm for building a distributional thesaurus (and other sketch engine developments). In *Proc. 45th ACL*, pages 41–44, Prague, Czech Republic.

Hinrich Schütze. 1993. Word space. In *Advances in Neural Information Processing Systems 5*, pages 895–902. Morgan Kaufmann.

Ming Tan, Wenli Zhou, Lei Zheng, and Shaojun Wang. 2012. A scalable distributed syntactic, semantic, and lexical language model. *Computational Linguistics*, 38(3):631–671.

P. D. Turney and P. Pantel. 2010. From frequency to meaning: vector space models of semantics. *J. Artif. Int. Res.*, 37(1):141–188.

A. J. Viterbi. 1967. Error bounds for convolutional codes and an asymptotically optimum decoding algorithm. *IEEE Transactions on Information Theory*, 13(2):260–269.

Understanding seed selection in bootstrapping

Yo Ehara†∗ **Issei Sato**‡ **Hidekazu Oiwa**†∗ **Hiroshi Nakagawa**‡
† Graduate School of Information Science and Technology ‡ Information Technology Center
The University of Tokyo / 7-3-1 Hongo, Bunkyo-ku, Tokyo, Japan
∗ JSPS Research Fellow
Kojimachi Business Center Building, 5-3-1 Kojimachi, Chiyoda-ku, Tokyo, Japan
{ehara@r., sato@r., oiwa@r., nakagawa@}dl.itc.u-tokyo.ac.jp

Abstract

Bootstrapping has recently become the focus of much attention in natural language processing to reduce labeling cost. In bootstrapping, unlabeled instances can be harvested from the initial labeled "seed" set. The selected seed set affects accuracy, but how to select a good seed set is not yet clear. Thus, an "iterative seeding" framework is proposed for bootstrapping to reduce its labeling cost. Our framework iteratively selects the unlabeled instance that has the best "goodness of seed" and labels the unlabeled instance in the seed set. Our framework deepens understanding of this seeding process in bootstrapping by deriving the dual problem. We propose a method called expected model rotation (EMR) that works well on not well-separated data which frequently occur as realistic data. Experimental results show that EMR can select seed sets that provide significantly higher mean reciprocal rank on realistic data than existing naive selection methods or random seed sets.

1 Introduction

Bootstrapping has recently drawn a great deal of attention in natural language processing (NLP) research. We define bootstrapping as a method for harvesting "instances" similar to given "seeds" by recursively harvesting "instances" and "patterns" by turns over corpora using the distributional hypothesis (Harris, 1954). This definition follows the definitions of bootstrapping in existing NLP papers (Komachi et al., 2008; Talukdar and Pereira, 2010; Kozareva et al., 2011). Bootstrapping can greatly reduce the cost of labeling instances, which is especially needed for tasks with high labeling costs.

The performance of bootstrapping algorithms, however, depends on the selection of seeds. Although various bootstrapping algorithms have been proposed, randomly chosen seeds are usually used instead. Kozareva and Hovy (2010) recently reports that the performance of bootstrapping algorithms depends on the selection of seeds, which sheds light on the importance of selecting a good seed set. Especially a method to select a seed set considering the characteristics of the dataset remains largely unaddressed. To this end, we propose an "iterative seeding" framework, where the algorithm iteratively ranks the goodness of seeds in response to current human labeling and the characteristics of the dataset. For iterative seeding, we added the following two properties to the bootstrapping;

- criteria that support iterative updates of goodness of seeds for seed candidate unlabeled instances.
- iterative update of similarity "score" to the seeds.

To invent a "criterion" that captures the characteristics of a dataset, we need to measure the influence of the unlabeled instances to the model. This model, however, is not explicit in usual bootstrapping algorithms' notations. Thus, we need to reveal the model parameters of bootstrapping algorithms for explicit model notations.

To this end, we first reduced bootstrapping algorithms to label propagation using Komachi et al.

(2008)'s theorization. Komachi et al. (2008) shows that simple bootstrapping algorithms can be interpreted as label propagation on graphs (Komachi et al., 2008). This accords with the fact that many papers such as (Talukdar and Pereira, 2010; Kozareva et al., 2011) suggest that graph-based semi-supervised learning, or label propagation, is another effective method for this harvesting task. Their theorization starts from a simple bootstrapping scheme that can model many bootstrapping algorithms so far proposed, including the "Espresso" algorithm (Pantel and Pennacchiotti, 2006), which was the most cited among the Association for Computational Linguistics (ACL) 2006 papers.

After reducing bootstrapping algorithms to label propagation, next, we will reveal the model parameters of a bootstrapping algorithm by taking the dual problem of bootstrapping formalization of (Komachi et al., 2008). By revealing the model parameters, we can obtain an interpretation of selecting seeds which helps us to create criteria for the iterative seeding framework. Namely, we propose expected model rotation (EMR) criterion that works well on realistic, and not well-separated data.

The contributions of this paper are summarized as follows.

- The iterative seeding framework, where seeds are selected by certain criteria and labeled iteratively.
- To measure the influence of the unlabeled instances to the model, we revealed the model parameters through the dual problem of bootstrapping.
- The revealed model parameters provides an interpretation of selecting seeds focusing on how well the dataset is separated.
- "EMR" criterion that works well on not well-separated data which frequently occur as realistic data. .

2 Related Work

Kozareva and Hovy (2010) recently shed light on the problem of improving the seed set for bootstrapping. They defined several goodness of seeds and proposed a method to predict these measures using support vector regression (SVR) for their doubly anchored pattern (DAP) system. However, Kozareva and Hovy (2010) does not show how effective the seed set selected by the goodness of seeds that they defined was for the bootstrapping process while they show how accurately they could predict the goodness of seeds.

Early work on bootstrapping includes that of (Hearst, 1992) and that of (Yarowsky, 1995). Abney (2004) extended self-training algorithms including that of (Yarowsky, 1995), forming a theory different from that of (Komachi et al., 2008). We chose to extend the theory of (Komachi et al., 2008) because it can actually explain recent graph-based algorithms including that of (Pantel and Pennacchiotti, 2006). The theory of Komachi et al. (2008) is also newer and simpler than that of (Abney, 2004).

The iterative seeding framework can be regarded as an example of active learning on graph-based semi-supervised learning. Selecting seed sets corresponds to sampling a data point in active learning. In active learning on supervised learning, the active learning survey (Settles, 2012) includes a method called expected model change, after which this paper's expected model rotation (EMR) is named. They share a basic concept: the data point that surprises the classifier the most is selected next. Expected model change mentioned by (Settles, 2012), however, is for supervised setting, not semi-supervised setting, with which this paper deals. It also does not aim to provide intuitive understanding of the dataset. Note that our method is for semi-supervised learning and we also made the calculation of EMR practical.

Another idea relevant to our EMR is an "angle diversity" method for support vector machines (Brinker, 2003). Unlike our method, the angle diversity method interprets each data point as data "lines" in a version space. The weight vector is expressed as a point in a version space. Then, it samples a data "line" whose angle formed with existing data lines is large. Again, our method builds upon different settings in that this method is only for supervised learning, while ours is for semi-supervised learning.

3 Theorization of Bootstrapping

This section introduces a theorization of bootstrapping by (Komachi et al., 2008).

3.1 Simple bootstrapping

Let $\mathcal{D} = \{(y_1, \boldsymbol{x}_1), \ldots, (y_l, \boldsymbol{x}_l), \boldsymbol{x}_{l+1}, \ldots, \boldsymbol{x}_{l+u}\}$ be a dataset. The first l data are labeled, and the following u data are unlabeled. We let $n = l + u$ for simplicity. Each $\boldsymbol{x}_i \in \mathbb{R}^m$ is an m-dimensional input feature vector, and $y_i \in C$ is its corresponding label where C is the set of semantic classes. To handle $|C|$ classes, for $k \in C$, we call an n-sized 0-1 vector $\boldsymbol{y}_k = (y_{1k}, \ldots, y_{nk})^\top$ a "seed vector", where $y_{ik} = 1$ if the i-th instance is labeled and its label is k, otherwise $y_{ik} = 0$.

Note that this multi-class formalization includes typical ranking settings for harvesting tasks as its special case. For example, if the task is to harvest animal names from all given instances, such as "elephant" and "zebra", C is set to be binary as $C = \{\text{animal}, \text{not animal}\}$. The ranking is obtained by the score vector resulting from the seed vector $\boldsymbol{y}_{\text{animal}} - \boldsymbol{y}_{\text{not animal}}$ due to the linearity.

By stacking row vectors $\boldsymbol{x}_i$, we denote $X = (\boldsymbol{x}_1, \ldots, \boldsymbol{x}_n)^\top$. Let X be an instance-pattern (feature) matrix where $(X)_{ij}$ stores the value of the jth feature in the ith datum. Note that we can almost always assume the matrix X to be sparse for bootstrapping purposes due to the language sparsity. This sparsity enables the fast computation.

The simple bootstrapping (Komachi et al., 2008) is a simple model of bootstrapping using matrix representation. The algorithm starts from $\boldsymbol{f}_0 \stackrel{\text{def}}{=} \boldsymbol{y}$ and repeats the following steps until $\boldsymbol{f}_c$ converges.

1. $\boldsymbol{a}_{c+1} = X^\top \boldsymbol{f}_c$. Then, normalize $\boldsymbol{a}_{c+1}$.

2. $\boldsymbol{f}_{c+1} = X\boldsymbol{a}_{c+1}$. Then, normalize $\boldsymbol{f}_{c+1}$.

The score vector after c iterations of the simple bootstrapping is obtained by the following equation.

$$\boldsymbol{f} = \left(\frac{1}{m}\frac{1}{n}XX^\top\right)^c \boldsymbol{y} \tag{1}$$

"Simplified Espresso" is a special version of the simple bootstrapping where $X_{ij} = \frac{\text{pmi}(i,j)}{\max \text{pmi}}$ and we normalize score vectors uniformly: $\boldsymbol{f}_c \leftarrow \boldsymbol{f}_c/n$, $\boldsymbol{a}_c \leftarrow \boldsymbol{a}_c/m$. Here, $\text{pmi}(i,j) \stackrel{\text{def}}{=} \log \frac{p(i,j)}{p(i)p(j)}$.

Komachi et al. (2008) pointed out that, although the scores $\boldsymbol{f}_c$ are normalized during the iterations in the simple bootstrapping, when $c \to \infty$, $\boldsymbol{f}_c$ converges to a score vector that does not depend on the seed vector $\boldsymbol{y}$ as the principal eigenvector of $\left(\frac{1}{m}\frac{1}{n}XX^\top\right)$ becomes dominant. For bootstrapping purposes, however, it is appropriate for the resulting score vector $\boldsymbol{f}_c$ to depend on the seed vector $\boldsymbol{y}$.

3.2 Laplacian label propagation

To make $\boldsymbol{f}$ seed dependent, Komachi et al. (2008) noted that we should use a power series of a matrix rather than a simple power of a matrix. As the following equation incorporates the score vectors $((-L)^c\boldsymbol{y})$ with both low and high c values, it provides a seed dependent score vector with taking higher c into account.

$$\sum_{c=0}^{\infty} \beta^c \left((-L)^c \boldsymbol{y}\right) = (I + \beta L)^{-1} \boldsymbol{y} \tag{2}$$

Instead of using $\left(\frac{1}{m}\frac{1}{n}XX^\top\right)$, Komachi et al. (2008) used $L \stackrel{\text{def}}{=} I - D^{-1/2}XX^\top D^{-1/2}$, a normalized graph Laplacian for graph theoretical reasons. D is a diagonal matrix defined as $D_{ii} \stackrel{\text{def}}{=} \sum_j (XX^\top)_{ij}$. This infinite summation of the matrix can be expressed by inverting the matrix under the condition that $0 < \beta < \frac{1}{\rho(L)}$, where $\rho(L)$ be the spectral radius of L.

Komachi et al. (2008)'s Laplacian label propagation is simply expressed as (3). Given $\boldsymbol{y}$, it outputs the score vector $\boldsymbol{f}$ to rank unlabeled instances. They reports that the resulting score vector $\boldsymbol{f}$ constantly achieves better results than those by Espresso (Pantel and Pennacchiotti, 2006).

$$\boldsymbol{f} = (I + \beta L)^{-1} \boldsymbol{y}. \tag{3}$$

4 Proposal: criteria for iterative seeding

This section describes our iterative seeding framework. The entire framework is shown in Algorithm 1.

Let g_i be the goodness of seed for an unlabeled instance i. We want to select the instance with the highest goodness of seed as the next seed added in the next iteration.

$$\hat{i} = \arg\max_i g_i \tag{4}$$

Algorithm 1 Iterative seeding framework

Require: y, X, the set of unlabeled instances U, the set of classes C.
  Initialize $g_{k,i'}; \forall k \in C, \forall i' \in U$
  repeat
    Select instance $\hat{i}$ by (4).
    Label $\hat{i}$. Let k' be $\hat{i}$'s class.
    $U \leftarrow U \backslash \{\hat{i}\}$
    for all $i' \in U$ **do**
      Recalculate $g_{k',i'}$
    end for
  until A sufficient number of seeds are collected.

Each seed selection criterion defines each goodness of seed g_i. To measure the goodness of seeds, we want to measure how an unlabeled instance will affect the model underlying Eq. (3). That is, we want to choose the unlabeled instance that would most influence the model. However, as the model parameters are not explicitly shown in Eq. (3), we first need to reveal them before measuring the influence of the unlabeled instances.

4.1 Scores as margins

This section reveals the model parameters through the dual problem of bootstrapping. We show that the score obtained by Eq. (3) can be regarded as the "margin" between each unlabeled data point and the hyperplane obtained by ridge regression; specifically, we can show that the i-th element of the resulting score vector obtained using Eq. (3) can be written as $f_i = \beta (y_i - \langle \hat{\mathbf{w}}, \phi(\mathbf{x}_i) \rangle)$, where $\hat{\mathbf{w}}$ is the optimal model parameter that we need to reveal (Figure 1). ϕ is a feature function mapping $\mathbf{x}_i$ to a feature space and is set to make this relation hold. Note that, for unlabeled instances, $y_i = 0$ holds, and thus f_i is simply $f_i = -\beta \langle \hat{\mathbf{w}}, \phi(\mathbf{x}_i) \rangle$. Therefore, $|f_i| \propto \| \langle \hat{\mathbf{w}}, \phi(\mathbf{x}_i) \rangle \|$ denotes the "margin" between each unlabeled data point and the underlying hyperplane.

Let Φ be defined as $\Phi \stackrel{\text{def}}{=} (\phi(\mathbf{x}_1), \ldots, \phi(\mathbf{x}_n))^\top$. The score vector $\mathbf{f}$ can be written using Φ as in (6). If we set Φ as Eq. (6), Eq. (5) is equivalent to Eq. (3).

$$\mathbf{f} = \left(I + \beta \Phi \Phi^\top\right)^{-1} \mathbf{y} \tag{5}$$

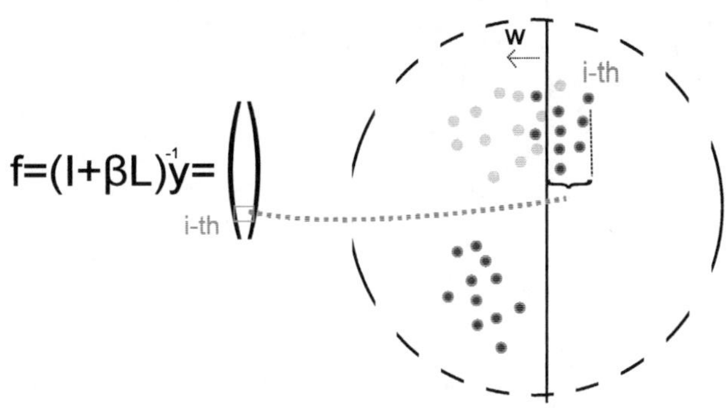

Figure 1: Scores as margins. The absolute values of the scores of the unlabeled instances are shown as the margin between the unlabeled instances and the underlying hyperplane in the feature space.

$$\Phi \Phi^\top = L = I - D^{-\frac{1}{2}} X X^T D^{-\frac{1}{2}} \tag{6}$$

By taking the diagonal of $\Phi\Phi^\top$ in Eq. (6), it is easy to see that $\|\phi(\mathbf{x}_i)\|^2 = \langle \phi(\mathbf{x}_i), \phi(\mathbf{x}_i) \rangle \leq 1$. Thus, the data points mapped into the feature space are within a unit circle in the feature space shown as the dashed circles in Figure 1-3. The weight vector is then represented by the classifying hyperplane that goes through the origin in the feature space. The classifying hyperplane views all the points positioned left of this hyperplane as the green class, and all the points positioned right of this hyperplane as the blue gray-stroked class. Note that all the points shown in Figure 1 are unlabeled, and thus the classifying hyperplane does not know the true classes of the data points. Due to the lack of space, the proof is shown in the appendix.

4.2 Margin criterion

Section 4.1 uncovered the latent weight vector for the bootstrapping model Eq. (3). A weight vector specifies a hyperplane that classifies instances into semantic classes. Thus, weight vector interpretation easily leads to an iterative seeding criterion: an unlabeled instance closer to the classifying hyperplane is more uncertain, and therefore obtains higher goodness of seed. We call this criterion the "margin criterion" (Figure 2).

First, we define $g_{k,i'} \stackrel{\text{def}}{=} |(\mathbf{f}_k)_{i'}| / s_k$ as the goodness of an instance i' to be labeled as k. s_k is the number of seeds labeled as class k in the current seed set. In the margin criterion, the goodness of the seed i' is then obtained by the difference between

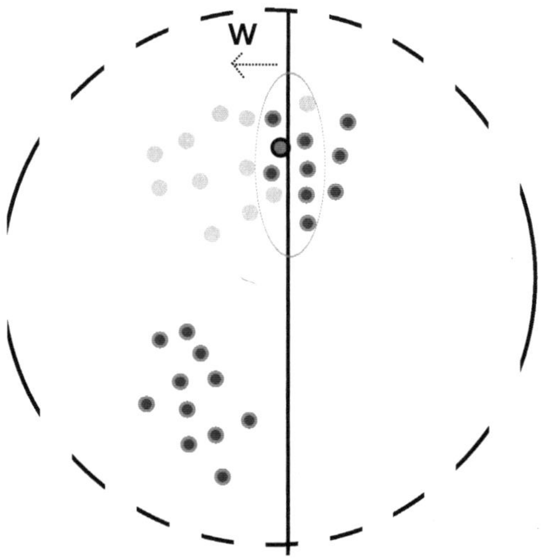

Figure 2: Margin criterion in binary setting. The instance closest to the underlying hyperplane, the red-and-black-stroked point, is selected. The part within the large gray dotted circle is not well separated. Margin criterion continues to select seeds from this part only in this example, and fails to sample from the left-bottom blue gray-stroked points. Note that all the points are unlabeled and thus the true classes of data points cannot be seen by the underlying hyperplane in this figure.

the largest and second largest $g_{k,i'}$ among all classes as follows:

$$g_i^{\text{Margin}} \stackrel{\text{def}}{=} -\left(\max_k g_{k,i'}^{\text{Margin}} - 2^{\text{nd}}\text{largest}_k g_{k,i'}^{\text{Margin}}\right). \tag{7}$$

The shortcoming of Margin criterion is that it can be "stuck", or jammed, or trapped, when the data are not well separated and the underlying hyperplanes goes right through the not well-separated part. In Figure 2, the part within the large gray dotted circle is not well separated. Margin criterion continues to select seeds from this part only in this example, and fails to sample from the left-bottom blue gray-stroked points.

4.3 Expected Model Rotation

To avoid Margin criterion from being stuck in the part where the data are not well separated, we propose another more promising criterion: the "Expected Model Rotation (EMR)". EMR measures the expected rotation of the classifying hyperplane (Figure 3) and selects the data point that rotates the un-

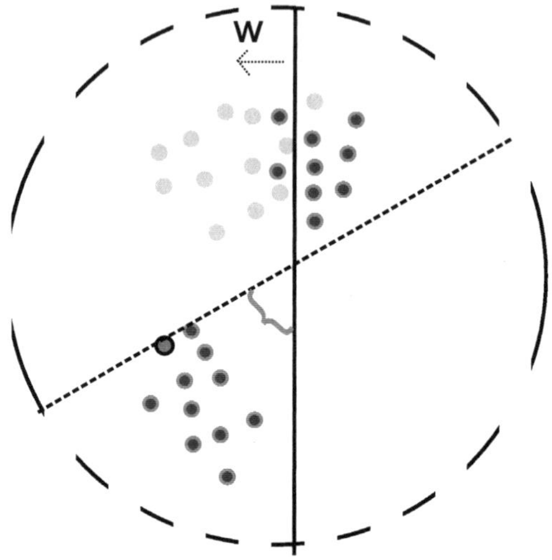

Figure 3: EMR criterion in binary setting. The instance that would rotate the underlying hyperplane the most is selected. The amount denoted by the purple brace "{" is the goodness of seeds in the EMR criterion. This criterion successfully samples from the left bottom blue points.

derlying hyperplane "the most" is selected. This selection method prevents EMR from being stuck in the area where the data points are not well separated. Another way of viewing EMR is that it selects the data point that surprises the current classifier the most. This makes the data points influential to the classification selected in early iteration in the iterative seeding framework. A simple rationale of EMR is that important information must be made available earlier.

To obtain the "expected" model rotation, in EMR, we define the goodness of seeds for an instance i', $g_{i'}$ as the sum of each per-class goodness of seeds $g_{k,i'}$ weighted by the probability that i' is labeled as k. Intuitively, $g_{k,i'}$ measures how the classifying hyperplane would rotate if the instance i' were labeled as k. Then, $g_{k,i'}$ is weighted by the probability that i' is labeled as k and summed. The probability for i' to be labeled as k can be obtained from the i'-th element of the current normalized score vector $p_{i'}(k) \stackrel{\text{def}}{=} \frac{|(\mathbf{f}_k)_{i'}/s_k|}{\sum_{k \in C}|(\mathbf{f}_k)_{i'}/s_k|}$, where s_k is the number of seeds labeled as class k in the current seed set.

$$g_{i'}^{\text{EMR}} \stackrel{\text{def}}{=} \sum_{k \in C} p_{i'}(k)\, g_{k,i'}^{\text{EMR}} \tag{8}$$

The per-class goodness of seeds $g_{k,i'}$ can be calculated as follows:

$$g_{k,i'}^{\text{EMR}} \stackrel{\text{def}}{=} 1 - \left| \frac{\mathbf{w}_k^\top}{||\mathbf{w}_k||} \frac{\mathbf{w}_{k,+i'}}{||\mathbf{w}_{k,+i'}||} \right|. \tag{9}$$

From Eq. (17) in the proof, $\mathbf{w} = \Phi^\top \mathbf{f}$. Here, $\mathbf{e}_{i'}$ is a unit vector whose i'-th element is 1 and all other elements are 0.

$$\mathbf{w}_k = \Phi^\top \mathbf{f}_k = \Phi^\top (I + \beta L)^{-1} \mathbf{y}_k \quad (10)$$

$$\mathbf{w}_{k,+i'} = \Phi^\top \mathbf{f}_{k,+i'} = \Phi^\top (I + \beta L)^{-1} (\mathbf{y}_k + \mathbf{e}_{i'}) \quad (11)$$

Although Eqs. (10) and (11) use Φ, we do not need to directly calculate Φ. Instead, we can use Eq. (6) to calculate these weight vectors as follows:

$$\mathbf{w}_k^\top \mathbf{w}_{k,+i'} = \mathbf{f}_k^\top \left(I - D^{-\frac{1}{2}} X X^T D^{-\frac{1}{2}} \right) \mathbf{f}_{k,+i'} \quad (12)$$

$$||\mathbf{w}|| = \sqrt{\mathbf{f}^\top \left(I - D^{-\frac{1}{2}} X X^T D^{-\frac{1}{2}} \right) \mathbf{f}}. \quad (13)$$

For more efficient computation, we cached $(I + \beta L)\, \mathbf{e}_{i'}$ to boost the calculation in Eqs. (10) and (11) by exploiting the fact that $\mathbf{y}_k$ can be written as the sum of $\mathbf{e}_i$ for all the instances in class k.

5 Evaluation

We evaluated our method for two bootstrapping tasks with high labeling costs. Due to the nature of bootstrapping, previous papers have commonly evaluated each method by using running search engines. While this is useful and practical, it also reduces the reproducibility of the evaluation. We instead used openly available resources for our evaluation.

First, we want to focus on the separatedness of the dataset. To this end, we prepared two datasets: one is "Freebase 1", a not well-separated dataset, and another is "sb-8-1", a well-separated dataset. We fixed $\beta = 0.01$ as Zhou et al. (2011) reports that $\beta = 0.01$ generally provides good performance on various datasets and the performance is not keen to β except extreme settings such as 0 or 1. In all experiments, each class initially has 1 seed and the seeds are selected and increased iteratively according to each criterion. The meaning of each curve is shared by all experiments and is explained in the caption of Figure 4.

"Freebase 1" is an experiment for information extraction, a common application target of bootstrapping methods. Based on (Talukdar and Pereira, 2010), the experiment setting is basically the same as that of the experiment Section 3.1 in their paper[1]. As 39 instances have multiple correct labels, however, we removed these instances from the experiment to perform the experiment under multi-class setting. Eventually, we had $31,143$ instances with $1,529$ features in 23 classes. The task of "Freebase 1" is bootstrapping instances of a certain semantic class. For example, to harvest the names of stars, given {Vega, Altair} as a seed set, the bootstrapping ranks Sirius high among other instances (proper nouns) in the dataset. Following the experiment setting of (Talukdar and Pereira, 2010), we used mean reciprocal rank (MRR) throughout our evaluation [2].

"sb-8-1" is manually designed to be well-separated and taken from 20 Newsgroup subsets[3]. It has $4,000$ instances with $16,282$ features in 8 classes.

Figure 4 and Figure 5 shows the results. We can easily see that "EMR" wins in "Freebase 1", a not well-separated dataset, and "Margin" wins in "sb-8-1", a well-separated dataset. This result can be regarded as showing that "EMR" successfully avoids being "stuck" in the area where the data are not well separated. In fact, in Figure 4, "Random" wins "Margin". This implies that the not well-separated part of this dataset causes the classifying hyperplane in "Margin" criterion to be stuck and make it lose against even simple "Random" criterion.

In contrast, in the "sb-8-1", a well-separated balanced dataset, "Margin" beats the other remaining two. This implies the following: When the dataset is well separated, uncertainty of a data point is the next important factor to select a seed set. As "Margin" exactly takes the data point that is the most uncertain to the current hyperplane, "Margin" works quite well in this example.

Note that all figures in all the experiments show the average of 30 random trials and win-and-lose relationships mentioned are statistically tested using Mann-Whitney test.

While "sb-8-1" is a balanced dataset, realistic data like "freebase 1" is not only not-well-separated, but also imbalanced . Therefore, we performed experiments "sb-8-1", an imbalanced well-separated dataset, and "ol-8-1", an imbalanced not-well sepa-

[1] *Freebase-1 with Pantel Classes*, `http://www.talukdar.net/datasets/class_inst/`

[2] MRR is defined as $MRR \stackrel{\text{def}}{=} \frac{1}{|Q|} \sum_{i \in Q} \frac{1}{r_i}$, where Q is the test set, $i \in Q$ denotes an instance in the test set Q, and r_i is the rank of the correct class among all $|C|$ classes.

[3] `http://mlg.ucd.ie/datasets/20ng.html`

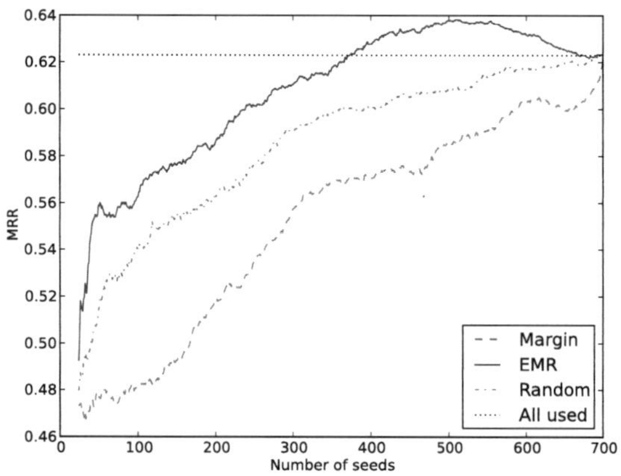

Figure 4: Freebase 1, a NOT well-separated dataset. Average of 30 random trials. "Random" and "Margin" are baselines. "Random" is the case that the seeds are selected randomly. "Margin" is the case that the seeds are selected using the margin criterion described in §4.2. "EMR" is proposed and is the case that the seeds are selected using the EMR criterion described in §4.3. At the rightmost point, all the curves meet because all the instances in the seed pool were labeled and used as seeds by this point. The MRR achieved by this point is shown as the line "All used". If a curve of each method crosses "All used", this can be intepretted as that iterative seeding of the curve's criterion can reduce the cost of labeling all the instances to the crossing point of the x-axis. "EMR" significantly beats "Random" and "Margin" where x-axis is 46 and 460 with p-value < 0.01.

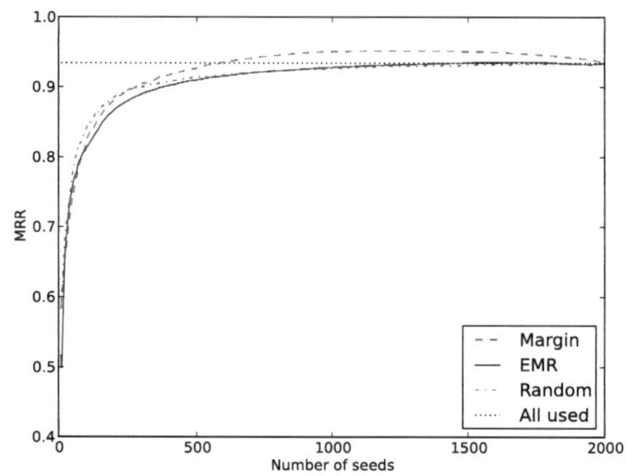

Figure 5: sb-8-1. A dataset manually designed to be well separated. Average of 30 random trials. Legends are the same as those in Figure 4. "Margin" beats "Random" and "EMR" where x-axis is 500 with p-value < 0.01.

rated dataset under the same experiment setting used for "sb-8-1". "sl-8-1" have $2,586$ instances with $10,764$ features. "ol-8-1" have $2,388$ instances with $9,971$ features. Both "sl-8-1" and "ol-8-1" have 8 classes.

Results are shown in Figure 6 and Figure 7. In Figure 6, "EMR" beats the other remaining two even though this is a well-separated data set. This implies that "EMR" can also be robust to the imbalancedness as well. In Figure 7, although the MRR of "Margin" eventually is the highest, the MRR of "EMR" rises far earlier than that of "Margin". This result can be explained as follows: "Margin" gets "stuck" in early iterations as this dataset is not well separated though "Margin" achieves best once it gets out of being stuck. In contrast, as "EMR" can avoid being stuck, it rises early achieving high performance with small number of seeds, or labeling. This result suggests that "EMR" is pereferable for reducing labeling cost while "Margin" can sometimes be preferable for higher performance.

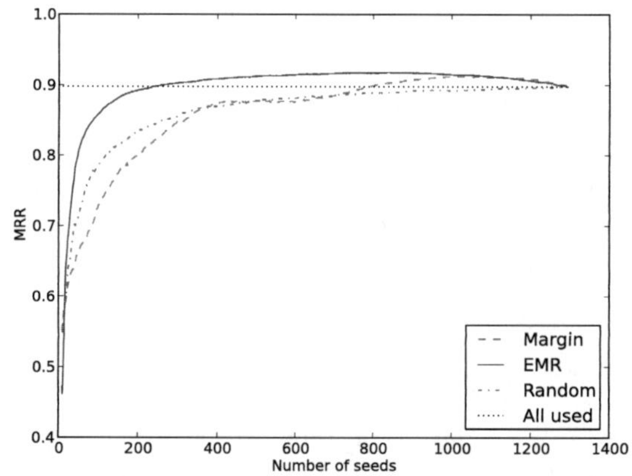

Figure 6: sl-8-1. An imbalanced well separated dataset. Average of 30 random trials. Legends are the same as those in Figure 4. "EMR" significantly beats "Random" and "Margin" where x-axis is 100 with p-value < 0.01.

6 Conclusion

Little is known about how best to select seed sets in bootstrapping. We thus introduced the iterative seeding framework, which provides criteria for selecting seeds. To introduce the iterative seeding framework, we deepened the understanding of the seeding process in bootstrapping through the dual problem by further extending the interpretation of bootstrapping as graph-based semi-supervised learning (Komachi et al., 2008), which generalizes

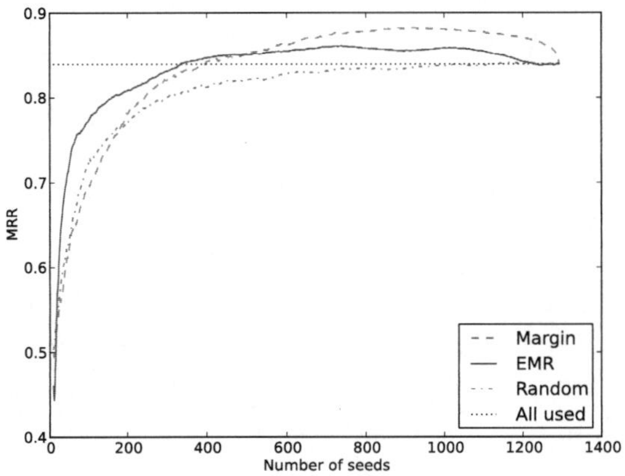

Figure 7: ol-8-1. An imbalanced NOT well separated dataset. Average of 30 random trials. Legends are the same as those in Figure 4. "EMR" significantly beats "Random" and "Margin" where x-axis is 100 with p-value < 0.01. "Margin" significantly beats "EMR" and "Random" where x-axis is $1,000$ with p-value < 0.01.

and improves Espresso-like algorithms.

Our method shows that existing simple "Margin" criterion can be "stuck" at the area when the data points are not well separated. Note that many realistic data are not well separated. To deal with this problem, we proposed "EMR" criterion that is not stuck in the area where the data points are not well separated.

We also contributed to make the calculation of "EMR" practical. In particular, we reduced the number of matrix inversions for calculating the goodness of seeds for "EMR". We also showed that the parameters for bootstrapping also affect the convergence speed of each matrix inversion and that the typical parameters used in other work are fairly efficient and practical.

Through experiments, we showed that the proposed "EMR" significantly beats "Margin" and "Random" baselines where the dataset are not well separated. We also showed that the iterative seeding framework with the proposed measures for the goodness of seeds can reduce labeling cost.

Appendix: Proof Consider a simple ridge regression of the following form where $0 < \beta < 1$ is a positive constant.

$$\min_{\mathbf{w}} \frac{\beta}{2} \sum_{i=1}^{n} \left\| y_i - \langle \mathbf{w}, \phi(\mathbf{x}_i) \rangle \right\|^2 + \|\mathbf{w}\|^2 . \quad (14)$$

We define $\xi_i = y_i - \langle \mathbf{w}, \phi(\mathbf{x}_i) \rangle$. By using ξ_i, we can rewrite Eq. (14) into an optimization problem with equality constraints as follows:

$$\min_{\mathbf{w}} \frac{\beta}{2} \sum_{i=1}^{n} \xi_i^2 + \|\mathbf{w}\|^2 \quad (15)$$

$$\text{s.t.} \forall i \in \{1, \dots, n\}; y_i = \mathbf{w}^\top \phi(\mathbf{x}_i) + \xi_i . \quad (16)$$

Because of the equality constraints of Eq. (16), we obtain the following Lagrange function h. Here, each bootstrapping score f_i occurs as Lagrange multipliers: $h(\mathbf{w}, \xi, \mathbf{f}) \stackrel{\text{def}}{=} \frac{1}{2}\|\mathbf{w}\|^2 + \frac{\beta}{2}\sum_{i=1}^{n} \xi_i^2 - \sum_{i=1}^{n} \left(\langle \mathbf{w}, \phi(\mathbf{x}_i) \rangle + \xi_i - y_i \right) f_i$.

By taking derivatives of h, we can derive $\hat{\mathbf{w}}$ by expressing it with the sum of each f_i and $\phi(\mathbf{x}_i)$.

$$\frac{\partial h}{\partial \mathbf{w}} = 0 \Rightarrow \hat{\mathbf{w}} = \sum_{i=1}^{n} f_i \phi(\mathbf{x}_i) \quad (17)$$

$$\frac{\partial h}{\partial \xi_i} = 0 \Rightarrow f_i = \beta \left(\xi_i = \beta y_i - \langle \hat{\mathbf{w}}, \phi(\mathbf{x}_i) \rangle \right) \quad (18)$$

Substituting the relations derived in Eqs. (17) and (18) to the equation $\frac{\partial h}{\partial f_i} = 0$ results in Eq. (19).

$$\frac{\partial h}{\partial f_i} = 0 \Rightarrow \sum_{j=1}^{n} f_j \phi(\mathbf{x}_i)^\top \phi(\mathbf{x}_j) + \frac{1}{\beta} f_i = y_i \quad (19)$$

Equation (19) can be written as a matrix equation using Φ defined as $\Phi \stackrel{\text{def}}{=} \left(\phi(\mathbf{x}_1), \dots, \phi(\mathbf{x}_n) \right)^\top$. From Eq. (20), we can easily derive the form of Eq. (3) as $\left(\Phi\Phi^\top + \frac{1}{\beta} I \right)^{-1} \mathbf{y} \propto \left(I + \beta \Phi\Phi^\top \right)^{-1} \mathbf{y}$.

$$\left(\Phi\Phi^\top + \frac{1}{\beta} I \right) \mathbf{f} = \mathbf{y} \quad (20)$$

□

References

Steven Abney. 2004. Understanding the yarowsky algorithm. *Computational Linguistics*, 30(3):365–395.

Klaus Brinker. 2003. Incorporating diversity in active learning with support vector machines. In *Proc. of ICML*, pages 59–66, Washington D.C.

Zelling S. Harris. 1954. Distributional structure. *Word*.

Marti A. Hearst. 1992. Automatic acquisition of hyponyms from large text corpora. In *Proc. of COLING*, pages 539–545.

Mamoru Komachi, Taku Kudo, Masashi Shimbo, and Yuji Matsumoto. 2008. Graph-based analysis of semantic drift in Espresso-like bootstrapping algorithms. In *Proc. of EMNLP*, pages 1011–1020, Honolulu, Hawaii.

Zornitsa Kozareva and Eduard Hovy. 2010. Not all seeds are equal: Measuring the quality of text mining seeds. In *Proc. of NAACL-HLT*, pages 618–626, Los Angeles, California.

Zornitsa Kozareva, Konstantin Voevodski, and Shanghua Teng. 2011. Class label enhancement via related instances. In *Proc. of EMNLP*, pages 118–128, Edinburgh, Scotland, UK.

Patrick Pantel and Marco Pennacchiotti. 2006. Espresso: Leveraging generic patterns for automatically harvesting semantic relations. In *Proc. of ACL-COLING*, pages 113–120, Sydney, Australia.

Burr Settles. 2012. *Active Learning*. Synthesis Lectures on Artificial Intelligence and Machine Learning. Morgan & Claypool Publishers.

Partha Pratim Talukdar and Fernando Pereira. 2010. Experiments in graph-based semi-supervised learning methods for class-instance acquisition. In *Proc. of ACL*, pages 1473–1481, Uppsala, Sweden.

David Yarowsky. 1995. Unsupervised word sense disambiguation rivaling supervised methods. In *Proc. of ACL*, pages 189–196, Cambridge, Massachusetts.

Xueyuan Zhou, Mikhail Belkin, and Nathan Srebro. 2011. An iterated graph laplacian approach for ranking on manifolds. In *Proc. of KDD*, pages 877–885.

Graph-Structures Matching for Review Relevance Identification

Lakshmi Ramachandran and **Edward F. Gehringer**
North Carolina State University
{lramach, efg}@ncsu.edu

Abstract

Review quality is determined by identifying the relevance of a review to a submission (the article or paper the review was written for). We identify relevance in terms of the semantic and syntactic similarities between two texts. We use a word order graph, whose vertices, edges and double edges help determine structure-based match across texts. We use WordNet to determine semantic relatedness. Ours is a lexico-semantic approach, which predicts relevance with an accuracy of 66% and f-measure of 0.67.

1 Introduction

Reviews play a critical role in making decisions, e.g., for grading students, accepting manuscripts for publication, or funding grants. Therefore, we must ensure that the decision-making party finds the review's content useful. Kuhne *et al.* (2010) found that authors were contented with reviewers who made an effort to understand their work. Nelson and Schunn (2009) found that reviews locating problems in the author's work, or providing suggestions for improvement help authors understand and use feedback effectively.

We investigated peer reviews from Expertiza, a web-based collaborative learning application (Gehringer, 2010). We found that reviewers provide comments such as, "Yes, it is good! It is very well organized." Such a review does not contain any unique information, or reference a specific concept or object in the author's submission. Such a generic review could work for *any* submission. Consider the comment, "I felt that some of the examples were clichéd." The reviewer criticizes the "examples" in the author's work but does not explain why they find the example "clichéd".

A review's quality may be assessed with the help of several metrics such as relevance of a review to the submission, its content type, coverage, tone, quantity of feedback provided (Ramachandran, 2011). In this paper we focus on the study of one review quality metric - *review relevance*.

A *relevant review* paraphrases the concepts described in a submission, with possible descriptions of problems identified in the author's work. Our aim is to identify whether a review is relevant to the work it was written for.

While paraphrasing, an idea may be restated by the reviewer with possible lexical and syntactic changes to the text. According to Liu *et al.* (2009), a good paraphrase, while preserving the original meaning of the text should contain some syntactic changes. According to Boonthum (2004) patterns followed commonly while paraphrasing include lexical synonymy, change in voice and change in sentence structure. Therefore, conventional text matching approaches, which look for exact matches, may not be good at identifying relevance.

2 Definition of Relevance

Definition Let S be the set of sentences in the text under review (the submission) and R be the set of review sentences. Let s and r represent a sentence in the submission and review respectively.

$$relevance(S,R) = \frac{1}{|R|} \sum_{\forall r \in R} \{ \underset{\forall s \in S}{\text{argmax}}(\textit{lexicoSemSim(s, r)}) \} \quad (1)$$

lexicoSemSim(s,r) represents the *lexico-semantic* match between s and r. Relevance is the average of the best lexico-semantic matches of a review's sentences with corresponding submission sentences. The meaning and usage of *lexicoSemSim* has been explained in detail in Section 6. We acknowledge that all review sentences may not have corresponding matches in the submission. Our aim is only to identify the proportion of review text that is lexico-semantically relevant to a submission.

Since our aim is to identify the lexico-semantic match between texts, we need a representation that captures the syntax or order of tokens in a text. Hence we use a word order graph. Word order graphs are suited for identifying lexical and voice changes, which are common among paraphrased text. Similarity should capture the degree of relatedness between texts. Hence we use a WordNet-based metric (Fellbaum, 1998).

Figure 1 contains a sample submission and three sample reviews. The first review has some instances of exact match with the submission and is therefore relevant to the submission. However, the relevance of the second review may not be determined by a text overlaps

Submission: The debate on internet radio centers around an initiated fee imposed upon the internet radio stations. Proponents of the fee claim that it is necessary because artists are losing money since their music can be listened to without purchase. This fee, the internet radio stations contend, will drive them out of business. Though many artists see the internet stations as a welcome marketing tool to get their music heard. The radio stations began a campaign that involved a day of silence to raise awareness and get users to write to congress in their support.

Relevant review (text overlaps with the submission): Start with a general article on Internet radio rather than a listing of stations. The list of stations can follow that.

Relevant review (lexico-semantically related to the submission): The article should include an article prominently featuring the artists' interests. Arguments imply that the fee would bankrupt the stations.

Non-relevant: The article does seem to treat differing viewpoints fairly exploring both the negative consequences of hate speech and the negative consequences of censoring it.

Figure 1: The figure contains a sample submission, two relevant reviews – one with overt text matches and another that is lexico-semantically similar to the submission, and a non-relevant review.

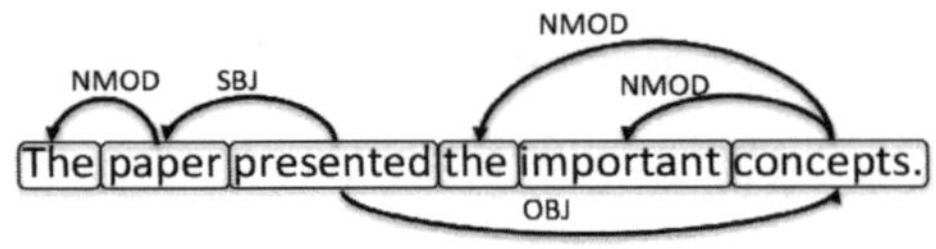

(a) Dependency tree

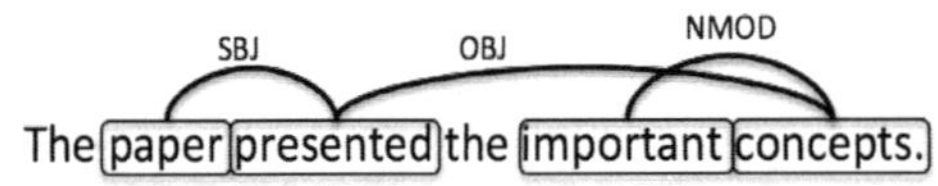

(b) Word order graph

Figure 2: Displaying the ordering difference between a dependency tree representation and a word order representation for the text "The paper presented the important concepts."

match. The third review is lexico-semantically distinct from the submission.

3 Related Work

There is little previous work in the area of identifying relevance between a review and a submission. Xiong and Litman (2011) use shallow metrics such as noun, verb count to identify review helpfulness. Their approach does not check for presence of paraphrases or summaries in a review. Ours is a pioneering effort in the application of relevance identification to the study of review helpfulness.

In this section we list some related work in the area of text matching, with a focus on approaches that use graphs such as lexical chains or dependency trees to represent text. Haghighi *et al.* (2005) use dependency trees to determine text entailment. They use node and path substitutions to compare text graphs.

Vertices in a dependency tree represent words, and edges capture the asymmetric dependency relationships between a head word and its modifier. Figure 2(a) contains a dependency tree representation (Bohnet, 2010) for the text "The paper presented the important concepts." We see that every token in the text is a vertex in the tree and edges depict governance relations (head → modifier). For example, "presented" is the root of this sentence and the edge between "presented" and "paper" signifies a subject relationship (SBJ). Dependency trees may not capture ordering information. For instance when we read the edges of the dependency tree in Figure 2(a) we get presented → paper, presented → concepts. The order of words in the edges is reversed, as in the case of presented → paper, although the actual order in the text is paper → presented.

The corresponding word order graph representation in Figure 2(b) captures the order of the words. The word order graph captures SBJ—OBJ ordering as in paper—presented—concepts, which the directed edges in a dependency tree do not capture. Thus dependency tree representations may not be a useful representation in studying lexical or word order changes across documents.

Mani and Bloedorn (1997) suggest a graph search and matching approach for multi-document summarization. The graph matching approach used by Mani and Bloedorn focuses on concept or topics-based matching (noun entities). The graph captures adjacency relations between concepts or topics. Their graph representation does not capture ordering information, which would be suited for tasks involving comparison of lexical-order changes. As noted earlier, text matching with possible changes in word order is essential for a task like relevance identification. Existing representations and matching techniques do not capture this information. Van *et al.* (2009) construct phrase nets using regular expressions. Phrase nets are constructed for specific relations between tokens e.g. "X at Y" may indicate location of object X. Phrase nets are used as a tool for visualizing relations between objects in literary texts.

The document index graph (DIG) used by Hammouda and Kamel (2002), capture phrases of a document. Although the DIG captures order of words within a phrase, it does not capture the order of phrases within a document. As a result this representation does not capture complete sentence structure information, which may be necessary to identify whether a review contains sentence structure changes.

Mihalcea (2004) uses a graph to perform sentence extraction and summarization. Vertices in the graph represent sentences in a document. Weighted graph edges represent the degree of overlap across content of the sentences.

Kauchak and Barzilay (2006) suggest an automated technique to create paraphrases for human and machine-translated text pairs, by substituting words in machine translated texts with their corresponding synonyms. They define paraphrases primarily in terms of synonyms of individual tokens.

Although there do exist independent research works that discuss graph-based summarization and paraphrasing techniques, they use content overlap or synonym matches to determine paraphrases. They do not consider context during text comparison. Our work is an amalgamation of existing research in the areas of text matching and paraphrase recognition.

4 Graph Representation

In a word order graph, edges represent relations between contiguous vertices. The graph captures word or phrase order of the text. Figure 2(b) contains the graph representation for a review.

A word order graph is suitable for applications that identify relevance or paraphrases across texts. Paraphrases may contain lexical changes and word or phrase shuffling across a text's length. Graph matches identify the presence or absence of lexical changes using the ordering and context that the word order graphs capture. A detailed description of the graph generation algorithm can be found in Ramachandran and Gehringer (2012).

1. The graph generator takes a piece of text as input and generates a graph as its output. We use period (.), semicolons (;) or exclamations (!) to break the text into multiple segments[1]. A text segment is a complete grammatical unit that can stand independent of the other clauses in the sentence in terms of its meaning.

2. The text is then tagged with parts-of-speech (POS) (NN, DT, VB, RB[2] etc.). We use the Stanford NLP POS tagger to generate the tagged text (Toutanova *et al.*, 2003). POS tags are useful in determining how to group words into phrases while still maintaining the order.

3. We use a heuristic phrase chunking technique[3] to group consecutive subject components (nouns, prepositions etc.) into a subject vertex, consecutive verbs (or modals) into a verb vertex, and similarly for adverb and adjective vertices. A graph vertex may contain a phrase or a token.

4. When a verb vertex is created the algorithm looks for the last created subject vertex to form an edge between the two. Ordering is maintained when an edge is created, i.e., if a subject vertex was formed before a verb vertex a subject—verb edge is created, else a verb—object edge is created. An adjective or an adverb is attached to the subject or verb vertex found in the sentence (i.e., subject—adjective or verb—adverb edge).

5. We tag graph edges with dependencies (Bohnet, 2010). We use the *anna* library available as part of the *mate tools* package to identify dependencies. Labels indicate the relation between words and their modifiers (e.g. SBJ – subject—verb relationship, OBJ – verb—object relationship). Post edge creation, we iterate through all edges to determine whether a dependency exists between the tokens representing the edge's vertices. We add an edge label if a dependency exists, e.g., "concepts—important" in Figure 2(b) captures the noun-modifier (NMOD) relation. Labels capture the grammatical role played by tokens in a text.

5 Semantic Relatedness

Match between two tokens could be one of: (1) exact, (2) synonym, (3) hypernym or hyponym (more generic or specific), (4) meronym or holonym (sub-part or whole) (5) presence of common parents (excluding generic parents such as "object", "entity"), and (6) overlaps across definitions or examples of compared tokens[4], or (7) distinct or non-match. Each match is given a weight value, which represents its *degree of importance*, e.g., exact matches are more important than synonym matches, which are in turn more important than hypernyms or hyponyms and so on. Weight values are in the [0-6] range, 0 being the lowest match (distinct) and 6 the best match (exact). Unlike other approaches, which capture just exact or synonymy matches, our approach captures semantic relatedness between tokens using a few types of matches (Ramachandran, 2013).

Each match is identified using WordNet. WordNet has been used successfully to measure relatedness by Agirre *et al.* (2009). We use WordNet because it is faster than querying a knowledge source such as Wikipedia, which contains more than a million articles, not all of which may be relevant.

6 Lexico-Semantic Matching

The degree of match between two graphs depends on the degree of match between their vertices and edges. In this section we describe three types of matches across graphs - (1) phrase or token matching, (2) context matching, and (3) sentence structure matching. Figure 3 contains an overview of our relevance identification approach.

6.1 Phrase or token matching

In phrase or token matching, vertices containing phrases or tokens are compared across graphs. This

[1]Approach used is similar to that of the deterministic sentence splitter used by the Stanford NLP sentence splitter. `http://nlp.stanford.edu/software/tokenizer.shtml`

[2]NN - noun, DT - determiner, VB(Z) - verb, RB - adverb

[3]Our chunker groups words based on the POS tags without the overhead of training a model to perform chunking.

[4]Using context to match tokens was an approach used by Lesk (1986) for word-sense disambiguation.

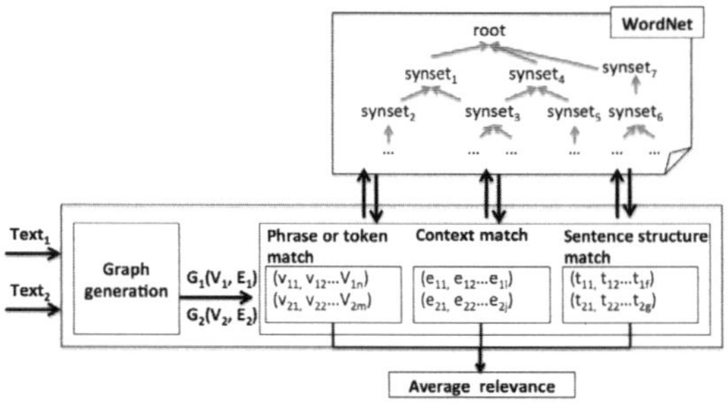

Figure 3: Overview of our approach for relevance identification task.

matching succeeds in capturing semantic relatedness between single or compound words. When vertices "concepts" and "points" are compared, a *common parents* match is found. This match would have been missed when using only an exact or synonym match.

$$\textit{Phrase(S, R)} = \frac{1}{|V_r|} \sum_{\forall r(v) \in V_r} \operatorname*{argmax}_{\forall s(v) \in V_s} \{\textit{match}(s(v), r(v))\} \tag{2}$$

An overall phrase match is determined by taking the average of the best match that every review phrase has with a corresponding submission phrase. Similarity between two vertices is calculated as the average of matches between their constituent words or phrases. Match could be one of those listed in Section 5. In Equation 2, $r(v)$ and $s(v)$ refer to review and submission vertices respectively, and V_r and V_s is the set of vertices in a review and a submission.

6.2 Context matching

Context matching compares edges with same and different syntax, and edges of different types across two text graphs. We refer to the match as *context* matching since contiguous phrases (vertices) are chosen from a graph for comparison with another, i.e., more context. Relatedness between edges is the average of the vertex matches. We compare edge labels for matches retaining word order. Edge labels capture grammatical relations, and play an important role in matching. Hence if edges have the same labels then the average match is retained, else the match is halved. Some of the context-based matches include:

- **Ordered match** - Ordered match preserves the order of phrases in a text. We compare same type edges[5] with the same vertex order. Figure 4(a) shows the comparison of single edges from two review graphs. A match is identified between edges "important—concepts" and "necessary—points", because they capture the noun-modifier relationship (NMOD), and because a relation exists between tokens "concepts" and "points".

- **Lexical change** - Lexical match flips the order of comparison, e.g., we compare subject—verb with verb—object edges or vice versa. The match identifies paraphrases, which involve lexical changes. Figure 4(b) depicts lexical change match. When comparing edge "paper—presented" with edge "included—points", we compare vertex "paper" with "points" and "presented" with "included". A match is found between tokens "paper" and "points", resulting in the edge pair getting a relatedness value greater than a *non-match*. Had it not been for the lexical change match, such a relation may have been missed.

- **Nominalization match** - The match identifies noun nominalizations - nouns formed from verbs or adjectives (e.g. abstract → abstraction, ambiguous → ambiguity).

  In an ordered and lexical change match we compare same types of vertices (of the compared edges). We compare vertices of different types, e.g., the subject and verb vertices or the subject and adjective vertices. This match also captures relations between nouns and their adjective forms (e.g. ethics → ethical), and nouns and their verb forms (e.g. confusion → to confuse).

  In Figure 4(b) when we compare the edge "paper—presented" with edge "presentation—included", we compare "paper" (NN) with "included" (VB) and "presented" (VB) with "presentation" (NN) . Token "presentation" is the nominalization of token "presented", as a result of which a match is identified between the two edges.

$$\begin{aligned}\textit{Context(S, R)} = \frac{1}{3|E_r|}\Bigg(& \sum_{r(e) \in E_r} \operatorname*{argmax}_{\forall s(e) \in E_s} \{\textit{match}_{ord}(s(e), r(e))\} + \\ & \sum_{r(e) \in E_r} \operatorname*{argmax}_{\forall s(e) \in E_s} \{\textit{match}_{lex}(s(e), r(e))\} + \\ & \sum_{r(e) \in E_r} \operatorname*{argmax}_{\forall s(e) \in E_s} \{\textit{match}_{nom}(s(e), r(e))\}\Bigg)\end{aligned} \tag{3}$$

In Equation 2, $r(e)$ and $s(e)$ refer to review and submission edges. The formula calculates the average best matches that review edges have with corresponding submission edges, for each of the above three types of matches $\textit{match}_{ord}$, $\textit{match}_{lex}$ and $\textit{match}_{nom}$. E_r and E_s represent the sets of review and submission edges respectively.

6.3 Sentence structure matching

Sentence structure matching compares double edges (two contiguous edges[6]), which constitute a complete segment[7] (e.g. subject—verb—object), across graphs.

[5]Same type edges are edges with same types of vertices.

[6]Two consecutive edges sharing a common vertex.

[7]In this work we only consider single and double edges, and not more contiguous edges (triple edges etc.), for text matching.

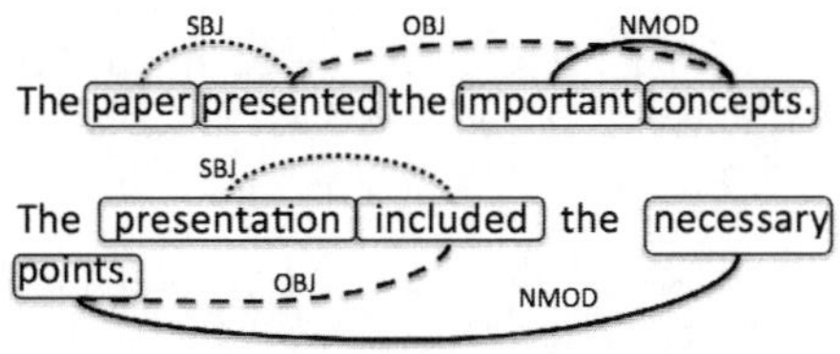

(a) Ordered match - similar edges are compared across the two reviews, i.e., SBJ with SBJ, OBJ with OBJ etc.

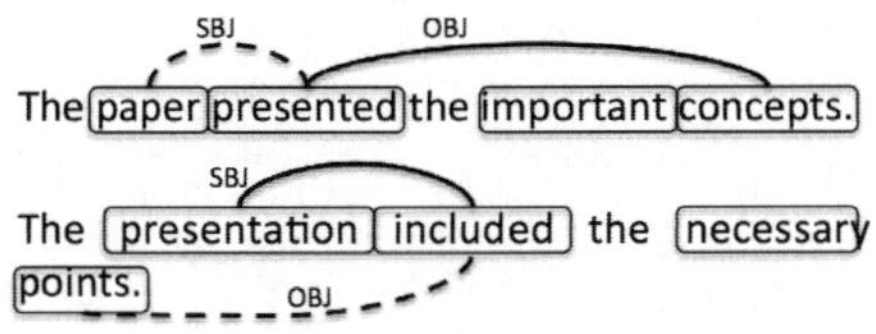

(b) Lexical change - edges of different types are compared, i.e., SBJ with OBJ and OBJ with SBJ respectively. Only the compared edges are shown in the graph representation.

Figure 4: Context matching across two text graphs.

The matching captures similarity across segments, and it captures voice changes. Relatedness between double edges is the average of the vertex matches. Edge labels are compared in ordered matching, and the average vertex match is halved if the edge labels are different. Some sentence structure matches are:

- **Ordered match** - Double edges capture more word order than single edges, hence this matching captures more context. In Figure 5(a) double edges "paper—presented—concepts" and "presentation—included—points" are compared. Vertices "paper", "presented" and "concepts" are compared with vertices "presentation", "included" and "points" respectively.

- **Voice change** - Voice match captures word or phrase shuffling. Change of voice from active to passive, or vice versa is common with paraphrased text. Vertices of the same type are compared across double edges. However, the order of comparison is flipped. Consider the comparison between active and passive texts "The author presented the important concepts." and "Necessary points were explained by the author." in Figure 5(b). We compare "author" and "author" (exact match), "presented" and "were explained" (synonym match), and "concepts" and "points" (common parents match). This results in a cumulative voice match value of 4[8]. Only a voice change match succeeds in capturing such a relationship across the length of a sentence segment.

[8]Average of the vertex match values - 6 for exact match, 5 for synonym match, 2 for common parents match. Edge labels are not compared since the order of comparison of the vertices is flipped.

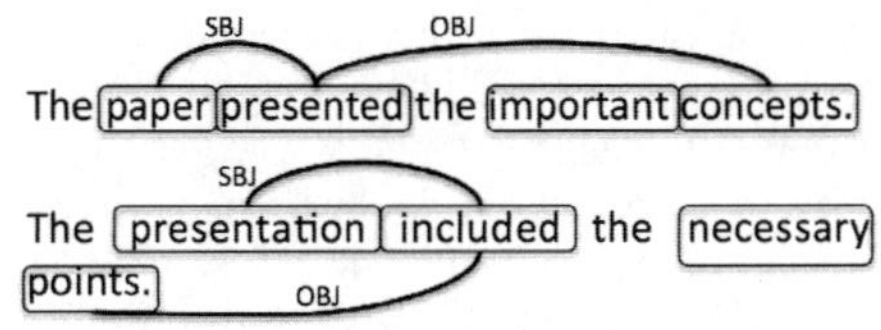

(a) Ordered sentence structure match.

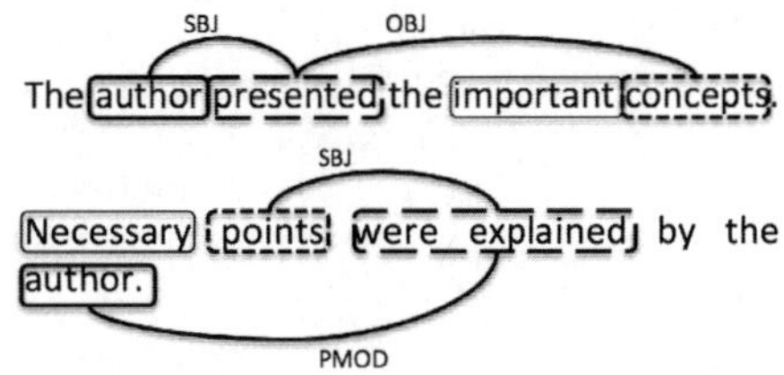

(b) Voice change match - Order of comparison of the vertices is flipped, i.e., "author" is compared with "author", "presented" with "were explained" and "concepts" with "points".

Figure 5: Matching sentence segments across two text graphs. Compared vertices are denoted by similar borders.

$$\textit{SentStruct(S, R)} = \frac{1}{2|T_r|}\Bigg(\sum_{r(t)\in T_r} \underset{\forall s(t)\in T_s}{\operatorname{argmax}}\{\textit{match}_{ord}(s(t), r(t))\} + \sum_{r(t)\in T_r} \underset{\forall s(t)\in T_s}{\operatorname{argmax}}\{\textit{match}_{voice}(s(t), r(t))\}\Bigg) \quad (4)$$

The cumulative sentence structure match in Equation 3 calculates the average of the best ordered ($\textit{match}_{ord}$) and voice change ($\textit{match}_{voice}$) matches that a review's double edges have with corresponding submission double edges. $r(t)$ and $s(t)$ refer to double edges, and T_r and T_s are the number of double edges in the review and submission respectively.

Relevance in Equation 1 can be re-written as the average of the lexico-semantic relatedness values calculated from phrase, context and sentence structure matches.

$$\textit{relevance(S, R)} = \frac{1}{3}(\textit{Phrase(S, R)} + \textit{Context(S, R)} + \textit{SentStruct(S, R)}) \quad (5)$$

7 Experiments

We evaluate the performance of our graph matching approach in identifying the relevance of a review. We also study the performance of each match - *Phrase, Context* and *SentStruct* to determine whether the matches add value, and help improve the overall performance of our approach.

7.1 Data and method

We select review-submission pairs from assignments completed using Expertiza (Gehringer, 2010). Each review is compared with its respective submission, and in order to include some explicit non-relevant cases reviews are compared with other submission texts. For the sake of evaluation we identify whether a review is relevant or not relevant to a submission. We chose 986 review-submission pairs containing an equal number of relevant and non-relevant reviews for our study. Relevance thresholds for the different matches are determined based on the averages. Two annotators labeled 19% of randomly selected data as *relevant* or *non-relevant*. We found an 80% agreement, and a Spearman correlation of 0.44 (significance $p < .0001$) between the two annotators' ratings. We use labels from the first annotator for testing due to the high percent agreement.

7.2 Results

Table 1 contains the accuracy and f-measure values of our approach in identifying relevance. A phrase or token matching contains no context. Consider the sample review "I would retitle 'Teaching, Using and Implementing Ethics' to 'Teaching and Using Codes of Ethics'." This review gets a good phrase match value of 3.3 with a submission (in Figure 1) discussing different codes of ethics. However, this review is not fully relevant to the content of the submission, since it is suggesting a change in title, and does not discuss the submission's content. Thus a simple non context-based phrase match tends to magnify the degree of relatedness between two texts. Thus although a phrase match is important, the lack of context may inflate relevance.

In the case of context matching, we found that lexical and nominalization matches produce lower match values than an ordered match. This happens because not all reviews contain word order changes or nominalizations, and flipping the order of matching results in a lower match when compared to that from an ordered match. The lower values decrease the average context matching, thus rendering a review non-relevant to a submission. This phenomenon explains the dip in context matching's accuracy and f-measure.

We observed a similar trend with sentence structure matches, where voice match produced a lower value than the ordered match in some of the cases. However the average *SentStruct* match in Equation 3, with an accuracy of 65%, shows an improvement over both phrase and context matches (Table 1).

Relevance is identified with an accuracy of 66% and f-measure of 0.67 (Table 1). Our approach has a high recall of 0.71, indicating a good degree of agreement with human relevance ratings. Thus the average of the phrase, context and sentence structure matches shows an improvement over each of the individual matches. This indicates that the addition of context (ordering) from edges and double edges contributes to an improvement in performance.

Dependency trees perform best for phrase matching (Table 1). Accuracy and f-measure of identifying relevance decreases for context, sentence structure and overall relevance matches. This is likely because edges in dependency trees capture only governance (head $\rightarrow$ modifier relation), and not word order.

Dependency trees contain more vertices and edges than our graph, which results in an increase in the time taken to carry out pairwise comparison between the review and submission texts. We randomly selected 4% of the data to study the time taken to identify relevance by dependency trees, and by our graph. We found that in most cases dependency trees take more time than our graph (Figure 6). Thus our graph has a better performance, and is also faster than a dependency tree representation.

Table 1: Comparing accuracy, precision, recall and f-measure values of our word order graph with those of a dependency-tree representation.

Metric	Phrase	Context	Sentence Structure	Relevance
Word order graph				
accuracy	64%	62%	65%	**66%**
precision	0.64	0.63	**0.65**	0.64
recall	0.67	0.60	0.63	**0.71**
***f*-measure**	0.65	0.62	0.64	**0.67**
Dependency tree				
accuracy	64%	50%	52%	61%
precision	0.63	0.50	0.52	0.6
recall	0.7	0.40	0.41	0.65
***f*-measure**	0.66	0.44	0.46	0.62

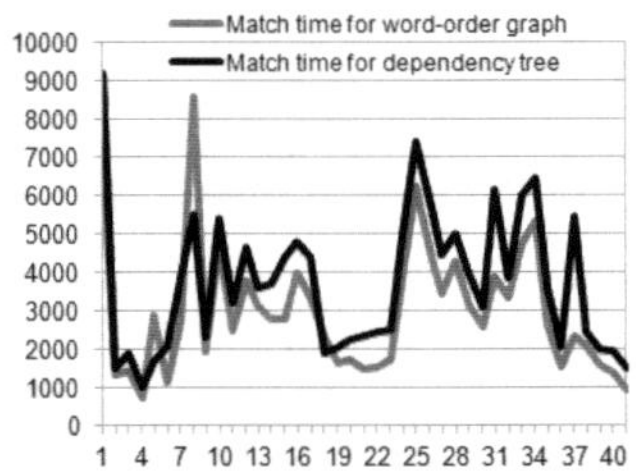

Figure 6: Identifying relevance with dependency trees takes more time (in milliseconds) than with word order graphs.

7.2.1 Comparison with a text overlap-based approach

We compare our approach with an overlap-based relevance identification approach. For this measure we consider the average of 1 to 4-gram overlaps between a review and a submission's texts to determine relevance. This is a precision-based metric, similar to the one used by Papineni *et al.* (2002).

$relevance_{overlap} = \frac{overlap(R,S)}{|R|}$, where *overlap* calculates the number of tokens in the review (R) that overlap with tokens in submission (S), and $|R|$ indicates the number of tokens in the review. Stopwords and frequent words are excluded from the numerator and denominator during overlap calculation.

This approach classifies a majority 62% of the records as non-relevant, and has an f-measure value of 0.59. The overlap approach has a high false negative

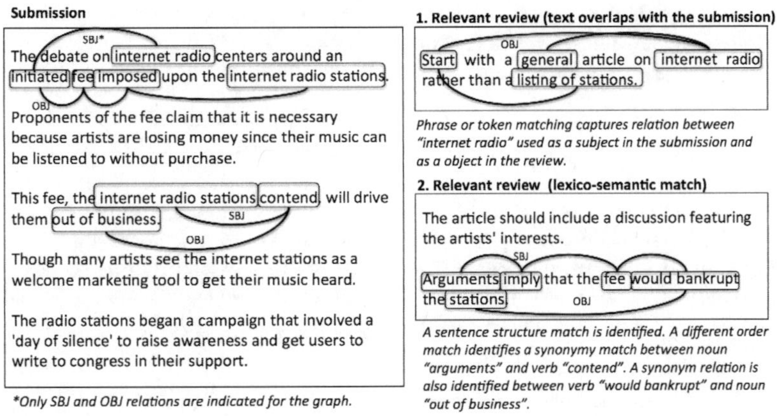

Figure 7: Example of phrase or token matching and sentence structure match between a review and a submission.

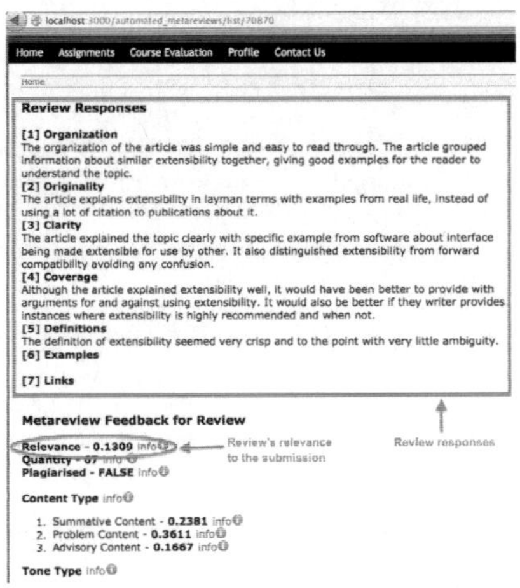

Figure 8: Output from our review assessment system displaying relevance value of reviews. Review's contents are relevant to article on "software extensibility".

rate i.e., several relevant reviews were wrongly classified as non-relevant (recall of 0.52). A simple text overlap, which does not capture the relations our approach succeeds in capturing, does not outperform our approach.

Figure 7 contains two sample reviews displaying phrase and sentence structure matching with sentences from a sample submission. The first review has some instances of exact match with the submission and its relevance may be easy to identify. However, relevance of the second review may not be determined by a text overlaps match. Our order-based matching and semantic relatedness metric help capture the relevance between the second review and the submission.

8 Feedback to Reviewers

A screenshot of the output from our review assessment system can be seen in Figure 8. In this example we have a review written for an article on *software extensibility*[9]. The sample review in Figure 8 has a relevance of 0.1309 (on a scale of 0–1). As can be seen from the screenshot, our automated assessment system provides feedback on not just relevance but on other metrics such as quantity, content and tone types too. However, a discussion of the approach involved in calculating each of these metrics is beyond the scope of this paper.

Our aim with this review assessment system is to motivate reviewers to update their review and make it more relevant to the text under review. This would help authors to better understand details of the review, and use the review to fix and improve their work.

In the future we are planning to improve the format of this output by providing textual feedback in addition to the numeric feedback. The feedback will point to specific instances of the review that need improvement. This may make it easy for reviewers to interpret the numeric score, and maybe further motivate reviewers to use the information to improve their reviews.

9 Conclusion

Assessment of reviews is an important problem in education, science and human resources, and so it is worthy of serious attention. In this paper we use a graph-based approach to determine whether a review is relevant to a piece of submission. Some important findings from our experiments are:

1. Additional context from graph edges and sentence structures helps improve the accuracy and f-measure of predicting relevance.

2. Our approach produces higher f-measure than a text overlap-based approach, that takes the average of 1 to 4-gram overlaps between review and submission texts to determine relevance.

[9]Software Extensibility `https://en.wikipedia.org/wiki/Extensibility`

3. Our approach produces higher accuracy and f-measure than dependency trees, which capture word-modifier information and not word order information.

References

Aria D. Haghighi, Andrew Y. Ng and Christopher D. Manning. 2005. Robust textual inference via graph matching. In *Proceedings of the conference on Human Language Technology and Empirical Methods in Natural Language Processing.* Vancouver, British Columbia, Canada 387–394.

Bernd Bohnet. 2010. Very high accuracy and fast dependency parsing is not a contradiction. In *Proceedings of the 23rd International Conference on Computational Linguistics (COLING).* Beijing, China. 89–97.

Bing Quan Liu and Shuai Xu and Bao Xun Wang. 2009. A combination of rule and supervised learning approach to recognize paraphrases. In *Proceedings of the International Conference on Machine Learning and Cybernetics.* July. 110–115.

Christiane Fellbaum. 1998. WordNet: An Electronic Lexical Database. *MIT Press, Cambridge, MA.*

Chutima Boonthum. 2004. iSTART: paraphrase recognition. In *Proceedings of the ACL 2004 workshop on Student research (ACLstudent).* Barcelona, Spain.

Conny Kuhne and Klemens Bohm and Jing Zhi Yue. 2010. Reviewing the reviewers: A study of author perception on peer reviews in computer science. *CollaborateCom.* 1–8.

David Kauchak and Regina Barzilay. 2006. Paraphrasing for automatic evaluation. In *Proceedings of the main conference on Human Language Technology Conference of the North American Chapter of the Association of Computational Linguistics (HLT-NAACL '06).* New York, New York. 455–462.

Edward F. Gehringer. 2010. Expertiza: Managing Feedback in Collaborative Learning. *Monitoring and Assessment in Online Collaborative Environments: Emergent Computational Technologies for E-Learning Support.* 75–96.

Eneko Agirre, Enrique Alfonseca, Keith Hall, Jana Kravalova, Marius Paşca and Aitor Soroa. 2009. A study on similarity and relatedness using distributional and WordNet-based approaches. In *Proceedings of Human Language Technologies: The 2009 Annual Conference of the North American Chapter of the Association for Computational Linguistics.* Boulder, Colorado. 19–27.

Frank Van Ham, Martin Wattenberg and Fernanda B Viégas. 2009. Mapping text with phrase nets. *IEEE Transactions on Visualization and Computer Graphics* 15(6):1169–1176.

Inderjeet Mani and Eric Bloedorn. 1997. Multi-document summarization by graph search and matching. In *Proceedings of the fourteenth national conference on artificial intelligence and ninth conference on Innovative applications of artificial intelligence (AAAI '97).* Providence, Rhode Island. 622–628.

Khaled M. Hammouda and Mohamed S. Kamel. 2002. Phrase-based Document Similarity Based on an Index Graph Model. In *Proceedings of the 2002 IEEE International Conference on Data Mining (ICDM).*

Kishore Papineni, Salim Roukos, Todd Ward and Wei-Jing Zhu. 2002. BLEU: a method for automatic evaluation of machine translation. In *Proceedings of the 40th Annual Meeting on Association for Computational Linguistics (ACL).* Philadelphia, Pennsylvania. 311–318.

Kristina Toutanova, Dan Klein, Christopher D. Manning and Yoram Singer. 2003. Feature-Rich Part-of-Speech Tagging with a Cyclic Dependency Network. In *Proceedings of HLT-NAACL 2003*, 252–259.

Lakshmi Ramachandran and Edward F. Gehringer. 2011. Automated assessment of review quality using latent semantic analysis. *11th IEEE International Conference on Advanced Learning Technologies.* July. 136–138.

Lakshmi Ramachandran and Edward F. Gehringer. 2012. A Word-Order Based Graph Representation For Relevance Identification [poster]. *CIKM 2012, 21st ACM Conference on Information and Knowledge Management.* Maui, Hawaii. October.

Lakshmi Ramachandran and Edward F. Gehringer. 2013. An Ordered Relatedness Metric for Relevance Identification. In *proceedings of the Seventh IEEE International Conference on Semantic Computing (ICSC) 2013.*

Melissa M. Nelson and Christian D. Schunn. 2009. The nature of feedback: How different types of peer feedback affect writing performance. *Instructional Science.* 27(4):375–401.

Michael Lesk. 1986. Automatic sense disambiguation using machine readable dictionaries: how to tell a pine cone from an ice cream cone. In *Proceedings of the 5th annual international conference on System documentation (SIGDOC).* Toronto, Ontario, Canada. 24–26.

Rada Mihalcea. 2004. Graph-based ranking algorithms for sentence extraction, applied to text summarization. In *Proceedings of the ACL 2004 on Interactive poster and demonstration sessions (ACL demo).* Stroudsburg, PA, USA.

Wenting Xiong and Diane Litman. 2011. Automatically predicting peer-review helpfulness. In *Proceedings of the 49th Annual Meeting of the Association for Computational Linguistics: Human Language Technologies: short papers (HLT) - Volume 2.* Portland, Oregon. 502–507.

Automatic Extraction of Reasoning Chains from Textual Reports

Gleb Sizov and Pinar Öztürk
Department of Computer Science
Norwegian University of Science and Technology
Trondheim, Norway
{sizov, pinar}@idi.ntnu.no

Abstract

Many organizations possess large collections of textual reports that document how a problem is solved or analysed, e.g. medical patient records, industrial accident reports, lawsuit records and investigation reports. Effective use of expert knowledge contained in these reports may greatly increase productivity of the organization. In this article, we propose a method for automatic extraction of reasoning chains that contain information used by the author of a report to analyse the problem at hand. For this purpose, we developed a graph-based text representation that makes the relations between textual units explicit. This representation is acquired automatically from a report using natural language processing tools including syntactic and discourse parsers. When applied to aviation investigation reports, our method generates reasoning chains that reveal the connection between initial information about the aircraft incident and its causes.

1 Introduction

Success of an organization is highly depend on its knowledge which is generated and accumulated by its employees over years. However, unless made explicit and shareable, organizations have the risk of losing this knowledge because employees may change jobs at any time, or retire. It is common to document such experience, also for evidence purpose in case of legal problems and governmental regulations. Consequently, many companies and institutions have large collections of textual reports documenting their organizational experience on a particular task, a client or a problem. Industrial incident reports, law suit reports, electronic patient records and investigation reports are the most intuitive examples. The effective use of the knowledge contained in these reports can save substantial time and resources. For example, incident reports can be used to identify possible risks and prevent future incidents, law suit reports constitute precedences for future cases, and patient records might help to diagnose and find an appropriate treatment for a patient with similar symptoms.

Existing search engines are effective at finding relevant documents. However, after retrieval, interpretation and reasoning with knowledge contained in these documents is still done manually with no computer assistance other than basic keyword-based search. In our research, we are aiming to develop methods that will assist users in interpretation and reasoning with knowledge contained in textual reports. The rationale behind our approach is that experts' line of reasoning for understanding and solving a problem can be reused for the analysis of a similar problem. Reasoning knowledge can be extracted from a report by analysing its syntactic and rhetorical structure. When extracted and represented in a computer-friendly way, this knowledge can be used for automatic and computer-assisted reasoning.

In this article, we propose a method for automatic extraction of reasoning chains from textual reports. A reasoning chain is defined as a sequence of transitions from one piece of information to another starting from the *problem description* and leading to its *solution*. Our model is based on a novel graph-based text representation, called Text Reasoning Network (TRN), which decomposes a document into text units, discovers the connections between these text units and makes them explicit. TRN is acquired automatically from text using natural language processing tools including a syntactic parser, a discourse parser and a semantic similarity measure.

We tested our method on aviation investigation reports from Transportation Board of Canada. These reports are produced as a result of investigation of aircraft incidents where experts are assigned the task of analysing an incident and writing down their understanding of what and why it happened. Reasoning chains extracted from the investigation reports reveal the connection between initial information about the incident and its causes. When visualized, this connection can be interpreted and analysed.

The rest of the paper is organized as follows. Section 2 provides an overview of the related research. In section 3, TRN representation is described. Generation of reasoning chains from aviation investigation reports is explained in section 4. Interesting examples of reasoning chains generated by our system are demonstrated and analysed in section 5. In section 6, we discuss the results and elaborate on future work.

2 Related Work

To our knowledge, automatic extraction of reasoning chains from text has not been attempted before. However, we were able to find several papers dealing with text processing tasks relevant to our goal that make use of graph-based representations.

The work done by Pechsiri and Piriyakul (2010) is focused on extraction of causal relations from text and construction of an explanation graph. The relations are extracted between clauses based on mined cause-effect verb pairs, e.g. "If the [aphids infest rice pants], [the leaves will become yellow]." with cause verb "infest" and effect verb "become". The explanation graph is constructed directly from the extracted relations, which is different from our approach where reasoning chains are extracted as paths from the graph-based representation of a report. There is only one example of the explanation graph presented in the paper. This graph is generated from plant disease technical papers capturing part of the domain knowledge. Manual inspection of the graph revealed few mistakes.

An interesting research was conducted by Berant (2012) for his PhD thesis. Unlike Pechsiri and Piriyakul (2010), his approach relies on textual entailment instead of causal relations. Entailment relations are obtained between propositional patterns, e.g. $(X \xleftarrow{subj} desire \xrightarrow{obj} Y, X \xleftarrow{subj} want \xrightarrow{obj} Y)$, using a classifier trained on distributional similarity features. The focus of their work is to exploit transitive nature of entailment relations in learning of entailment graphs. As an application, the authors developed a novel text exploration tool, where a user can drill down/up from one statement to another through the entailment graph. Entailment relations alone, i.e. $text \xrightarrow{entails} hypothesis$, are not sufficient for extraction of reasoning chains because the *hypothesis* often contains the information which is already present in the *text*, making it impossible to create a path from the problem description to the solution. However, when combined with other types of relations they might be useful for out task.

In the paper by Jin and Srihari (2007), authors generate and evaluate evidence trails between concepts across documents. An evidence trail is a path connecting two concepts in a graph where nodes are concepts that correspond to named entities and noun phrases participating in subject-verb-object constructs. Three variations of the representation are tested, each with edges capturing different types of information. In the first one, edges capture word order in text. The second one captures co-occurrence of concepts. The third variation contains edges with weights corresponding to the similarity between contexts of the concepts. Vector space model is used to represent and measure the similarity between the contexts. The concept-based representation is substantially different from TRN but the idea of finding a shortest path between nodes and use it as the evidence is similar. There is one example of the evidence trail shown in the paper: "bush - afghanistan - qaeda - bin ladin", which reveals the connection between topics rather than concrete pieces of information.

A graph-based representation similar to (Jin and Srihari, 2007) have been applied for Textual Case-

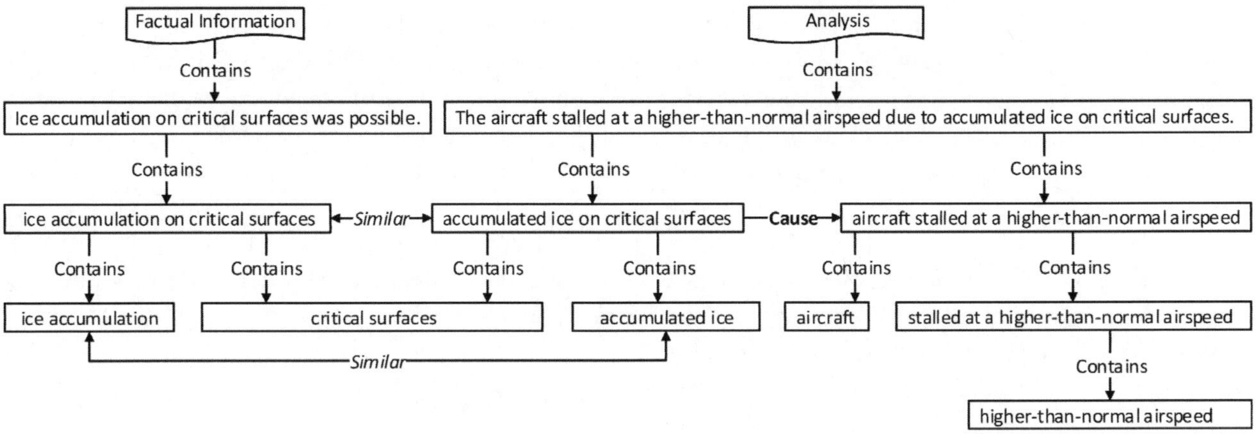

Figure 1: Two sentences represented as Text Reasoning Network.

Based Reasoning (TCBR) (Lenz and Burkhard, 1996; Cunningham et al., 2004), a task of automatically solving a new problem given a collection of reports describing previous problems with solutions. The dataset we use in our research can be considered a TCBR dataset, since each report contains a problem description and a solution part. Problem-solving based on knowledge represented in textual form is a tough task and in practice TCBR approaches either do classification of a problem into predefined classes or retrieve a report that describes a problem similar to a query problem. In the later case, information retrieval methods are utilized, including graph-based representations for computing similarity between documents as it is done by Cunningham et al. (2004). Their representation, inspired by Schenker et al. (2003), contains terms as nodes and edges connecting the adjacent terms in text. Nodes and edges are labelled with the frequency of their appearance and with the section where they appear, i.e. title or text. Infrequent terms are removed. In addition, domain knowledge is introduced as a list of important domain terms that are preserved even if their frequency is low. The similarity used is based on maximum common sub-graph. When tested on summary documents from a law firm handling insurance cases, the results show improvement over vector space model representations.

3 Text Reasoning Network

In our approach, a reasoning chain is extracted as a path from the graph-based text representation. An appropriate representation is crucial because chains extracted from it are only as good as the representation itself. In this section we introduce a novel graph-based text representation, called Text Reasoning Network (TRN), which is a graph with two types of nodes: text nodes and section nodes; and three types of edges: structural, similarity and causal. Figure 1 shows two sentences from a report represented as TRN with section nodes on the top and all the text nodes below them. The representation is acquired automatically from text by the following procedure: (1) syntax trees obtained from a syntactic parser are added to the graph, (2) section nodes are attached to sentence nodes, (3) similarity edges are added between similar text nodes, (4) cause relations identified by a discourse parser are added. The rest of this section provides details on the structure of TRN and methods used to generate it from text.

3.1 Nodes and Structural Relations

We are aiming to extract chains that capture the information used by the author of a report to reason about the problem at hand. Graph-based text representations described in section 2 use individual terms or short phrases as nodes. Small text units such as these are unable to capture sufficient information for our purpose. Another popular choice for a node in a textual graph is a sentence, which captures a more or less complete piece of information and is easy to interpret. However, a complex sentence may contain several pieces of information where only one is used in a reasoning chain.

A syntax tree provides a natural decomposition of

a sentence into its constituents. Since it is hard to determine beforehand the size of constituents that would be useful in a reasoning chain, we decided to incorporate all the S (sentence, clause), NP (noun phrase) and VP (verb phrase) nodes from syntax trees produced by Stanford Parser (Klein and Manning, 2003). These nodes are referred to as *text nodes*. In addition to text nodes, the structure of a syntax tree is also retained by adding *structural relations Contains* and *PartOf* to TRN that correspond to relations between parent and children text units in the syntax tree. Figure 1 shows text nodes extracted from two sentences along with *Contains* relations between them. *PartOf* edges are not shown to avoid the clutter.

Graphs extracted from different sentences in a document are combined into one. Each node has a unique identity that is composed of a sequence of stemmed words with stopwords removed. The major implication of this is that if two sentences overlap, they will share one or several nodes, e.g. node "critical surfaces" in figure 1.

In addition to text nodes, there are also *section nodes* corresponding to parts of a document, e.g. "Factual Information" and "Analysis" nodes in figure 1. These nodes capture the structure of a document. Text nodes containing a complete sentence, also referred to as *sentence nodes*, are attached to section nodes by structural relations.

3.2 Similarity Relations

In addition to structural relations, text nodes are connected through similarity relations. To obtain these relations, a similarity value is computed for each pair of text nodes of the same category (S, VP, NP) that are not in the same sentence. *Similar* edges are added to the graph for node pairs with the similarity value above a predefined threshold, e.g. nodes "ice accumulation" and "accumulated ice" in figure 1.

Our similarity measure finds one-to-one alignment of words from two text units to maximize the total similarity between them. For words we compute *LCH* (Leacock et al., 1998) similarity, based on a shortest path between the corresponding senses in WordNet. A complete bipartite graph is constructed and the maximum weighted bipartite matching is computed using the Hungarian Algorithm (Kuhn, 1955). Nodes in this bipartite graph represent words from the text units while edges have weights that correspond to similarities between words. Maximum weighted bipartite matching finds a one-to-one alignment that maximizes the sum of similarities between aligned words. This sum is normalized to lie between 0 and 1 and is used as the final value for the similarity between text units. If the value is higher or equal 0.6 a *Similar* edge is added between the corresponding nodes.

3.3 Causal Relations

Causal relations are essential for analysis and decision making allowing inference about past and future events (Garcia-Retamero et al., 2007). As seen in (Pechsiri and Piriyakul, 2010) causal graphs extracted from domain-specific documents provide a powerful representation of expert knowledge.

State-of-the-art techniques for extraction of causal relations from text use automatic classifiers trained on lexical features to recognize relations between subject and object in a clause or between verbs of different clauses (Chang and Choi, 2005; Bethard and Martin, 2008). Causal relations are among discourse relations defined by Rhetorical Structure Theory (Mann and Thompson, 1988). Therefore, a discourse parser can be used to obtain them from text. The advantage of this approach is that a discourse parser recognizes relations between larger text units. Few discourse parsers are available that can parse an entire document. For our work we used PDTB-Styled End-to-End Discourse Parser by Lin et al. (2010), which makes use of machine learning techniques trained on Penn Discourse Treebank (PDTB) (Prasad et al., 2008). Cause relations identified by the parser are added to TRN graph by mapping arguments of the relations to text nodes and then adding *Cause* edges between them.

4 Generation of Reasoning Chains from Aviation Accident Reports

Generation of a reasoning chain from a report is a three-stage process: (1) a report is converted from text to a TRN graph, (2) given a start and an end node, several paths are extracted from the graph, (3) paths are combined, post-processed and visualized.

4.1 Dataset

In our work we use aviation investigation reports from Transportation Safety Board of Canada[1]. Each report in this collection documents an aircraft incident and contains the following sections: (1) "Summary" is a brief description of the incident, (2) "Factual Information" (further referred to as "Factual") contains details about the aircraft, pilot, weather conditions, terrain and communication with controllers (3) "Analysis" is a discussion of the incident with the purpose to explain it based on the information presented in the previous section, (4) "Findings as to Causes and Contributing Factor" (further referred to as "Causes") is a brief enumeration of findings that most likely caused the incident.

The reports were downloaded from Transportation Board of Canada website as html documents. Text and structure were extracted from html using a custom Java component developed based on manual analysis of the html source. Preprocessing steps including tokenization, sentence splitting and part-of-speech tagging were accomplished using ANNIE components in GATE NLP platform (Cunningham et al., 2002).

4.2 Extraction of Reasoning Chains

We define a reasoning chain as the shortest path through a TRN representation of a report starting from a sentence in "Summary" and ending at one of the sentences in "Causes" section. The rationale behind this decision is to reveal the author's reasoning line starting from the initial information about the incident contained in "Summary" and leading to incident causes in "Causes" section. Hence, the path finding process is constrained to follow the direction from "Summary" to "Causes" through "Factual" and "Analysis" sections. The reasoning chain path with constraints is defined by the following context-free grammar in Backus-Naur Form (optional items in [...]):

⟨*path*⟩ ::= ⟨*summary-path*⟩ [⟨*edge*⟩ ⟨*factual-path*⟩] [⟨*edge*⟩ ⟨*analysis-path*⟩] ⟨*edge*⟩ ⟨*causes-path*⟩

⟨*summary-path*⟩ ::= ⟨*summary-node*⟩
| ⟨*summary-node*⟩ ⟨*contains-edge*⟩ ⟨*summary-path*⟩

⟨*factual-path*⟩ ::= ⟨*factual-node*⟩
| ⟨*factual-node*⟩ ⟨*edge*⟩ ⟨*factual-path*⟩

⟨*analysis-path*⟩ ::= ⟨*analysis-node*⟩
| ⟨*analysis-node*⟩ ⟨*edge*⟩ ⟨*analysis-path*⟩

⟨*causes-path*⟩ ::= ⟨*causes-node*⟩
| ⟨*causes-node*⟩ ⟨*partof-edge*⟩ ⟨*causes-path*⟩

⟨*edge*⟩ ::= ⟨*partof-edge*⟩
| ⟨*contains-edge*⟩
| ⟨*similar-edge*⟩
| ⟨*cause-edge*⟩

Several paths are obtained for each "Summary" sentence, each of which starting at one of the text nodes contained in the sentence. These paths are then combined into a reasoning graph. Before visualization, a post-processing algorithm is applied to make the reasoning graph more compact. The algorithm collapses a sequence of structural edges of the same type into a single edge, e.g. $A \xrightarrow{contains} B \xrightarrow{contains} C$ is converted into $A \xrightarrow{contains} C$ if there is no other edge attached to B. The compressed graph (shown in figures 2, 3 and 4) is visualized using JGraphX library with hierarchical layout for automatic positioning of nodes.

5 Examples and Analysis

In this section we analyse three reasoning graphs generated by our system. These graphs were selected mainly because of their compact size and ease of interpretation even for someone who is not an aviation expert. Every chain starts with a sentence from "Summary" on the top of the figure and ends with one or several sentences in "Causes" on the bottom. For each node a contained text unit is displayed, followed by one or several letters in parenthesis indicating which section of the report this text node is observed in: S - "Summary", F - "Factual", A - "Analysis", C - "Causes".

Figure 2 shows the reasoning graph with one branch expressing that the captain's focus on "setting climb power" and the "landing gear" prevented him from paying attention to the "aircraft altitude" so the "sink rate was undetected and aircraft struck the ground". The start and the end sentences are not similar and it is the sentence from the "Analysis" section that connects these two.

[1] Aviation Investigation Reports are available at `http://goo.gl/k9mMV`

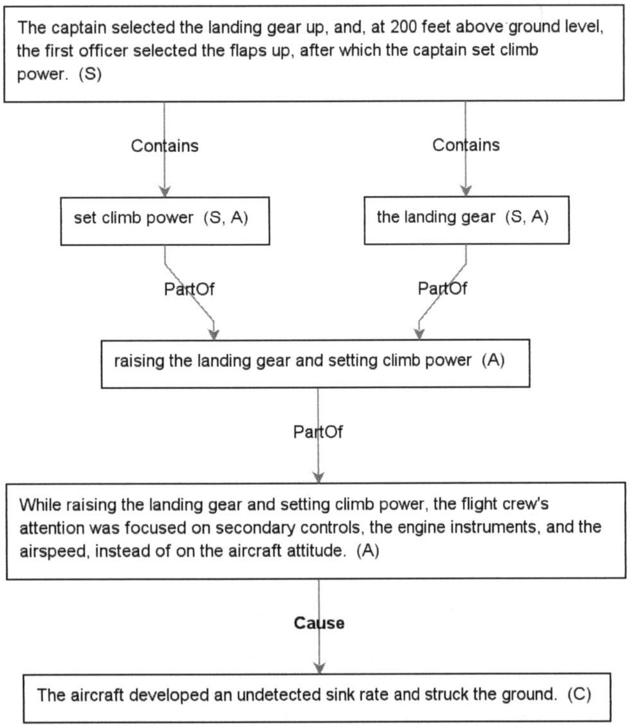

Figure 2: A reasoning graph from report A05O0225 (available at `goo.gl/SZpTS`)

The graph in figure 3 has two branches. The left branch directly points to a sentence with "the auxiliary fuel pump" but it does not explain "a poor electrical connection". The right branch, however, is longer and goes from "switched fuel tank" to "fuel flow" and then to "fuel pressure", which is part of a sentence in the "Cause" section that includes this text segment: "reduction of fuel pressure, preventing normal engine operation".

The graph in figure 4 contains two branches as well. The left branch picks up the location of the flight "Deer Lake" which relates to "icing conditions" although the text node suggesting "a lower altitude was requested to remain clear of icing conditions" makes this branch incoherent. The right branch provides a connection between "Provincial Airlines Limited" and "no requirement" in their "standard operating procedures" for a "method for ensuring the correct selection of AFCS climb modes". The chain goes through "an inappropriate AFCS mode" providing a good idea of the incident cause.

Reasoning chains extracted by the system provide a brief overview of the authors' reasoning line showing how a basic information about the incident is connected to its causes. However, some chains are less informative than others (left branch in figure 3) or incoherent (left branch of 4). In the former case the chain could be made more informative if the system will be queried to find evidence for "poor electrical connection" in addition to "the auxiliary fuel pump". In the latter case, the chain becomes incoherent because "icing conditions" is used in different contexts where the first sentence states the lack of "icing conditions" and the second the presence of "icing conditions". It is possible to account for this inconsistency by introducing a preference for larger text units capturing more context or by recognizing negations/absence.

6 Conclusion and Future Work

This paper presents a method for extraction of reasoning chains from textual reports. The method is based on a graph-based text representation that captures both the structure and the content of the report. Extracted reasoning chains provide a convenient way to visualize information used by a domain expert to reason about causes of an aircraft incident. It may help in analysis of future incidents and opens the possibility for automatic or computer-assisted analysis. The methods can be adapted to other domains and applications by defining appropriate start nodes, end nodes and constraints like it is done in section 4.2.

Extraction of reasoning chains is a new task and there are yet no evaluation measures available. One of the primary goals for our future work is to develop a formal evaluation procedure for this task. An intrinsic evaluation will require manually constructed reasoning chains as the gold standard to compare the automatically extracted ones with. For the extrinsic evaluation, reasoning chains can be used in TCBR task for solution retrieval and evaluated with TCBR evaluation measures (Raghunandan et al., 2008; Adeyanju et al., 2010). We also plan to continue our work on the representation by adding new types of relations to TRN and on the reasoning chain extraction algorithm by adapting flow networks instead of shortest path for extraction of reasoning chains.

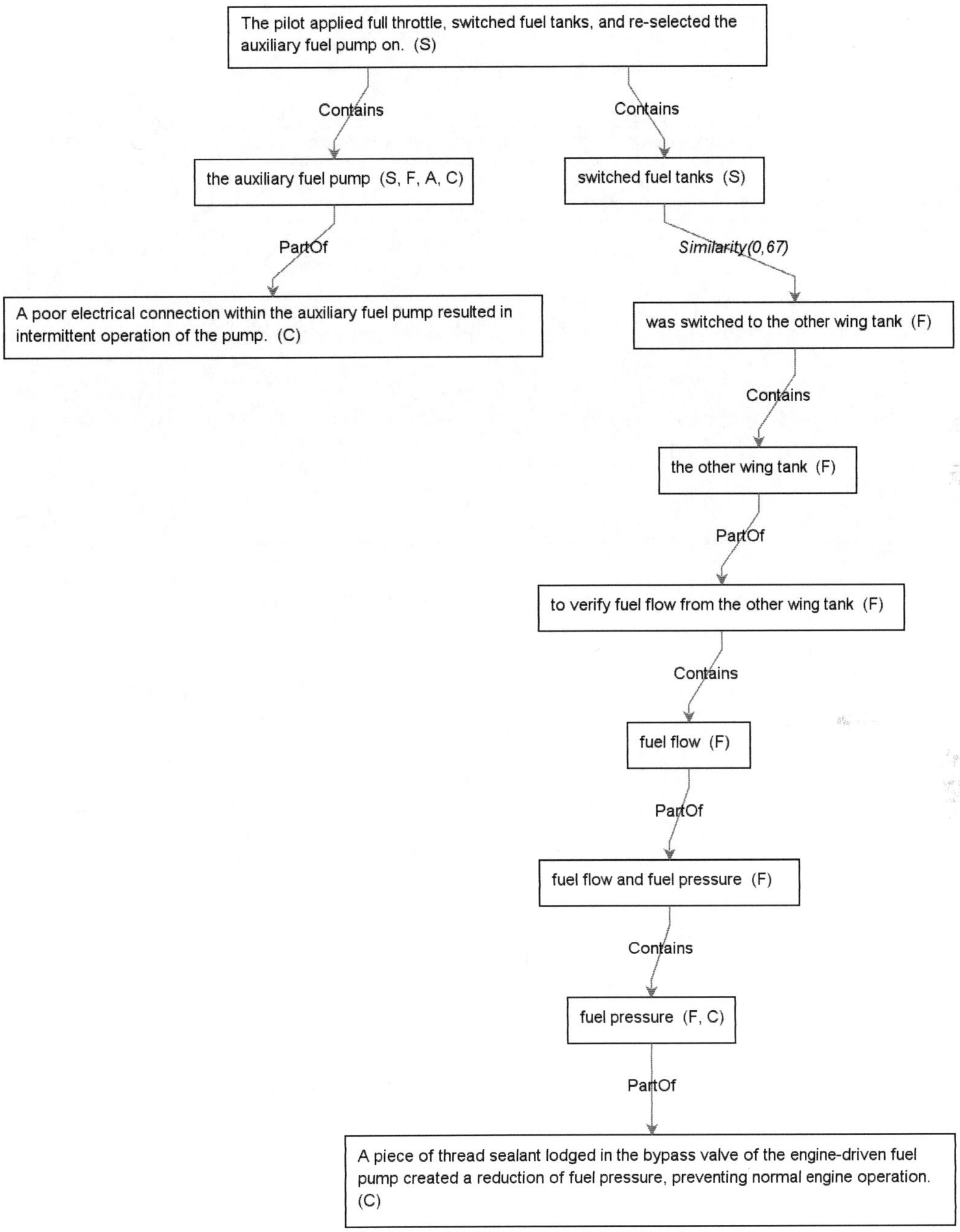

Figure 3: A reasoning graph from report A05O0146 (available at `goo.gl/MPMIq`)

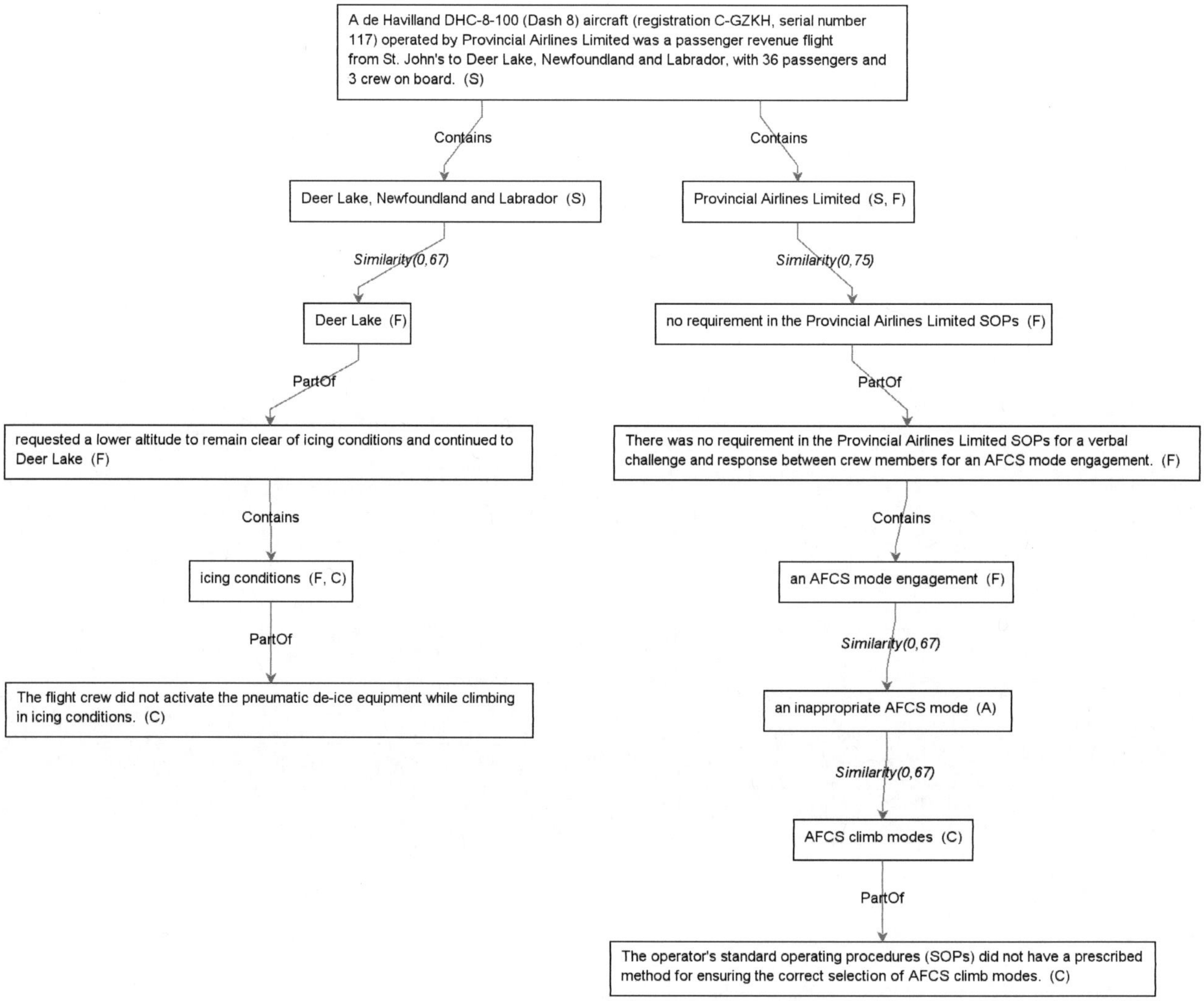

Figure 4: A reasoning graph from report A05A0059 (available at `goo.gl/u1CXI`)

References

Ibrahim Adeyanju, Nirmalie Wiratunga, Robert Lothian, and Susan Craw. 2010. Applying machine translation evaluation techniques to textual cbr. In *Case-Based Reasoning. Research and Development*, pages 21–35. Springer.

Jonathan Berant. 2012. *Global Learning of Textual Entailment Graphs*. Ph.D. thesis, Tel Aviv University.

Steven Bethard and James H Martin. 2008. Learning semantic links from a corpus of parallel temporal and causal relations. In *Proceedings of the 46th Annual Meeting of the Association for Computational Linguistics on Human Language Technologies: Short Papers*, pages 177–180. Association for Computational Linguistics.

Du-Seong Chang and Key-Sun Choi. 2005. Causal relation extraction using cue phrase and lexical pair probabilities. In *Natural Language Processing–IJCNLP 2004*, pages 61–70. Springer.

Hamish Cunningham, Diana Maynard, Kalina Bontcheva, and Valentin Tablan. 2002. Gate: an architecture for development of robust hlt applications. In *Proceedings of 40th Annual Meeting of the Association for Computational Linguistics*, pages 168–175, Philadelphia, Pennsylvania, USA, July. Association for Computational Linguistics.

Colleen Cunningham, Rosina Weber, Jason M Proctor, Caleb Fowler, and Michael Murphy. 2004. Investigating graphs in textual case-based reasoning. In *Advances in Case-Based Reasoning*, pages 573–586. Springer.

Rocio Garcia-Retamero, Annika Wallin, and Anja Dieckmann. 2007. Does causal knowledge help us be faster and more frugal in our decisions? *Memory & cognition*, 35(6):1399–1409.

Wei Jin and Rohini K. Srihari. 2007. Graph-based text representation and knowledge discovery. *Proceedings of the 2007 ACM symposium on Applied computing - SAC '07*, page 807.

Dan Klein and Christopher D Manning. 2003. Accurate unlexicalized parsing. In *Proceedings of the 41st Annual Meeting on Association for Computational Linguistics-Volume 1*, pages 423–430. Association for Computational Linguistics.

Harold W Kuhn. 1955. The hungarian method for the assignment problem. *Naval research logistics quarterly*, 2(1-2):83–97.

Claudia Leacock, George A Miller, and Martin Chodorow. 1998. Using corpus statistics and wordnet relations for sense identification. *Computational Linguistics*, 24(1):147–165.

Mario Lenz and Hans-Dieter Burkhard. 1996. Case retrieval nets: Basic ideas and extensions. In *KI-96: Advances in Artificial Intelligence*, pages 227–239. Springer.

Ziheng Lin, Hwee Tou Ng, and Min-Yen Kan. 2010. A pdtb-styled end-to-end discourse parser. Technical report, Cambridge Univ Press.

William C Mann and Sandra A Thompson. 1988. Rhetorical structure theory: Toward a functional theory of text organization. *Text*, 8(3):243–281.

Chaveevan Pechsiri and Rapepun Piriyakul. 2010. Explanation knowledge graph construction through causality extraction from texts. *Journal of Computer Science and Technology*, 25(5):1055–1070.

Rashmi Prasad, Nikhil Dinesh, Alan Lee, Eleni Miltsakaki, Livio Robaldo, Aravind K Joshi, and Bonnie L Webber. 2008. The penn discourse treebank 2.0. In *LREC*. Citeseer.

M. A. Raghunandan, Nirmalie Wiratunga, Sutanu Chakraborti, Stewart Massie, and Deepak Khemani. 2008. Evaluation measures for tcbr systems. In *Advances in Case-Based Reasoning*, pages 444–458. Springer.

A. Schenker, M. Last, H. Bunke, and A. Kandel. 2003. Clustering of web documents using a graph model. *Web Document Analysis: Challenges and Opportunities*, pages 1–16.

Graph-based Approaches for Organization Entity Resolution in MapReduce

Hakan Kardes, Deepak Konidena, Siddharth Agrawal, Micah Huff and **Ang Sun**
inome Inc.
Bellevue, WA, USA
{hkardes,dkonidena,sagrawal,mhuff,asun}@inome.com

Abstract

Entity Resolution is the task of identifying which records in a database refer to the same entity. A standard machine learning pipeline for the entity resolution problem consists of three major components: blocking, pairwise linkage, and clustering. The blocking step groups records by shared properties to determine which pairs of records should be examined by the pairwise linker as potential duplicates. Next, the linkage step assigns a probability score to pairs of records inside each block. If a pair scores above a user-defined threshold, the records are presumed to represent the same entity. Finally, the clustering step turns the input records into clusters of records (or profiles), where each cluster is uniquely associated with a single real-world entity. This paper describes the blocking and clustering strategies used to deploy a massive database of organization entities to power a major commercial People Search Engine. We demonstrate the viability of these algorithms for large data sets on a 50-node hadoop cluster.

1 Introduction

A challenge for builders of databases whose information is culled from multiple sources is the detection of duplicates, where a single real-world entity gives rise to multiple records (see (Elmagarmid, 2007) for an overview). Entity Resolution is the task of identifying which records in a database refer to the same entity. Online citation indexes need to be able to navigate through the different capitalization and abbreviation conventions that appear in bibliographic entries. Government agencies need to know whether a record for "Robert Smith" living on "Northwest First Street" refers to the same person as one for a "Bob Smith" living on "1st St. NW". In a standard machine learning approach to this problem all records first go through a cleaning process that starts with the removal of bogus, junk and spam records. Then all records are normalized to an approximately common representation. Finally, all major noise types and inconsistencies are addressed, such as empty/bogus fields, field duplication, outlier values and encoding issues. At this point, all records are ready for the major stages of the entity resolution, namely blocking, pairwise linkage, and clustering. Since comparing all pairs of records is quadratic in the number of records and hence is intractable for large data sets, the blocking step groups records by shared properties to determine which pairs of records should be examined by the pairwise linker as potential duplicates. Next, the linkage step assigns a score to pairs of records inside each block. If a pair scores above a user-defined threshold, the records are presumed to represent the same entity. The clustering step partitions the input records into sets of records called profiles, where each profile corresponds to a single entity.

In this paper, we focus on entity resolution for the organization entity domain where all we have are the organization names and their relations with individuals. Let's first describe the entity resolution for organization names, and discuss its significance and the challenges in more detail. Our process starts by collecting billions of personal records from three sources of U.S. records to power a major commercial People Search Engine. Example fields on these records might include name, address, birthday, phone number, (encrypted) social security number, relatives, friends, job title, universities attended, and organizations worked for. Since the data sources are heterogeneous, each data source provides different aliases of an organization including abbreviations, preferred names, legal names, etc. For example, Person A might have both "Microsoft", "Microsoft Corp", "Microsoft Corporation", and "Microsoft Research" in his/her profile's organization field. Person B might have "University of Washington", while Person C has "UW" as the organization listed in his/her profile. Moreover, some organizations change their names, or are acquired by other institutions and become subdivisions. There are also many organizations that share the same name or abbreviation. For instance, both "University of Washington", "University of Wisconsin Madison", "University of Wyoming" share the same abbreviation, "UW". Additionally, some of the data sources might be noisier than the others and there might be different kind of typos that needs to be addressed.

Addressing the above issues in organization fields is crucial for data quality as graphical representations of the data become more popular. If we show different representations of the same organization as separate institutions in a single person's profile, it will decrease the confidence of a customer about our data quality. Moreover, we should have a unique representation of organizations in order to properly answer more complicated graph-based queries such as "how am I connected to company X?", or "who are my friends that has a friend that works at organization X, and graduated from school Y?".

We have developed novel and highly scalable components for our entity resolution pipeline which is customized for organizations. The focus of this paper is the graph-based blocking and clustering components. In the remainder of the paper, we first describe these components in Section 2. Then, we evaluate the performance of our entity resolution framework using several real-world datasets in Section 3. Finally, we conclude in Section 4.

2 Methodology

In this section, we will mainly describe the blocking and clustering strategies as they are more graph related. We will also briefly mention our pairwise linkage model.

The processing of large data volumes requires highly scalable parallelized algorithms, and this is only possible with distributed computing. To this end, we make heavy use of the hadoop implementation of the MapReduce computing framework, and both the blocking and clustering procedures described here are implemented as a series of hadoop jobs written in Java. It is beyond the scope of this paper to fully describe the MapReduce framework (see (Lin, 2010) for an overview), but we do discuss the ways its constraints inform our design. MapReduce divides computing tasks into a map phase in which the input, which is given as (key,value) pairs, is split up among multiple machines to be worked on in parallel and a reduce phase in which the output of the map phase is put back together for each key to independently process the values for each key in parallel. Moreover, in a MapReduce context, recursion becomes iteration.

2.1 Blocking

How might we subdivide a huge number of organizations based on similarity or probability scores when all we have is their names and their relation with people? We could start by grouping them into sets according to the words they contain. This would go a long way towards putting together records that represent the same organization, but it would still be imperfect because organizations may have nicknames, abbreviations, previous names, or misspelled names. To enhance this grouping we could consider a different kind of information like soundex or a similar phonetic algorithm for indexing words to address some of the limitations of above grouping due to typos. We can also group together the organizations which appear in the same person's profile. This way, we will be able to block the different representations of the same organization to some extent. With a handful of keys like this we can build redundancy into our system to accommodate different types of error, omission, and natural variability. The blocks of records they produce may overlap, but this is desirable because it gives the clustering a chance to join records that blocking did not put together.

The above blocks will vary widely in size. For example, we may have a small set of records containing the word "Netflix" which can then be passed along immediately to the linkage component. However, we may have a set of millions of records containing the word "State" which still needs to be cut down to subsets with manageable sizes, otherwise it will be again impractical to do all pairwise computations in this block. One way to do this is to find other common properties to further subdivide this set. The set of all records containing not only "State" but also a specific state name like "Washington" is smaller than the set of all records containing the word "State", and intuitively records in this set will be more likely to represent the same organization. Additionally we could block together all the "State" records with the same number of words, or combination of the initials of each word. As with the original blocks, overlap between these sub-blocks is desirable. We do not have to be particularly artful in our choice of sub-blocking criteria: any property that seems like it might be individuating will do. As long as we have an efficient way to search the space, we can let the data dynamically choose different sub-blocking strategies for each oversize block. To this end, we use the ordering on block keys to define a binomial tree where each node contains a list of block keys and is the parent of nodes that have keys that come later in the ordering appended to the list. Figure 1 shows a tree for the oversize top-level set tTkn1 with three sub-blocking tokens sTkn1 $<$ sTkn2 $<$ sTkn3. With each node of the tree we can associate a block whose key is the list of blocks keys in that node and whose records are the intersection of the records in those blocks, e.g. the tTkn1 $\cap$ sTkn1 $\cap$ sTkn2 node represents all the records for organizations containing all these tokens. Because the cardinality of an intersected set is less than or equal to the cardinalities of the sets that were intersected, every block

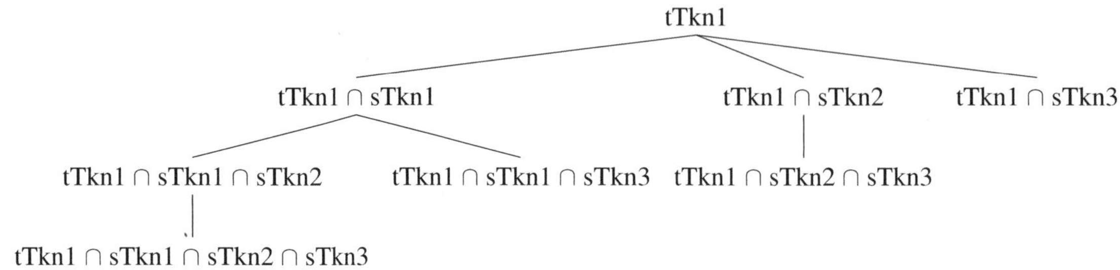

Figure 1: The root node of this tree represents an oversized block for the name Smith and the other nodes represent possible sub-blocks. The sub-blocking algorithm enumerates the tree breadth-first, stopping when it finds a correctly-sized sub-block.

in the tree is larger than or equal to any of its children. We traverse the tree breadth-first and only recurse into nodes above the maximum block size. This allows us to explore the space of possible sub-blocks in cardinality order for a given branch, stopping as soon as we have a small enough sub-block.

The algorithm that creates the blocks and sub-blocks takes as input a set of records and a maximum block size M. All the input records are grouped into blocks defined by the top-level properties. Those top-level blocks that are not above the maximum size are set aside. The remaining oversized blocks are partitioned into sub-blocks by sub-blocking properties that the records they contain share, and those properties are appended to the key. The process is continued recursively until all sub-blocks have been whittled down to an acceptable size. The pseudo code of the blocking algorithm is presented in Figure 2. We will represent the key and value pairs in the MapReduce framework as $< key; value >$. The input organization records are represented as $< INPUT\_FLAG, ORG\_NAME >$. For the first iteration, this job takes the organization list as input. In later iterations, the input is the output of the previous blocking iteration. In the first iteration, the mapper function extracts the top-level and sub-level tokens from the input records. It combines the organization name and all the sub-level tokens in a temp variable called $newValue$. Next, for each top-level token, it emits this top-level token and the newValue in the following format: $< topToken, newValue >$. For the later iterations, it combines each sub level token with the current blocking key, and emits them to the reducer. Also note that the lexicographic ordering of the block keys allows separate mapper processes to work on different nodes in a level of the binomial tree without creating redundant sub-blocks (e.g. if one mapper creates a International ∩ Business ∩ Machines block another mapper will not create a International ∩ Machines ∩ Business one). This is necessary because individual MapReduce jobs run independently without shared memory or other runtime communication mechanisms. In the reduce phase, all the records will be grouped together for each block key. The reducer function iterates over all the records in a newly-created sub-block, counting them to determine whether or not the block is small enough or needs to be further subdivided. The blocks that the reducer deems oversized become inputs to the next iteration. Care is taken that the memory requirements of the reducer function are constant in the size of a fixed buffer because otherwise the reducer runs out of memory on large blocks. Note that we create a black list from the high frequency words in organization names, and we don't use these as top-level properties as such words do not help us with individuating the records.

More formally, this process can be understood in terms of operations on sets. In a set of N records there are $\frac{1}{2}N(N-1)$ unique pairs, so an enumeration over all of them is $O(N^2)$. The process of blocking divides this original set into k blocks, each of which contains at most a fixed maximum of M records. The exhaustive comparison of pairs from these sets is $O(k)$, and the constant factors are tractable if we choose a small enough M. In the worst case, all the sub-blocks except the ones with the very longest keys are oversize. Then the sub-blocking algorithm will explore the powerset of all possible blocking keys and thus have exponential runtime. However, as the blocking keys get longer, the sets they represent get smaller and eventually fall beneath the maximum size. In practice these two countervailing motions work to keep this strategy tractable.

2.2 Pairwise Linkage Model

In this section, we give just a brief overview of our pairwise linkage system as a detailed description and evaluation of that system is beyond the scope of this paper.

We take a feature-based classification approach to predict the likelihood of two organization names $< o_1, o_2 >$ referring to the same organization entity. Specifically, we use the OpenNLP[1] maximum entropy (maxent) package as our machine learning tool. We choose to work with maxent because the training is fast and it has a good support for classification. Regarding the features, we mainly have two types: surface string features and context features. Examples of surface string features are edit dis-

[1] http://opennlp.apache.org/

```
Blocking Iterations
map(key, value)
  if(key.equals(EntityName)
    String[] tokens ← value.split(" ")
    sublevelTokenSet ← ∅
    toplevelTokenSet ← ∅
    for each (token ∈ tokens)
      sublevelTokenSet.add(token.hashCode())
    if(notExist(blackList, token))
      toplevelTokenSet.add(token.hashCode())
    String newValue ← value
    for each (sToken ∈ sublevelTokenSet)
      newValue ← newValue.append(STR + sToken)
    for each (tToken ∈ toplevelTokenSet)
      emit(tToken, newValue)
  else
    String[] keyTokens ← key.split(STR)
    String[] valueTokens ← value.split(STR)
    for each (token ∈ valueTokens)
      if(token > keyTokens[keyTokens.length − 1])
        emit(key.append(STR + token), value)

reduce(key, < iterable > values)
    buffer ← ∅
  for each (value ∈ values)
    buffer.add(value)
    if(buffer.length ≥ MAXBLOCKSIZE)
      break
  if(buffer.length ≥ MAXBLOCKSIZE)
    for each (ele ∈ buffer)
      emit(key, ele)
    for each (value ∈ values)
      emit(key, value)
  elseif(buffer.length ≥ 1)
    blocks.append(key, buffer)
```

Figure 2: Alg.1 - Blocking

tance of the two names, whether one name is an abbreviation of the other name, and the longest common substring of the two names. Examples of context features are whether the two names share the same url and the number of times that the two names co-occur with each other in a single person record.

2.3 Clustering

In this section, we present our clustering approach. Let's, first clarify a set of terms/conditions that will help us describe the algorithms.

Definition (Connected Component): Let G = (V, E) be an undirected graph where V is the set of vertices and E is the set of edges. C = $(C_1, C_2, ..., C_n)$ is the set of disjoint connected components in this graph where $(C_1 \cup C_2 \cup ... \cup C_n)$ = V and $(C_1 \cap C_2 \cap ... \cap C_n)$ = $\emptyset$. For each connected component $C_i \in C$, there exists a path in G between any two vertices v_k and v_l where $(v_k, v_l) \in C_i$. Additionally, for any distinct connected component $(C_i, C_j) \in C$, there is no path between any pair v_k and v_l where $v_k \in C_i$, $v_l \in C_j$. Moreover, the problem of finding all connected components in a graph is finding the C satisfying the above conditions. □

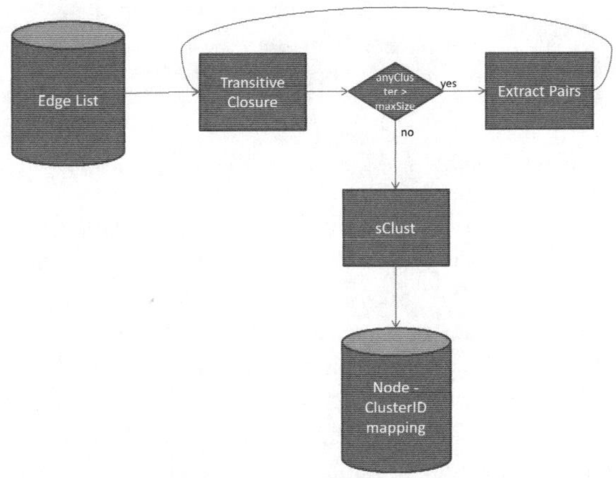

Figure 3: Clustering Component

Definition (Component ID): A component id is a unique identifier assigned to each connected component.

Definition (Max Component Size): This is the maximum allowed size for a connected component. □

Definition (Cluster Set): A cluster set is a set of records that belong to the same real world entity. □

Definition (Max Cluster Size): This is the maximum allowed size for a cluster. □

Definition (Match Threshold): Match threshold is a score where pairs scoring above this score are said to represent the same entity. □

Definition (No-Match Threshold): No-Match threshold is a score where pairs scoring below this score are said to represent different entities. □

Definition (Conflict Set): Each record has a conflict set which is the set of records that shouldn't appear with this record in any of the clusters. □

The naive approach to clustering for entity resolution is transitive closure by using only the pairs having scores above the match threshold. However, in practice we might see many examples of conflicting scores. For example, (a,b) and (b,c) pairs might have scores above match threshold while (a,c) pair has a score below no-match threshold. If we just use transitive closure, we will end up with a single cluster with these three records (a,b,c). Another weakness of the regular transitive closure is that it creates disjoint sets. However, organizations might share name, or abbreviation. So, we need a soft clustering approach where a record might be in different clusters.

On the other hand, the large volume of our data requires highly scalable and efficient parallelized algorithms. However, it is very hard to implement par-

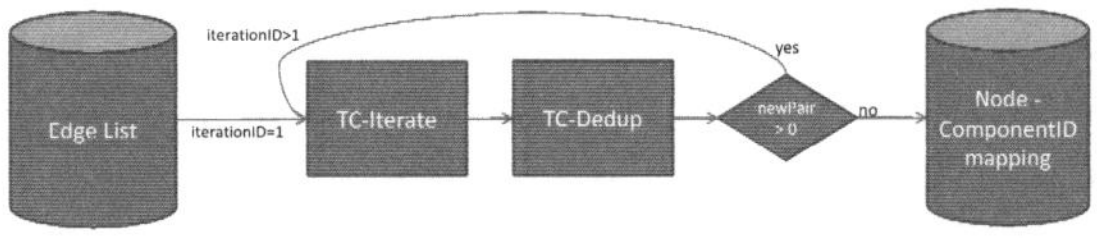

Figure 4: Transitive Closure Component

allelized clustering approaches with high precision for large scale graphs due to high time and space complexities (Bansal, 2003). So, we propose a two-step approach in order to build both a parallel and an accurate clustering framework. The high-level architecture of our clustering framework is illustrated in Figure 3. We first find the connected components in the graph with our MapReduce based transitive closure approach, then further, partition each connected component in parallel with our novel soft clustering algorithm, sClust. This way, we first combine similar record pairs into connected components in an efficient and scalable manner, and then further partition each connected component into smaller clusters for better precision. Note that there is a dangerous phenomenon, black hole entities, in transitive closure of the pairwise scores (Michelson, 2009). A black hole entity begins to pull an inordinate amount of records from an increasing number of different true entities into it as it is formed. This is dangerous, because it will then erroneously match on more and more records, escalating the problem. Thus, by the end of the transitive closure, one might end up with black hole entities with millions of records belonging to multiple different entities. In order to avoid this problem, we define a black hole threshold, and if we end up with a connected component above the size of the black hole threshold, we increment the match threshold by a delta and further partition this black hole with one more transitive closure job. We repeat this process until the sizes of all the connected components are below the black hole threshold, and then apply sClust on each connected component. Hence at the end of the entire entity resolution process, the system has partitioned all the input records into cluster sets called profiles, where each profile corresponds to a single entity.

2.4 Transitive Closure

In order to find the connected components in a graph, we developed the *Transitive Closure* (TC) module shown in Figure 4. The input to the module is the list of all pairs having scores above the match threshold. As an output from the module, what we want to obtain is the mapping from each node in the graph to its corresponding componentID. For simplicity, we use the smallest node id in each connected component as the identifier of that component. Thus, the module should output a mapping table from each node in the graph to the smallest node id in its corresponding connected component. To this end, we designed a chain of two MapReduce jobs, namely, TC-Iterate, and TC-Dedup, that will run iteratively till we find the corresponding componentIDs for all the nodes in the graph.

```
Transitive Closure Iterate
map(key, value)
  emit(key, value)
  emit(value, key)

reduce(key, < iterable > values)
  minValue ← values.next()
  if(minValue < key)
    emit(key, minValue)
    for each (value ∈ values)
      Counter.NewPair.increment(1)
      emit(value, minValue)
```

(a) Transitive Closure - Iterate

```
Transitive Closure Dedup
map(key, value)
  emit(key.append(STR + value), null)

reduce(key, < iterable > values)
  String[] keyTokens ← key.split(STR)
  emit(keyTokens[0], keyTokens[1])
```

(b) Transitive Closure - Dedup

Figure 5: Alg.3 - Transitive Closure

TC-Iterate job generates adjacency lists $AL = (a_1, a_2, ..., a_n)$ for each node v, and if the node id of this node v_{id} is larger than the min node id a_{min} in the adjacency list, it first creates a pair (v_{id}, a_{min}) and then a pair for each (a_i, a_{min}) where $a_i \in AL$, and $a_i \neq a_{min}$. If there is only one node in AL, it means we will generate the pair that we have in previous iteration. However, if there is more than one node in AL, it means we might generate a pair that we didn't have in the previous iteration, and one more iteration is needed. Please note that, if v_{id} is smaller than a_{min}, we don't emit any pair.

The pseudo code of TC-Iterate is given in Figure 5-(a). For the first iteration, this job takes the pairs having scores above the match threshold from the initial edge list as input. In later iterations, the input is the output of TC-Dedup from the previous iteration. We first start with the initial edge list to construct the first degree neighborhood of each node. To this end, for each edge $< a; b >$, the mapper emits both $< a; b >$, and $< b; a >$ pairs so that a should be in the adjacency list of b and vice versa. In the reduce phase, all the adjacent nodes will be grouped together for each node. Reducers don't receive the values in a sorted order. So, we use a secondary sort approach to pass the values to the reducer in a sorted way with custom partitioning (see (Lin, 2010) for details). This way, the first value becomes the minValue. If the minValue is larger than the key, we don't emit anything. Otherwise,

```
Bring together all edges for each partition
Phase-1
map(key, value)
  if(key.equals(ConflationOutput))
    if ((value.score ≤ NO_MATCH_THR)||
      (value.score ≥ MATCH_THR))
        emit(value.entity1, value)
  else          //TCDedupOutput
    temp.entity1 ← value
    temp.entity2 ← null
    temp.score ← null
    emit(key, temp)
    emit(value, temp)
reduce(key, < iterable > values)
  valueList ← ∅
  for each (value ∈ values)
    if(value.entity2 = null)
      clusID ← value.entity1
    else
      valueList.add(value)
  for each (value ∈ valueList)
    emit(clusID, value)

Phase-2
map(key, value)
  emit(key, value)
reduce(key, < iterable > values)
  valueList ← ∅
  for each (value ∈ values)
    valueList.add(value)
  emit(key, valueList)
```

Figure 6: Alg.3 - Bring together all edges for each partition

we first emit the $< key; minValue >$ pair. Next, we emit a pair for all other values as $< value; minValue >$, and increase the global NewPair counter by 1. If the counter is 0 at the end of the job, it means that we found all the components and there is no need for further iterations.

During the TC-Iterate job, the same pair might be emitted multiple times. The second job, TC-Dedup, just deduplicates the output of the CCF-Iterate job. This job increases the efficiency of TC-Iterate job in terms of both speed and I/O overhead. The pseudo code for this job is given in Figure 5-(b).

The worst case scenario for the number of necessary iterations is d+1 where d is the diameter of the network. The worst case happens when the min node in the largest connected component is an end-point of the largest shortest-path. The best case scenario takes d/2+1 iterations. For the best case, the min node should be at the center of the largest shortest-path.

2.5 sClust: A Soft Agglomerative Clustering Approach

After partitioning the records into disjoint connected components, we further partition each connected component into smaller clusters with sClust approach. sClust is a soft agglomerative clustering approach, and its main difference from any other hierarchical clustering method is the "conflict set" term that we described above. Any of the conflicting nodes cannot appear in a cluster with this approach. Additionally, the maximum size of the clusters can be controlled by an input parameter.

First as a preprocessing step, we have a two-step MapReduce job (see Figure 6) which puts together and sorts all the pairwise scores for each connected component discovered by transitive closure. Next, sClust job takes the sorted edge lists for each connected component as input, and partitions each connected component in parallel. The pseudo-code for sClust job is given in Figure 7. sClust iterates over the pairwise scores twice. During the first iteration, it generates the node structures, and conflict sets for each of these structures. For example, if the pairwise score for (a, b) pair is below the no-match threshold, node a is added to node b's conflict set, and vice versa. By the end of the first iteration, all the conflict sets are generated. Now, one more pass is needed to build the final clusters. Since the scores are sorted, we start from the highest score to agglomeratively construct the clusters by going over all the scores above the match threshold. Let's assume we have a pair (a, b) with a score above the match threshold. There might be 4 different conditions. First, both node a and node b are not in any of the clusters yet. In this case, we generate a cluster with these two records and the conflict set of this cluster becomes the union of conflict sets of these two records. Second, node a might already be assigned to a set of clusters C' while node b is not in any of the clusters. In these case, we add node b to each cluster in C' if it doesn't conflict with b. If there is no such cluster, we build a new cluster with nodes a and b. Third is the opposite version of the second condition, and the procedure is the same. Finally, both node a and node b might be in some set of clusters. If they already appear in the same cluster, no further action needed. If they just appear in different clusters, these clusters will be merged as long as there is no conflict between these clusters. If there are no such unconflicting clusters, we again build a new cluster with nodes a and b. This way, we go over all the scores above the match threshold and build the cluster sets. Note that if the clusters are merged, their conflict sets are also merged. Additionally, if the max cluster size parameter is defined, this condition is also checked before merging any two clusters, or adding a new node to an existing cluster.

```
Clustering
map(key, valueList)
  for each (value ∈ valueList)
    if(value.score ≥ MATCH_THR)
      nodes.insert(value.entity1)
      nodes.insert(value.entity2)
    else
      node1Index ← find(value.entity1, nodes)
      node2Index ← find(value.entity2, nodes)
      nodes[node1Index].conflictSet.insert(node2Index)
      nodes[node2Index].conflictSet.insert(node1Index)
  for each (value ∈ valueList)
    if(value.score ≥ MATCH_THR)
      node1Index ← find(value.entity1, nodes)
      node2Index ← find(value.entity2, nodes)
      node1ClusIDLength ← nodes[node1Index].clusIDs.length
      node2ClusIDLength ← nodes[node2Index].clusIDs.length
      if((node1ClusIDLength = 0) && (node2ClusIDLength = 0))
        clusters[numClusters].nodes[0] ← node1Index
        clusters[numClusters].nodes[1] ← node2Index
        clusters[numClusters].confSet ←
            mergeSortedLists(nodes[node1Index].confSet, nodes[node2Index].confSet)
        nodes[node1Index].clusIDs.insert(numClusters)
        nodes[node2Index].clusIDs.insert(numClusters)
        numClusters++
      elseif(node1ClusIDLength = 0)
        for each (node2ClusID ∈ nodes[node2Index].clusIDs)
          if(notContain(clusters[node2ClusID].confSet, node1Index))
            insertToSortedList(clusters[node2ClusID].nodes, node1Index)
            clusters[node2ClusID].confSet ←
                mergeSortedLists(clusters[node2ClusID].confSet, nodes[node1Index].confSet)
            nodes[node1Index].clusIDs.insert(node2ClusID)
      elseif(node2ClusIDLength = 0)
        for each (node1ClusID ∈ nodes[node1Index].clusIDs)
          if(notContain(clusters[node1ClusID].confSet, node2Index))
            insertToSortedList(clusters[node1ClusID].nodes, node2Index)
            clusters[node1ClusID].confSet ←
                mergeSortedLists(clusters[node1ClusID].confSet, nodes[node2Index].confSet)
            nodes[node2Index].clusIDs.insert(node1ClusID)
      elseif(notIntersect(clusters[node1ClusID].clusIDs, clusters[node2ClusID].clusIDs))
        for each (node1ClusID ∈ nodes[node1Index].clusIDs)
          for each (node2ClusID ∈ nodes[node2Index].clusIDs)
            if( notIntersect(clusters[node1ClusID].confSet, clusters[node2ClusID].nodes) &&
                  notIntersect(clusters[node2ClusID].confSet, clusters[node1ClusID].nodes) )
              clusters[node1ClusID].nodes ←
                  mergeSortedList(clusters[node1ClusID].nodes, clusters[node2ClusID].nodes)
              clusters[node1ClusID].confSet ←
                  mergeSortedLists(clusters[node1ClusID].confSet, clusters[node2ClusID].confSet)
              for each (nodeIndex ∈ clusters[node2ClusID].nodes)
                  nodes[nodeIndex].clusIDs.insert(node1ClusID)
              clusters[node2ClusID].isRemoved ← true
              clusters[node2ClusID].nodes ← null
              clusters[node2ClusID].confSet ← null
```

Figure 7: Alg.4 - Clustering

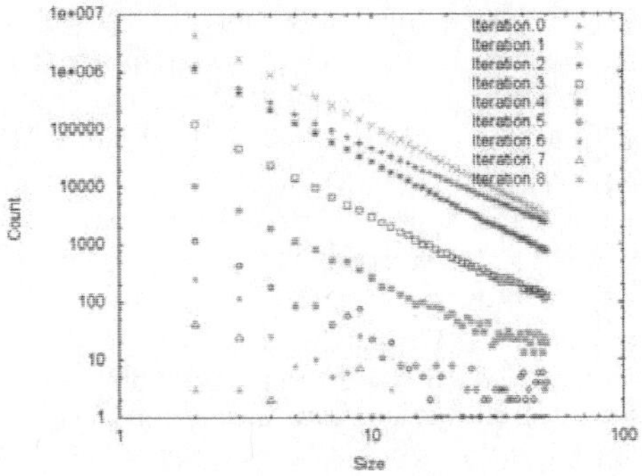

(a) Block Dist. (iterations)

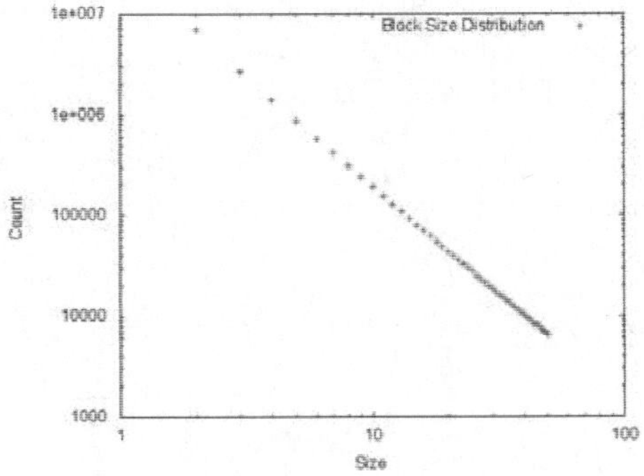

(b) Block Dist. (overall)

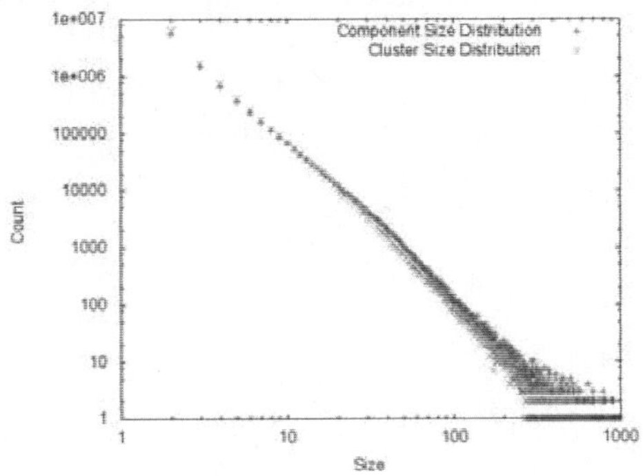

(c) Component & Cluster Size Dist.

Figure 8: Size Distributions

3 Evaluation

In this section, we present the experimental results for our entity resolution framework. We ran the experiments on a hadoop cluster consisting of 50 nodes, each with 8 cores. There are 10 mappers, and 6 reducers available at each node. We also allocated 3 Gb memory for each map/reduce task.

We used two different real-world datasets for our experiments. The first one is a list of 150K organizations along with their aliases provided by freebase[2]. By using this dataset, we both trained our pairwise linkage model and measured the precision and recall of our system. We randomly selected 135K organizations from this list for the training. We used the rest of the organizations to measure the performance of our system. Next, we generated positive examples by exhaustively generating a pair between all the aliases. We also randomly generated equal number of negative examples among pairs of different organization alias sets. We trained our pairwise classifier with the training set, then ran it on the test set and measured its performance. Next, we extracted all the organization names from this set, and ran our entire entity resolution pipeline on top of this set. Table 1 presents the performance results. Our pairwise classifier has 97% precision and 63% recall when we use a match threshold of 0.65. Using same match threshold, we then performed transitive closure. We also measured the precision and recall numbers for transitive closure as it is the naive approach for the entity resolution problem. Since transitive closure merges records transitively, it has very high recall but the precision is just 64%. Finally, we performed our sClust approach with the same match threshold. We set the no-match threshold to 0.3. The pairwise classifier has slightly better precision than sClust but sClust has much better recall. Overall, sClust has a much better f-measure than both the pairwise classifier and transitive closure.

	precision	recall	f-measure
Pairwise Classifier	97	63	76
Transitive Closure	64	98	77
sClust	95	76	84

Table 1: Performance Comparison

Second, we used our production set to show the viability of our framework. In this set, we have 68M organization names. We ran our framework on this dataset. Blocking generated 14M unique blocks, and there are 842M unique comparisons in these blocks. The distribution of the block sizes presented in Figure 8-(a) and (b). Blocking finished in 42 minutes. Next, we ran our pairwise classifier on these 842M pairs and it finished in 220 minutes. Finally, we ended up with 10M clusters at the end of the clustering stage which took 3 hours. The distribution of the connected components and final clusters are presented in Figure 8-(c).

4 Conclusion

In this paper, we presented a novel entity resolution approach for the organization entity domain. We have implemented this in the MapReduce framework with low memory requirements so that it may scale to large scale datasets. We used two different real-world datasets in our experiments. We first evaluated the performance of our approach on truth data provided by freebase. Our clustering approach, sClust, significantly improved the recall of the pairwise classifier. Next, we demonstrated the viability of our framework on a large scale dataset on a 50-node hadoop cluster.

[2]http://www.freebase.com/

References

A. K. Elmagarmid, P. G. Iperirotis, and V. S. Verykios. Duplicate record detection: A survey. In *IEEE Transactions on Knowledge and Data Engineering*, pages 1–16, 2007.

J. Lin and C. Dyer. *Data-Intensive Text Processing with MapReduce*. Synthesis Lectures on Human Langugage Technologies. Morgan & Claypool, 2010.

N. Bansal, A. Blum and S. Chawla Correlation Clustering. *Machine Learning*, 2003.

M. Michelson and S.A. Macskassy Record Linkage Measures in an Entity Centric World. *In Proceedings of the 4th workshop on Evaluation Methods for Machine Learning*, Montreal, Canada, 2009.

N. Adly. Efficient record linkage using a double embedding scheme. In R. Stahlbock, S. F. Crone, and S. Lessmann, editors, *DMIN*, pages 274–281. CSREA Press, 2009.

A. N. Aizawa and K. Oyama. A fast linkage detection scheme for multi-source information integration. In *WIRI*, pages 30–39. IEEE Computer Society, 2005.

R. Baxter, P. Christen, and T. Churches. A comparison of fast blocking methods for record linkage, 2003.

M. Bilenko and B. Kamath. Adaptive blocking: Learning to scale up record linkage. In *Data Mining, 2006. ICDM'*, number December, 2006.

P. Christen. A survey of indexing techniques for scalable record linkage and deduplication. *IEEE Transactions on Knowledge and Data Engineering*, 99(PrePrints), 2011.

T. de Vries, H. Ke, S. Chawla, and P. Christen. Robust record linkage blocking using suffix arrays. In *Proceedings of the 18th ACM conference on Information and knowledge management*, CIKM '09, pages 305–314, New York, NY, USA, 2009. ACM.

T. de Vries, H. Ke, S. Chawla, and P. Christen. Robust record linkage blocking using suffix arrays and bloom filters. *ACM Trans. Knowl. Discov. Data*, 5(2):9:1–9:27, Feb. 2011.

M. A. Hernandez and S. J. Stolfo. Real-world data is dirty. data cleansing and the merge/purge problem. *Journal of Data Mining and Knowledge Discovery*, pages 1–39, 1998.

L. Jin, C. Li, and S. Mehrotra. Efficient record linkage in large data sets. In *Proceedings of the Eighth International Conference on Database Systems for Advanced Applications*, DASFAA '03, pages 137–, Washington, DC, USA, 2003. IEEE Computer Society.

A. McCallum, K. Nigam, and L. H. Ungar. Efficient clustering of high-dimensional data sets with application to reference matching. In *Proceedings of the ACM International Conference on Knowledge Discover and Data Mining*, pages 169–178, 2000.

J. Nin, V. Muntes-Mulero, N. Martinez-Bazan, and J.-L. Larriba-Pey. On the use of semantic blocking techniques for data cleansing and integration. In *Proceedings of the 11th International Database Engineering and Applications Symposium*, IDEAS '07, pages 190–198, Washington, DC, USA, 2007. IEEE Computer Society.

A. D. Sarma, A. Jain, and A. Machanavajjhala. CBLOCK: An Automatic Blocking Mechanism for Large-Scale Deduplication Tasks. Technical report, 2011.

M. Weis, F. Naumann, U. Jehle, J. Lufter, and H. Schuster. Industry-scale duplicate detection. *Proc. VLDB Endow.*, 1(2):1253–1264, Aug. 2008.

S. E. Whang, D. Menestrina, G. Koutrika, M. Theobald, and H. Garcia-Molina. Entity resolution with iterative blocking. In *Proceedings of the 35th SIGMOD international conference on Management of data*, SIGMOD '09, pages 219–232, New York, NY, USA, 2009. ACM.

W. Winkler. Overview of record linkage and current research directions. Technical report, U.S. Bureau of the Census, 2006.

S. Yan, D. Lee, M.-Y. Kan, and L. C. Giles. Adaptive sorted neighborhood methods for efficient record linkage. In *Proceedings of the 7th ACM/IEEE-CS joint conference on Digital libraries*, JCDL '07, pages 185–194, New York, NY, USA, 2007. ACM.

L. Kolb, and E. Rahm. Parallel entity resolution with Dedoop. Datenbank-Spektrum (2013): 1-10.

B. McNeill, H. Kardes, and A. Borthwick. Dynamic Record Blocking: Efficient Linking of Massive Databases in MapReduce. In *QDB* (2012).

A Graph-Based Approach to Skill Extraction from Text*

Ilkka Kivimäki[1], **Alexander Panchenko**[4,2], **Adrien Dessy**[1,2], **Dries Verdegem**[3], **Pascal Francq**[1], **Cédrick Fairon**[2], **Hugues Bersini**[3] **and Marco Saerens**[1]
[1]ICTEAM, [2]CENTAL, Université catholique de Louvain, Belgium
[3]IRIDIA, Université libre de Bruxelles, Belgium
[4] Digital Society Laboratory LLC, Russia

Abstract

This paper presents a system that performs skill extraction from text documents. It outputs a list of professional skills that are relevant to a given input text. We argue that the system can be practical for hiring and management of personnel in an organization. We make use of the texts and the hyperlink graph of Wikipedia, as well as a list of professional skills obtained from the LinkedIn social network. The system is based on first computing similarities between an input document and the texts of Wikipedia pages and then using a biased, hub-avoiding version of the Spreading Activation algorithm on the Wikipedia graph in order to associate the input document with skills.

1 Introduction

One of the most difficult tasks of an employer can be the recruitment of a new employee out of a long list of applicants. Another challenge of the employer is to keep track of the skills and know-how of their employees in order to direct the right people to work on things they know. In the scientific community, editors of journals and committees of conferences always face the task of assigning suitable reviewers for a tall pile of submitted papers. The tasks described above are example problems of *expertise retrieval* (Balog et al., 2012). It is a subfield of information retrieval that focuses on inferring associations between people, expertise and information content, such as text documents.

In this paper, we propose a method that makes a step towards a solution of these problems. We describe an approach for the extraction of professional skills associated with a text or its author. The goal of our system is to automatically extract a set of skills from an input text, such as a set of articles written by a person. Such technology can be potentially useful in various contexts, such as the ones mentioned above, along with expertise management in a company, analysis of professional blogs, automatic meta-data extraction, etc.

For succeeding in our goal, we exploit Wikipedia, a list of skills obtained from the LinkedIn social network and the mapping between them. Our method consists of two phases. First, we analyze a query document with a vector space model or a topic model in order to associate it with Wikipedia articles. Then, using these initial pages, we use the Spreading Activation algorithm on the hyperlink graph of Wikipedia in order to find articles that correspond to LinkedIn skills and are related or central to the initial pages.

One difficulty with this approach is that it often results in some skills, which can be identified as hubs of the Wikipedia graph, constantly being retrieved, regardless of what the input is. In order to avoid this pitfall, we bias the activation to avoid spreading to general, or popular nodes. We try different measures of node popularity to redirect the spreading and perform evaluative experiments which show that this biasing in fact improves retrieval results.

We have built a web service that enables anyone to test our skill extraction system. The name of the system is `Elisit`, an abbreviation from "Expertise Localization from Informal Sources and Information

*Part of this work has been funded by projects with the "Région wallonne". We thank this institution for giving us the opportunity to conduct both fundamental and applied research. In addition, we thank Laurent Genard and Stéphane Dessy for their contributions for the work.

Technologies" and conveying the idea of trying to elicit, i.e. draw forth latent information about expertise in a target text. According to the best of our knowledge, we are the first to propose such a system and describe openly the method behind it.

2 Related work

The recent review of Balog et al. (2012) gives a thorough presentation of the problems of expertise retrieval and of the methodology used for solving them. They classify these problems in subcategories of *expert retrieval* and *expert profiling*. The former means the task of providing a name of a person who is an expert in a field that is presented as a query, while the latter means assigning expertise to a person, or some other entity based on information that is available of that entity. Recent expertise retrieval research has focused on the TREC enterprise track, which uses the TREC W3C and CERC corpora (Balog et al., 2008). These datasets contain annotated crawls of websites. The task in the TREC enterprise challenge is to build a model that performs expert retrieval and document retrieval based on a set of query topics, which correspond to expertise areas.

Our approach is quite different from the one used in the TREC challenge, as we focus on a fixed list of skills gathered from the LinkedIn website. Thus, we were not able to directly compare our system to the systems participating in the TREC enterprise track. Our problem shares some resemblance with the INEX entity-ranking track (Demartini et al., 2010), where the goal was to rank Wikipedia pages related to queries about a given topic. Our skill retrieval task can also be seen as an entity ranking task, where the entities are Wikipedia pages that correspond to skills.

LinkedIn has developed methods for defining skills and for finding relations between them (Skomoroch et al., 2012). These techniques are used in their service, for example, for recommending job opportunities to the users. The key difference of our technology is that it allows a user to search for skills by submitting an arbitrary text, instead of only searching for skills related to a certain skill. Although expertise retrieval has been an active research topic for some time, there have not been many methods for explicitly assigning particular skills to text content or people producing text content.

Our method consists of two steps. First, we apply a text similarity method to detect the relevant Wikipedia pages. Second, we enrich the results with graph mining techniques using the hyperlink graph of Wikipedia. We have not found a similar combination being applied for skill extraction before, although both parts have been well studied in similar contexts before. For instance, Steyvers et al. (2004) proposed the Author-Topic Model, a graphical model based on LDA (Blei et al., 2003), that associates authors of texts with topics detected from those texts.

Wikipedia has been already used in NLP research both as a corpus and as a semantic network. Its hyperlink graph is a collaboratively constructed network, as opposed to manually crafted networks such as WordNet (Miller, 1995). Gabrilovich and Markovitch (2007) introduced Explicit Semantic Analysis (ESA), where the words of a document are represented as mixtures of concepts, i.e. Wikipedia pages, according to their occurence in the body texts of the pages. The experimental results show that this strategy works very well and outranks, for example, LSA (Landauer and Dumais, 1997) in the task of measuring document similarity. ESA was later extended by taking into account the graph structure provided by the links in Wikipedia (Yeh et al., 2009). The authors of this work used a PageRank-based algorithm on the graph for measuring word and document similarity. This approach was coined *WikiWalk*.

Associating the elements of a text document under analysis with Wikipedia pages involves itself already many problems often encountered in NLP. The process where certain words and multiword expressions are associated with a certain Wikipedia page has been called *Wikification* (Mihalcea and Csomai, 2007). In our work, we take a more general approach, and try to associate the full input text to a set of Wikipedia pages according to different vector space models. The models and the details of this strategy are explained in section 3.3.

The `Elisit` system uses the Spreading Activation algorithm on the Wikipedia graph to establish associations between texts and skills. We chose to use Spreading Activation, as it tries to simulate a cognitive associative memory (Anderson, 1983), and the Wikipedia hyperlink network can be understood as an associative network. The simulation works by finding associations in a network of concepts by spreading pulses of activation from concepts into their neighbours. In the context of NLP, the Spreading Activation algorithm has been traditionally used for word sense disambiguation (Hirst, 1988) and information retrieval (Crestani, 1997). Gouws et al. (2010) have shown that this algorithm, applied to the Wikipedia graph, can also be used to measure conceptual and document similarity.

3 Methodology

In this section, we will explain how the `Elisit` skill extraction system works. We will first explain how the system uses data from Wikipedia and LinkedIn. Then, we will describe the two main components of the system, the `text2wiki` module, which associates a query document with related Wikipedia pages, and the `wiki2skill` module, which aims to associate the Wikipedia pages found by the `text2wiki` module with Wikipedia pages that correspond to skills.

3.1 Wikipedia texts and links

Each page in Wikipedia contains a text that may include hyperlinks to other pages. We make the assumption that there is a meaningful semantic relationship between the pages that are linked with each other and that the Wikipedia hyperlink graph can be exploited as an associative network. The properties of the hyperlink structure of Wikipedia and the nature of the information contained in the links have been investigated by Koolen (2011).

In addition to the encyclopedia pages, Wikipedia also contains, among others, category, discussion and help pages. In our system, we are only interested in the encyclopedia pages and the hyperlinks between them. We are using data downloaded[1] on May 2nd 2012. This dump encompasses 3,983,338 pages with 247,560,469 links, after removal of the redirect pages. The Wikipedia graph consists of a giant Strongly Connected Component (SCC) of 3,744,419 nodes, 4130 SCC's of sizes from 61 to 2 nodes and 228,881 nodes that form their own SCC's.

[1] `http://dumps.wikimedia.org/`

3.2 LinkedIn skills

We gathered a list of skills from the LinkedIn social network[2]. The list includes skills which the users can assign to their profiles. This enables the site to recommend new contacts or open job opportunities to each user. The skills in the list have been generated by an automated process developed by LinkedIn (Skomoroch et al., 2012). The process decides, whether a word or a phrase or a skill suggested by a user is actually a skill through an analysis of the text contained in the user profile pages.

Each LinkedIn skill has its own webpage that contains information about the skill. One piece of information contained in most of these pages is a link to a Wikipedia article. According to Skomoroch et al. (2012), LinkedIn automatically builds this mapping. However, some links are manually verified through crowdsourcing. Not all skill pages contain a link to Wikipedia, but these skills are often either very specific or ambiguous. Thus, we decided to remove these skills from our final list. The list of skills used in the system was extracted from the LinkedIn site in September 2012. After removal of the skills without a link to Wikipedia, the list contained 27,153 skills.

3.3 `text2wiki` module

The goal of the `text2wiki` module is to retrieve Wikipedia articles that are relevant to an input text.

The output of the module is a vector of similarities between the input document and all articles of the English Wikipedia that contain at least 300 characters. There are approximately 3.3 million such pages. We only retrieve the 200 Wikipedia pages that are most similar to the input document. Thus, each input text is represented as a sparse vector $\mathbf{a}(0)$, which has 200 non-zero elements out of 3,983,338 dimensions corresponding to the full list of Wikipedia pages. Each non-zero value $a_i(0)$ of this vector is a semantic similarity of the query with the i-th Wikipedia article. This approach stems from ESA, mentioned above. The vector $\mathbf{a}(0)$ is given as input to the second module `wiki2skill`.

The `text2wiki` module relies on the `Gensim` library (Řehůřek and Sojka, 2010)[3]. In particular,

[2] `http://www.linkedin.com/skills`

[3] `http://radimrehurek.com/gensim`

we have used four different text similarity functions, based respectively on the classical Vector Space Models (VSM's) (Berry et al., 1994), LSA and LDA:

(a) TF-IDF (300,000 dimensions)
(b) LogEntropy (300,000 dimensions)
(c) LogEntropy + LSA (200 dimensions)
(d) LogEntropy + LDA (200 topics)

First, each text is represented as a vector $\mathbf{x}$ in a space of the 300,000 most frequent terms in the corpus, each appearing at least in 10% of the documents (excluding stopwords). We limited the number of dimensions to 300,000 to reduce computational complexity. The models (a) and (b) directly use this representation, while for (c) and (d) this initial representation is transformed to a vector $\mathbf{x}'$ in a reduced space of 200 dimensions/topics. For LSA and LDA, the number of dimensions is often empirically selected from the range $[100 - 500]$ (Foltz, 1996; Bast and Majumdar, 2005). We followed this practice. From the vector representations ($\mathbf{x}$ or $\mathbf{x}'$), the similarity between the input document and each Wikipedia article is computed using the cosine similarity.

Pairwise comparison of a vector of 300,000 dimensions against 3.3 million vectors of the same size has a prohibitive computational cost. To make our application practical, we use an inverted index of `Gensim` to efficiently retrieve articles semantically related to an input document.

3.4 `wiki2skill` module

The `wiki2skill` module performs the Spreading Activation algorithm using the initial activations provided by the `text2wiki` module and returns a vector of final activations of all the nodes of the network and a vector containing the activations of only the nodes corresponding to skills.

The basic idea of Spreading Activation is to initially activate a set of nodes in a network and then iteratively spread the activation into the neighbouring nodes. This can actually be interpreted in many ways opening up a wide space of algorithms that can lead to different results. One attempt for an exact definition of the Spreading Activation algorithm can be found in the work of Shrager et al. (1987). Their formulation states that if $\mathbf{a}(0)$ is a vector containing the initial activations of each node of the network, then after each iteration, or time step, or pulse t, the vector of activations is

$$\mathbf{a}(t) = \gamma\mathbf{a}(t-1) + \lambda\mathbf{W}^{\mathsf{T}}\mathbf{a}(t-1) + \mathbf{c}(t), \quad (1)$$

where $\gamma \in [0, 1]$ is a *decay factor* which controls the conservation of activation during time, $\lambda \in [0, 1]$ is a *friction factor*, which controls the amount of activation that nodes can spread to their neighbors, $\mathbf{c}(t)$ is an *activation source vector* and $\mathbf{W}$ is a weighted adjacency matrix, where the weights control the amount of activation that flows through each link in the network. In some cases, iterating eq. (1) leads to a converged activation state, but often, especially when dealing with large networks, it is more practical to set the number of pulses, T, to some fixed, low number.

As already stated, this formulation of Spreading Activation spans a wide space of different algorithms. In particular, this space contains many random walk based algorithms. By considering the case where $\gamma = 0, \lambda = 1, \mathbf{c}(t) = \mathbf{0}$ and where the matrix $\mathbf{W}$ is row-stochastic, the Spreading Activation model boils down to a random walk model with a transition probability matrix $\mathbf{W}$, where $\mathbf{a}(t)$ contains the proportion of random walkers at each node when the initial proportions are given by $\mathbf{a}(0)$. When the situation is changed by choosing $\mathbf{c}(t) = (1-\lambda)\mathbf{a}(0)$, we obtain a bounded Random Walk with Restart model (Pan et al., 2004; Mantrach et al., 2011).

Early experiments with the first versions of the algorithm revealed an activation bias towards nodes that correspond to very general Wikipedia pages (e.g. the page "ISBN", which is often linked to in the References section of Wikipedia pages). These nodes have a high input degree, but are often not relevant for the given query. This problem is often encountered when analysing large graphs with random walk based measures. It is known that they can be dominated by the stationary distribution of the corresponding Markov Chain (Brand, 2005).

To tackle this problem, we assign link weights according to *preferential transition probabilities*, which define biased random walks that try to avoid hub nodes. They have been studied e.g. in the context of stochastic routing of packages in scale-free networks (Fronczak and Fronczak, 2009). These weights are given by

$$w^*_{ij} = \frac{\pi_j^\alpha}{\sum\limits_{k:(i,k)\in E} \pi_k^\alpha}, \quad (2)$$

where π_j is a *popularity index* and α is a *biasing parameter*, which controls the amount of activation that flows from node i to node j based on the popularity of node j. For the popularity index, we considered three options. First, we tried simply the input degree of a node. As a second option, we used the PageRank score of the node (Page et al., 1999) which corresponds to the node's weight in the stationary distribution of a *random surfer* that surfs Wikipedia by clicking on hyperlinks randomly. As a third popularity index, we used a score based on the HITS algorithm (Kleinberg, 1999), which is similar to PageRank, but instead assigns two scores, an authority score and a hub score. In short, a page has a high authority score, if it is linked to by many hub pages, and vice versa. In the case of HITS, the popularity index was defined as the product of the authority and hub scores of the node. When $\alpha = 0$, w_{ij} is equal for all links leaving from node i, but when $\alpha < 0$, activation will flow more to less popular nodes and less to popular nodes. We included the selection of a suitable value for α as a parameter to be tuned along with the rest of the spreading strategy in quantitative experiments that are presented in section 5.2. These experiments show that biasing the activation to avoid spreading to popular nodes indeed improves retrieval results.

We also decided to investigate whether giving more weight to links that exist in both directions would improve results. The Wikipedia hyperlink graph is directed, but in some cases two pages may contain a link to each other. We thus adjust the link weights w_{ij} so that $w_{ij} = \delta w^*_{ij}$ if $(j, i) \in E$ and $w_{ij} = w^*_{ij}$ otherwise, where $\delta \geq 1$ is a *bidirectional link weight*. With large values of δ, more activation will flow through bidirectional links than links that exist only in one direction. After this weighting, the final link weight matrix $\mathbf{W}$ is obtained by normalizing each element with its corresponding row sum to make the matrix row-stochastic. This makes the model easier to interpret by considering random walks. However, in a traditional Spreading Activation model the matrix $\mathbf{W}$ is not required to be row-stochastic. We plan to investigate in the future, how much the normalization affects the results.

The large size of the Wikipedia graph challenges the use of Spreading Activation. In order to provide a usable web service, we would need the system to provide results fast, preferably within fractions of seconds. So far, we have dealt with this issue within the `wiki2skill` module by respresenting the link weight matrix $\mathbf{W}$ of the whole Wikipedia graph using the sparse matrix library `SciPy`[4]. Each iteration of the Spreading Activation is then achieved by simple matrix arithmetic according to eq. (1). As a result, the matrix $\mathbf{W}$ must be precomputed from the adjacency matrix for a given value of the biasing parameter α and the bidirectional link weight δ when the system is launched. Thus, they cannot be selected separately for each query from the system. Currently, the system can perform one iteration of spreading activation within less than one second, depending on the sparsity of the activation vector. Our experiments indicate that the results are quite stable after five spreading iterations, meaning that we normally get results with the `wiki2skill` module in about one to three seconds.

4 The `Elisit` skill extraction system

The `Elisit` system integrates the `text2wiki` and the `wiki2skill` modules. We have built a web application[5] which lets everyone try our method and use it from third-party applications. Due to this web service, the `Elisit` technology can be easily integrated into systems performing skill search, email or document analysis, HR automatization, analysis of professional blogs, automatic meta-data extraction, etc. The web interface presents the user the result of the skill extraction (a list of skills) as well as the result of the `text2wiki` module (a list of Wikipedia pages). Each retrieved skill also contains a link to the corresponding Wikipedia page.

Figure 1 presents an example of results provided by the `Elisit` system. It lists skills extracted from the abstract of the chapter *Support vector machines and machine learning on documents* from

[4] `http://www.scipy.org/`

[5] GUI: `http://elisit.cental.be/`; RESTful web service: `http://elisit.cental.be:8080/`.

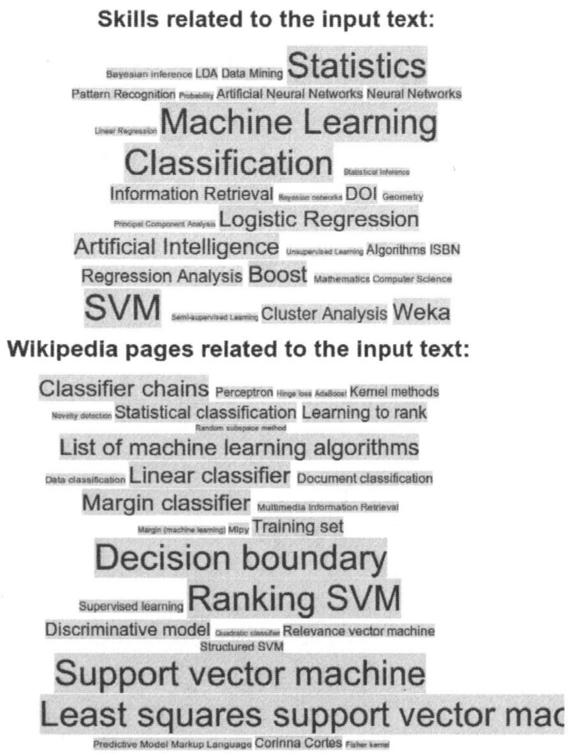

Figure 1: Skills extracted from a text about text document categorization.

Introduction to Information Retrieval by Manning et al. (2008). As one can observe, the Wikipedia pages found by the `text2wiki` module represent many low-level topics, such as "Desicion boundary", "Ranking SVM" or "Least square SVM". On the other hand, the skills retrieved after using the `wiki2skill` module provide high-level topics relevant to the input text, such as "SVM", "Machine Learning" or "Classification". These general topics are more useful, since a user, such as an HR manager, may be confused by too low-level skills.

5 Experiments & results

5.1 Evaluation of the `text2wiki` module

In order to compare the four text similarity functions, we collected $p = 200,000$ pairs of semantically related documents from the "See also" sections of Wikipedia articles. A good model is supposed to assign a high similarity to these pairs. However, since the distribution of similarity scores depends on the model, one cannot simply compare the mean similarity $\bar{s}$ over the set of pairs. Thus, we used a

Model	z-score
TF-IDF	8459
LogEntropy	4370
LogEntropy + LDA	2317
LogEntropy + LSA	2143

Table 1: Comparison of different text similarity functions on the Wikipedia "See also" dataset.

z-score as evaluation metric. The z-scores are computed as

$$z = \frac{\bar{s} - \hat{\mu}}{\sqrt{\hat{\sigma}^2 / p}} \tag{3}$$

where $\hat{\mu}$ and $\hat{\sigma}$ are sample estimates of mean and standard deviation of similarity scores for a given model. These sample estimates have been calculated from a set of 1,000,000 randomly selected pairs of articles. Table 1 presents the results of this experiment. It appears that more complex models (LSA, LDA) are outperformed on this task by the simpler vector space models (TF-IDF, LogEntropy). This can be just a special case with this experimental setting and perhaps another choice of the number of topics could give better results. Thus, further meta-parameter optimization of LSA and LDA is one approach for improving the performance of the `text2wiki` module.

5.2 Evaluation of the `wiki2skill` module

In order to find the optimal strategy of applying Spreading Activation, we designed an evaluation protocol relying on *related skills* listed on each LinkedIn skill page. These are automatically selected by computing similarities between skills from user profiles (Skomoroch et al., 2012). Each skill page contains at most 20 related skills.

For the evaluation procedure, we choose an initial node i, corresponding to a LinkedIn skill, and activate it by setting $\mathbf{a}(0) = \mathbf{e}_i$, that is a vector containing 1 in its i-th element and zeros elsewhere. Then, we compute $\mathbf{a}(T)$ with some spreading strategy and for some number of steps T, filter out the skill nodes and rank them according to their final activations. To measure how well the related skills are represented in this ranked list of skills, we use Precision at 1, 5 and 10, and R-Precision to evaluate the accuracy of the first ranked results and Recall at 100 to see how well the algorithm manages to activate all of the related skills.

There are many LinkedIn skills that are not well represented in the Wikipedia graph, because of ambiguity issues, for instance. To prevent these anomalies from causing misguiding results, we selected a fixed set of 16 representative skills for the evaluation. These skills were "Statistics", "Hidden Markov Models", "Telecommunications", "MeeGo", "Digital Printing", "OCR", "Linguistics", "Speech Synthesis", "Classical", "Impressionist", "Education", "Secondary Education", "Cinematography", "Executive producer", "Social Sciences", "Political Sociology".

Developing a completely automatic optimisation scheme for this model selection task would be difficult because of the number of different parameters, the size of the Wikipedia graph and the heuristic nature of the whole methodology. Thus, we decided to rely on a manual evaluation of the results.

Exploring the whole space of algorithms spanned by eq. (1) would be too demanding as well. That is why we have so far tested only a few models. In the preliminary experiments that we conducted with the system, we observed that using a friction factor λ smaller than one had little effect on the results, and thus we decided to always use $\lambda = 1$. Otherwise, we experimented with three models, which we will simply refer to as models 1, 2 and 3 and which we define as follows

- model 1: $\gamma = 0$ and $\mathbf{c}(t) = \mathbf{0}$;
- model 2: $\gamma = 1$ and $\mathbf{c}(t) = \mathbf{0}$;
- model 3: $\gamma = 0$ and $\mathbf{c}(t) = \mathbf{a}(0)$.

In model 1, activation is not conserved in a node but only depends on the activation it has received from its neighbors after each pulse. In contrast, the activation that a node receives is completely conserved in model 2. Model 3 corresponds to the Random Walk with Restart model, where the initial activation is fed to the system at each pulse. Models 1 and 2 eventually converge to a stationary distribution that is independent of the initial activation vector. This can be beneficial in situations where some of the initially activated nodes are noisy, or irrelevant, because it allows the initial activation to die out, or at least become lower than the activation of other, possibly more relevant nodes. With Model 3, the initially activated nodes remain always among the most activated nodes, which is not necessarily a robust choice.

The outcomes of the experiments demonstrated that model 2 and model 3 perform equally well. Indeed, these models are very similar, and apparently their small differences do not affect the results much. However, model 1 provided constantly worse results than the two other models. Thus, we decided to use model 3, corresponding to the Random Walk with Restart model, in the system and in selecting the rest of the spreading strategy.

We also evaluated different settings for the link weighting scheme. Here, we faced a startling result, namely that increasing the bidirectional link weight δ all the way up to the value $\delta = 15$ kept improving the results according to almost all evaluation measures. This would indicate that links that exist in only one direction do not convey a lot of semantic relatedness. However, we assume that this is a phenomenon caused by the nature of the experiment and the small subset of skills used in it, and not necessarily a general phenomenon for the whole Wikipedia graph. In our experiments, the improvement was more drastic in the range $\delta \in [1, 5]$ after which a damping effect can be observed. For this reason, we decided to set the bidirectional link weight in the `Elisit` system to $\delta = 5$.

We observed a similar phenomenon for the number of pulses T. Increasing its value up to $T = 8$ improved constantly the results. However, again, there was no substantial change in the results in the range $T \in [5, 8]$. In the web service, the number of pulses of the spreading activation can be determined by the user.

In addition to the parameters discussed above, the link weighting involves the popularity index π_j and the biasing parameter α. An overview of the effect of these two choices can be seen in Table 2, which presents the results with the different evaluation measures. These results were obtained by setting parameters as described earlier in this section. First, we can see from this table that using negative values for α in the weighting improves results compared to the natural random walk, i.e. the case $\alpha = 0$. This indicates that our strategy of biasing the spreading of activation to avoid popular nodes indeed improves the results. We can also see

	Pre@1			**Pre@5**			**Pre@10**			**R-Pre**			**Rec@100**		
α	d_{in}	PR	HITS	d_{in}	PR	HITS	d_{in}	PR	HITS	d_{in}	PR	HITS	d_{in}	PR	HITS
0	0	0	0	0.119	0.119	0.119	0.156	0.156	0.156	0.154	0.154	0.154	0.439	0.439	0.439
-0.2	0	0	0	0.206	0.238	0.206	**0.222**	0.216	0.213	0.172	0.193	0.185	0.469	0.469	0.494
-0.4	0	0	0	0.225	**0.263**	0.169	0.203	0.200	0.150	0.185	**0.204**	0.148	0.503	0.498	0.476
-0.6	0	0	**0.063**	0.238	0.225	0.119	0.200	0.197	0.141	0.186	0.193	0.119	0.511	0.517	0.418
-0.8	0	0	0	0.213	0.181	0.075	0.191	0.197	0.113	0.171	0.185	0.109	0.515	**0.524**	0.384
-1	0	0	0	0.169	0.156	0.063	0.178	0.197	0.091	0.154	0.172	0.097	0.493	0.518	0.336

Table 2: The effect of the biasing parameter α and the choice of popularity index on the results in the evaluation of the `wiki2skill` module.

that using Pagerank as the popularity index provided overall better results than using the input degree, which again yielded better results than using HITS. Thus, biasing according to the input connections of nodes seems more preferable than biasing according to co-citation or co-reference connections. The low scores with Precision@1 are understandable, because of the low number of positives (at most 20 related skills) in comparison to the total number of skills (over 27,000). In the `Elisit` system, we use the Pagerank score as the popularity index and set the value of the biasing parameter to $\alpha = -0.4$.

5.3 Evaluation of the whole `Elisit` system

We adapted the evaluation procedure used for the `wiki2skill` module, described in the previous section, in order to test the whole `Elisit` system. This time, instead of activating the node of a given skill, we activated the nodes found by the `text2wiki` module when fed with the Wikipedia article corresponding to the skill. We run the Spreading Activation algorithm with the setup presented in the previous section. To make the evaluation more realistic, the initial activation of the target skill node is set to zero (instead of 1, i.e. the cosine of a vector with itself).

The system allows its user to set the number of initially activated nodes. We investigated the effect of this choice by measuring Precision and Recall according to the related skills, and by looking at the average rank of the target skill on the list of final activations. However, there was no clear trend in the results when testing with 1-200 initially activated nodes. Nevertheless, we have noticed that using more than 20 initially activated nodes rarely improves the results. We must also emphasize that the choice of the number of initially activated nodes depends on the query, especially its length.

We also wanted to compare the different VSM's

VSM	Pre@1	Pre@5	Pre@10	R-Pre	Rec@100
TF-IDF	0.042	**0.231**	**0.214**	0.190	0.516
LogEntropy	**0.068**	0.216	0.212	**0.193**	**0.525**
LogEnt + LSA	0.042	0.180	0.181	0.163	0.491
LogEnt + LDA	0.089	0.193	0.174	0.159	0.470

Table 3: Comparison of the different models of the `text2wiki` module in the performance of the whole `Elisit` system.

of the `text2wiki` module when using the whole `Elisit` system. We did this by comparing Precision and Recall at different ranks w.r.t. the related skills of the target skill found on LinkedIn. Thus, this experiment combines the experiments introduced in sections 5.1, where the evaluation was based on the "See also" pages, and 5.2, where we used a set of 16 target skills and their related skills. Table 3 reports the Precision and Recall values obtained with the different VSM's. These values result from an average over 12 different numbers of initially activated nodes. They confirm the conclusion drawn from the experiment in section 5.1, namely that the LogEntropy and TF-IDF models outperform LSA and LDA models for this task.

6 Conclusion and future work

We have presented a method for skill extraction based on Wikipedia articles, their hyperlink graph, and a set of skills built by LinkedIn. We have also presented the `Elisit` system as a reference implementation of this method. This kind of a system has many potential applications, such as knowledge management in a company or recommender systems of websites. We have demonstrated with examples and with quantitative evaluations that the system indeed extracts relevant skills from text. The evaluation experiments have also allowed us to compare and finetune different strategies and parameters of the system. For example, we have shown that using a bias to avoid the spreading of activation to popular nodes of the graph improves retrieval results.

This work is still in progress, and we have many goals for improvement. One plan is to compute link weights based on the contents of linked pages using their vector space representation in the `text2wiki` module. The method and system proposed in the paper could also be extended to other languages. Finally, our methodology can potentially be used to different problems than skill extraction by substituting the LinkedIn skills with a list of Wikipedia pages from another domain.

References

John R Anderson. 1983. A spreading activation theory of memory. *Journal Of Verbal Learning And Verbal Behavior*, 22(3):261–295.

Krisztian Balog, Paul Thomas, Nick Craswell, Ian Soboroff, Peter Bailey, and Arjen P De Vries. 2008. Overview of the trec 2008 enterprise track. Technical report, DTIC Document.

Krisztian Balog, Yi Fang, Maarten de Rijke, Pavel Serdyukov, and Luo Si. 2012. Expertise retrieval. *Foundations and Trends in Information Retrieval*, 6(2-3):127–256.

Holger Bast and Debapriyo Majumdar. 2005. Why spectral retrieval works. In *Proceedings of the 28th annual international ACM SIGIR conference on Research and development in information retrieval*, pages 11–18. ACM.

Michael W. Berry, Susan T. Dumais, and Gavin W. O'Brien. 1994. Using linear algebra for intelligent information retrieval. Technical Report UT-CS-94-270.

David M. Blei, Andrew Y. Ng, and Michael I. Jordan. 2003. Latent dirichlet allocation. *Journal of Machine Learning Research*, 3:993–1022, March.

Matthew Brand. 2005. A random walks perspective on maximizing satisfaction and profit. *Proceedings of the 2005 SIAM International Conference on Data Mining*.

Fabio Crestani. 1997. Application of spreading activation techniques in information retrieval. *Artificial Intelligence Review*, 11(6):453–482.

Gianluca Demartini, Tereza Iofciu, and Arjen P De Vries. 2010. Overview of the inex 2009 entity ranking track. In *Focused Retrieval and Evaluation*, pages 254–264. Springer.

Peter W Foltz. 1996. Latent semantic analysis for text-based research. *Behavior Research Methods, Instruments, & Computers*, 28(2):197–202.

Agata Fronczak and Piotr Fronczak. 2009. Biased random walks in complex networks: The role of local navigation rules. *Physical Review E*, 80(1):016107.

Evgeniy Gabrilovich and Shaul Markovitch. 2007. Computing semantic relatedness using wikipedia-based explicit semantic analysis. In *IJCAI'07: Proceedings of the 20th international joint conference on Artifical intelligence*, pages 1606–1611, San Francisco, CA, USA. Morgan Kaufmann Publishers Inc.

Stephan Gouws, G-J van Rooyen, and Herman A. Engelbrecht. 2010. Measuring conceptual similarity by spreading activation over wikipedia's hyperlink structure. In *Proceedings of the 2nd Workshop on The People's Web Meets NLP: Collaboratively Constructed Semantic Resources*, pages 46–54, Beijing, China, August. Coling 2010 Organizing Committee.

Graeme Hirst. 1988. Semantic interpretation and ambiguity. *Artificial Intelligence*, 34(2):131–177.

Jon M. Kleinberg. 1999. Authoritative sources in a hyperlinked environment. *Journal of the ACM*, 46(5):604–632.

Marijn Koolen. 2011. *The Meaning Of Structure: the Value of Link Evidence for Information Retrieval*. Ph.D. thesis, University of Amsterdam, The Netherlands.

Thomas K. Landauer and Susan T. Dumais. 1997. A solution to plato's problem: The latent semantic analysis theory of acquisition, induction, and representation of knowledge. *Psych. review*, 104(2):211.

Christopher D Manning, Prabhakar Raghavan, and Hinrich Schütze. 2008. *Introduction to information retrieval*, volume 1. Cambridge University Press Cambridge.

Amin Mantrach, Nicolas van Zeebroeck, Pascal Francq, Masashi Shimbo, Hugues Bersini, and Marco Saerens. 2011. Semi-supervised classification and betweenness computation on large, sparse, directed graphs. *Pattern Recognition*, 44(6):1212–1224.

Rada Mihalcea and Andras Csomai. 2007. Wikify!: linking documents to encyclopedic knowledge. In Mário J. Silva, Alberto H. F. Laender, Ricardo A. Baeza-Yates, Deborah L. McGuinness, Bjørn Olstad, Øystein Haug Olsen, and André O. Falcão, editors, *CIKM*, pages 233–242. ACM.

George A Miller. 1995. Wordnet: a lexical database for english. *Communications of the ACM*, 38(11):39–41.

Lawrence Page, Sergey Brin, Rajeev Motwani, and Terry Winograd. 1999. The pagerank citation ranking: Bringing order to the web. *Technical Report 1999-0120, Computer Science Department, Stanford University*.

Jia-Yu Pan, Hyung-Jeong Yang, Christos Faloutsos, and Pinar Duygulu. 2004. Automatic multimedia cross-modal correlation discovery. In *Proceedings of the tenth ACM SIGKDD international conference on Knowledge discovery and data mining*, pages 653–658. ACM.

Radim Řehůřek and Petr Sojka. 2010. Software Framework for Topic Modelling with Large Corpora. In *Proceedings of the LREC 2010 Workshop on New Challenges for NLP Frameworks*, pages 45–50, Valletta, Malta, May. ELRA.

Jeff Shrager, Tad Hogg, and Bernardo A Huberman. 1987. Observation of phase transitions in spreading activation networks. *Science*, 236(4805):1092–1094.

Peter N Skomoroch, Matthew T Hayes, Abhishek Gupta, and Dhanurjay AS Patil. 2012. Skill customization system, January 24. US Patent App. 13/357,360.

Mark Steyvers, Padhraic Smyth, Michal Rosen-Zvi, and Thomas Griffiths. 2004. Probabilistic author-topic models for information discovery. In *Proceedings of the 10th ACM International Conference on Knowledge Discovery and Data Mining*. ACM Press.

Eric Yeh, Daniel Ramage, Christopher D. Manning, Eneko Agirre, and Aitor Soroa. 2009. Wikiwalk: Random walks on wikipedia for semantic relatedness. In *Graph-based Methods for Natural Language Processing*, pages 41–49. The Association for Computer Linguistics.

Author Index